BROADCAST
NEWSWRITING

BROADCAST NEWSWRITING

DAVID KEITH COHLER

PRENTICE HALL
Englewood Cliffs, New Jersey 07632

Library of Congress Cataloging-in-Publication Data

COHLER, DAVID KEITH.
    Broadcast newswriting.

    Includes index.
    1. Television broadcasting of news.   2. Television
authorship.   3. Radio journalism.   4. Radio authorship.
5. Broadcast journalism—Authorship.   I. Title.
PN4784.T4C57 1990   808'.06607   89-8750
ISBN 0-13-083528-5

Editorial/production supervision and interior design: KATHLEEN SCHIAPARELLI
Cover design: BEN SANTORA
Manufacturing buyer: CAROL BYSTROM

© 1990 by Prentice-Hall, Inc.
A division of Simon & Schuster
Englewood Cliffs, New Jersey 07632

Printed in the United States of America

10   9   8   7   6   5   4   3   2   1

ISBN 0-13-083528-5

Prentice-Hall International (UK) Limited, *London*
Prentice-Hall of Australia Pty. Limited, *Sydney*
Prentice-Hall Canada Inc., *Toronto*
Prentice-Hall Hispanoamericana, S.A., *Mexico*
Prentice-Hall of India Private Limited, *New Delhi*
Prentice-Hall of Japan, Inc., *Tokyo*
Simon & Schuster Asia Pte. Ltd., *Singapore*
Editora Prentice-Hall do Brasil, Ltda., *Rio de Janeiro*

For Esther Zion Cohler,
in loving memory.

Contents

Preface

The aim of this book is to introduce journalism students to the essentials of broadcast newswriting. Because the technology of gathering and producing broadcast news has grown so complex, basic writing skills are often overwhelmed in a maze of colored lights and electronic beeps. The result is a rush of sounds and pictures lacking clear communication of the import of current events.

The best (and perhaps only) place to rectify this blurring of journalism's goal—which is to inform and enlighten—is the classroom, where instructors and students can devote time and attention to writing. With rare exceptions, on-the-job training in newswriting simply does not exist. Because of modern technology's speed and the relentless nature of competition, few working journalists have the time to drill newcomers in basic skills. At the same time, these skills are supposed to be second nature to broadcast newsrooms. Therefore, this book is devoted predominantly to writing in broadcast style—simply, clearly, and directly. The classroom may be the budding broadcast journalist's first and last exposure to the luxury of time—time to read, time to write, time to think.

Writing for the Ear

To make a career in broadcast news, it helps to look like Peter Jennings or Diane Sawyer. But there's not much you can do about the face you were born with.

It helps to have a deep, resonant, or (if you're a woman) husky voice. But there's a limit to the flexibility of your vocal cords.

It helps to have a famous parent or marry the boss's son or daughter. But nepotism is comparatively rare in news broadcasting.

It helps to be able to write as well as Charles Osgood or Charles Kuralt. No buts. Writing is the backbone of journalism. Writing ability is so important that by developing your verbal skills and nose for news you can effectively overcome any perceived deficiencies in looks and voice.

In sum, your substantive skills as a journalist are far more important in the long run than cosmetic appearances.

Often, what you see and hear on your local news programs seems to contradict this. Yes, it's true that some stations do rely on cosmetics over substance, the pretty face over journalistic skill. But a great many stations, perhaps most, stress the substance.

Make no mistake about it, though: Except for government-supported public radio and television, stations are in business to make money, and the news, at least on the local level, is expected to show a profit. That means the more viewers or listeners a station can attract, the more money it can charge advertisers. Such bottom-line financing means many stations will not hesitate to hire a "pretty face" over a solid journalist where profitability is concerned.

This is the nature of most news broadcasting in the United States. It differs from systems in many countries where broadcasting is government-run or there is a mix of state-run and privately run stations. In the overwhelmingly profit-oriented U.S. system, station managements want newscasts to grab and hold the audience, to keep the audience from tuning out or, worse, switching to a competing station. Thus, while a newscast in a state-run system can afford to be dull or visually static, a newscast in a commercial system must be unflaggingly *interesting*. It must strive to compel the audience's attention.

You might argue that the news itself is inherently interesting—and most working journalists would agree with you. But they would also caution that the news does not "tell itself." No matter how intrinsically interesting a story might be, it requires a trained journalist, an effective writer and communicator, to preserve and impart that interest to a general audience.

Fortunately, many U.S. broadcasting companies recognize that the news is a vital service for an informed and democratic citizenry. So for every "pretty face" there are dozens of talented, hard-working journalists—writers, reporters, editors, producers, researchers, camera crews, and so forth. However, because broadcast news has become an attractive career for young people, and despite the expansion of news programming in recent times, the competition for jobs is very stiff. Newcomers are expected to know how to write well (and sometimes operate electronic equipment) before they are offered jobs.*

THE WAY PEOPLE TALK

The first words humans ever spoke were probably no more than inflected grunts, perhaps reactions to stepping on a sharp rock or to biting into a tasty hunk of raw zebra meat. Comedy writer–director Mel Brooks, in an old routine called "The 2,000-Year-Old Man," muses that the first word was in "rock-talk," as in, "Hey, don't t'row dat rock!"

The point is, the first word was *spoken,* not chiseled in stone at Cave Man U. Chiseling—writing, that is—came much later in our cultural development.

Skipping ahead to modern days, we come to the broadcast news business, in which the natural order is reversed: Words are written first, then spoken. More exactly, they are written to be spoken. The structure of the written sentences follows the cadences of oral speech—short and simple.

Broadcast newswriting has also been described as "writing for the ear" instead of for the eye. The eye can pause, skip forward and backward, ponder words, meanings, and sentence structure. The ear cannot. A listener of broadcast news gets only one chance. If a word, phrase, or sentence is not immediately clear on first hearing, listeners may become lost and unable to understand the

---

*A recent study for the Radio-Television News Directors Association (RTNDA) estimated the number of news department jobs at U.S. commercial stations at a total of 40,000—21,000 in radio, 19,000 in television. The study also estimated annual turnover at about 12,000, or 30 percent. While most of the turnover was a result of staffers changing jobs from one station to another, many of those hired were young people on their first jobs. Unfortunately, figures are virtually impossible to obtain on the exact number of entry-level positions in broadcast news.

rest of the story. In short, broadcast newswriting is a form of oral storytelling in which the words committed to paper or computer screen have no reality until given a human voice.

Many of you may already have been trained to write in newspaper style. If so, you were taught to make your first sentence (the lead sentence) a capsule version of the entire story. You were taught to cram the most significant elements of the story (Who, What, When, Where, Why, and How) into the lead sentence and into the sentences immediately following. This gave your story an "inverted pyramid" structure that enabled a copyeditor to trim from the end and fit your story into the available space.

In newspaper journalism, the result is often a convoluted and artificial kind of writing distant from human speech. If newspaper writing style were imposed on, say, the story of Little Red Riding Hood, the lead might go something like this:

> THE WOODS, Oct. 31—An eight-year-old girl narrowly missed serious injury when she was rescued by a woodsman who snatched her from the claws of a transvestite wolf who had already devoured her grandmother, forest rangers reported Thursday.

That sort of writing is known as "journalese." It rearranges a natural, chronological series of events into a formalized structure digested via the eye. It is very useful when your job is editing a newspaper.

But it has nothing to do with broadcast news. As broadcasters, our job is to grab people by the ears. How? Well, suppose we begin by saying,

```
A remarkable rescue in the Woods today...
```

Do we have people's attention? You bet we do. Very simply, we have begun to tell a story. We have not attempted to tell the whole story right off the bat. We have not even used a complete sentence. But we have found a good starting point. And now, step by step, we are going to tell the rest of the story in a way that allows listeners to stay with us. No jargon, no journalese, no verbal overload.

News stories, of course, are not like fairy tales. Instead, they are about a reality that is often ugly and complex. You can't start a broadcast news story by saying, "Once upon a time there was a brutal murder. . . ." But you can start by saying, "A brutal murder on the West Side today. . . ." That is a legitimate and effective way to grab people's attention. There are many other ways, and in a later chapter we will examine them. But for the moment let's try to think of broadcast newswriting as old-fashioned, sit-around-the-campfire storytelling—with a strong beginning.

A word of caution at this point: While it's true that broadcast newswriting is supposed to be conversational and follow the cadences of oral speech, it's also true that it should be correct in grammar, vocabulary, and syntax. We must be careful to omit the mistakes many people make in casual speech. In ordinary conversation, people do not pause to diagram their sentences or whip out a pocket dictionary. They often get their facts wrong, garble their syntax, say "lay down" when they mean "lie down," mistake "infer" for "imply," confuse "flaunt" and "flout," and so on. So let's put it this way: Broadcast newswriting is writing the way people talk when they use language correctly and get the facts straight.

BROADCAST NEWS VOCABULARY

In addition to using conversational language, broadcast journalists use a simplified vocabulary. The vocabulary of print journalism is small—around 10,000 words. The vocabulary of broadcast journalism is even smaller. Adjectives, for example, are short: a "spherical" object becomes *round* or *shaped like a ball;* a "lanky" person becomes *thin;* a "flaxen-haired" person is *blond;* "coniferous" trees become *evergreens* and "deciduous" trees become *leafy* trees; and so on.

Verbs, too, are short and active: "regarding" something becomes *watching* something; to "participate" becomes to *take part;* to "extinguish" a fire becomes to *put out* a fire; "assert," "opine," "recount," "state," "declare," "explicate," "elucidate," "avow," "expound," and "aver" become *say, tell,* or *explain;* "hasten" becomes *hurry;* "inculcate" becomes *teach;* "make a determination" becomes *decide;* "purchase" becomes *buy;* and so forth.

And let's not forget nouns: a "residence" or "domicile" becomes a *house, home,* or *apartment;* an "octogenarian" becomes an *80-year-old;* "mnemonics" becomes *memory improvement;* etc.

Some critics of broadcast news say its limited vocabulary leads to the impoverishment of language and, in effect, helps to promote functional illiteracy. That might be true if the aim of broadcast newswriting were to be literary. But that is not its aim. Its aim is to make the news clear to a mass audience—immediately and without complication.

Hence, if the choice is between a long word and a short one, choose the short one.

WYSWYS (WHAT YOU SEE IS WHAT YOU SAY)

Another characteristic of broadcast newswriting is that the copy you type on the page or computer screen should reflect the way it is to be spoken on the air. This often requires you to type words or phrases that do not appear in a printed story.

For example, if the U.S. trade deficit in a given month is "$15.3 billion," that looks fine on the printed page. But a broadcast news script—including the "$"—must be read aloud. Thus, the figure should be written as "15-point-3 billion dollars." Similarly, the figure "7.5%" should be written as "Seven-point-five percent" or, better, "Seven-and-a-half percent." (Notice the hyphens linking the parts of the number.)

A similar copy-appearance problem arises in quoting people's words, especially if the words constitute an opinion or moral judgment. In print journalism, you can bracket the words in quotation marks: "All men are created equal,"

Jefferson said. Looks fine on the printed page. But what happens when you read it aloud? No one can *see* the quotation marks. Thus, you must often provide "aural" quotation marks—by writing something on the order of,

```
Jefferson said--and these are his words--"All men are created

equal."
```

The foregoing illustrates yet another aspect of broadcast style. In print, the attribution (the name of the speaker or source of the information) is generally given at the end of the sentence, preceded by a comma:

```
    WASHINGTON (AP)--Higher postage rates, including a
25-cent charge for first-class mail, will begin April 3, the
Postal Service announced Tuesday.
```

Read aloud, it becomes evident that such placement does not follow the cadences of oral speech. In normal speech, who-said-it comes first. Therefore, in broadcast news the attribution is placed at the *start* of the sentence:

```
The Postal Service says postage rates will go up on April Third.  It

says first class stamps will cost a quarter.
```

. . . or in the middle:

```
The Postal Service says postage rates will go up on April Third.  A

first class letter, the Service says, will cost 25 cents.
```

Another matter is pronunciation. Suppose someone named "Myschkly-czevskinov" must be named or quoted. In print that looks difficult enough. When a newscaster or reporter has to *say* it, it becomes downright terrifying. So broadcast news copy must include visual aids to help the news anchor pronounce unfamiliar names and places. In this case, the writer would include, right after the actual spelling, a phonetic spelling: Mizz-kluh-SHEFFS-kin-off.

Most of these matters require rather simple adjustments for newswriters, and they soon become second nature. Far more difficult adjustments are necessitated by the very nature of radio and TV news, which exists not in space, but in *time*. The clock is a very cruel master.

THE LIMITATIONS OF TIME

Newspapers must shorten (or sometimes lengthen) stories to fit the available space. But that space is flexible. The number of pages may be increased or decreased each day, or even between editions, to suit the combined needs of the editorial and advertising departments.

Radio and television have no such flexibility. All departments must go by the clock. Much as they might wish it otherwise, there are only 24 hours in each day, 60 minutes in each hour, and 60 seconds in each minute—period.

To demonstrate the effects of the clock's tyranny on broadcast news, let's pick an actual newspaper story as our model:

JERUSALEM—Declaring that certain deeds "can never be forgiven in law or in the hearts of men," a Jerusalem court Monday sentenced retired Cleveland auto worker John Demjanjuk to death by hanging for World War II crimes at the Treblinka extermination camp in Poland.

The sentence, only the second death penalty announced in Israel's 40-year history, was greeted by prolonged applause, dancing and singing in the converted theater that has served for the last 14 months as Demjanjuk's courtroom.

"The Nation of Israel Lives!" the joyous spectators sang while three Treblinka survivors, who had identified Demjanjuk as the cruel camp guard known as "Ivan the Terrible," wept in the front row.

The condemned man reacted to the decision with an almost imperceptible shake of his head but was otherwise expressionless.

In convicting him a week ago, the court concluded—"unequivocally, without the slightest doubt"—that Demjanjuk, 68, is Ivan. The burly, bespectacled Ukrainian, who emigrated to the United States and settled in the Cleveland area in 1952, maintains that he is the victim of mistaken identity.

"I am innocent!" he shouted in Hebrew as he was wheeled into the courtroom early Monday afternoon to hear Judge Zvi Tal pronounce sentence. Demjanjuk was in a wheelchair because of persistent back problems.

The sentence means that the verdict will now go automatically before the country's High Court of Appeals under an Israeli law that provides for such a review in any case involving capital punishment.

The condemned man's son, John Demjanjuk Jr., termed the decision an "injustice" that will "shame the Israeli government, the Israeli Justice department, the U.S. Justice Department and, most unfortunately, the 6 million murdered in the Holocaust."

Demjanjuk was extradited from the United States to Israel in February, 1986, to face the Jewish state's first war crimes trial since that of Adolf Eichmann. Eichmann was convicted of masterminding Nazi Germany's systematic extermination of 6 million European Jews and was hanged in 1962.

The three-judge panel that heard Demjanjuk's case deliberated for more than three hours. Reading their decision, Judge Tal acknowledged that "almost 50 years have elapsed since Treblinka. We have established a new life, and we ask ourselves if time alleviates the crime; if time dulls the pain, and a person who has changed his course in life need not be punished as harshly.

"This holds true for some crimes," Tal said, "but not for those listed in the verdict. . . . These crimes can never be forgiven in law or in the hearts of men. These crimes can never be obliterated from memory. It is as though Treblinka continues to exist, as though the blood of the victims still cries out to us."

The court ruled last week that Demjanjuk operated the gas chambers at Treblinka in which about 850,000 individuals, most of them Jews, were put to death.

"We have not heard any extenuating circumstances from the defense," Tal said. And while acknowledging "the perils of an irrevocable sentence," he reminded the court of the sweeping certainty with which the panel had last week found Demjanjuk guilty. "In light of all the above, we sentence him to the punishment of death," Tal said.

Citing the Eichmann precedent, chief

prosecutor Yona Blattman had argued earlier that the death penalty was mandatory under Israel's Nazi and Nazi Collaborators Act—a position that Chief Judge Dov Levin rejected.

"The accused stood at the gateway to the inferno and went about his duties with unparalleled zeal and enthusiasm," Blattman argued in support of capital punishment. "The accused was no small cog. He was a major criminal against humanity.... He committed the most heinous acts with his very own hands, killing hundreds of thousands of people with utmost brutality."

As Blattman spoke, Demjanjuk, a member of the Ukrainian Orthodox (Christian) Church, crossed himself several times.

In his counterargument, chief defense attorney John Gill cited several instances in which people have been executed for crimes it was later learned they did not commit. New evidence continues to emerge related to his client's case, Gill said, and that presented during the trial "did not meet the required level of exactness needed to impose the death penalty."

"The taking of any innocent human life is a holocaust," Gill added, to the obvious displeasure of the bench.

Speaking briefly in his native Ukrainian, Demjanjuk said in his own defense that it was "very painful for me to sit here and hear the terrible tragedy that befell the Jewish people." He said he has no argument that "the atrocities perpetrated at Treblinka did take place, and that there is a hangman named Ivan, and he did brutalize the people."

However, Demjanjuk added, the court had made "a very grave mistake, because I am not 'Ivan the terrible.'... I do not deserve this. I am innocent, innocent, innocent, as God is my witness."

Trial spokesman Yossi Hasin said the date for the automatic appeal of the Demjanjuk verdict is uncertain. However, he noted, in order to give both prosecution and defense enough time to review the 444-page verdict and prepare arguments, it is unlikely that an appelate court will begin proceedings until at least the summer.

(Dan Fisher, © 1988 *Los Angeles Times*, reprinted with permission.)

By modern newspaper standards, that story is of moderate length, containing about 800 words. It takes a minute or two for the average person to read silently.

But radio and television news is read *aloud*, and by that standard it would take more than five minutes to read the story!

Now, there are a few news broadcasts that would spend five minutes on this story, or even longer, but they are almost exclusively on noncommercial public radio (NPR) and television (PBS). The overwhelming majority of U.S. news broadcasts are on commercial stations where *brevity* is the rule. Thus, the story you have just read would typically be allotted from 20 seconds to a maximum of one minute on radio, and from 20 seconds to at most a minute and a half on television (provided there were enough pictures to sustain the maximum length).

(There's no law that says stories must be told so briefly. It's just the way U.S. broadcast news is presented. If you think news stories should be told at greater length, just about the only way you'll ever make it happen is to own your own station or become the controlling shareholder of a broadcasting company.)

I hope you noticed a few of the matters we looked at earlier that need reworking for a broadcast version—making clear who said what, moving the attribution to the start of sentences, spelling out numbers ("World War *Two*," for example), and providing pronouncing help ("Dem-YAHN-yook"), and so on.

But those are minor matters compared to the major one: How do you reduce a 5-minute story to 20 seconds or one minute? How do you decide which facts to include and which to leave out? The way you answer those questions and the editorial decisions you make will depend, eventually, on how good a broadcast journalist you become, on your "news judgment." For the time being, here are some guidelines:

1. You should assume at the outset that people who are interested in the story's wealth of details will read newspapers—because they know they won't get those details on radio or TV. Let's not kid ourselves: A radio or TV newscast that promises to deliver "all" the day's news is misrepresenting itself.

2. You should reduce the story to its bare bones—in this case the sentencing to death (What) of John Demjanjuk (Who), plus Where (Israel), When (today), and Why (for the mass murder of Jews at a World War Two death camp in Poland). In a 20-second version, that's all you'll have time for. In a longer version you can include Demjanjuk's reaction (he says he's innocent), add details relevant to your listening audience (Demjanjuk spent more than 30 years in the U.S.), and tell what will happen next (an appeal).

3. You should eliminate the historical background except for those few facts that make the latest development significant.

4. You should try to eliminate the direct quotes (from the judge, the prosecution, the defense, the plaintiff's son, and the courtroom spectators). You'll find it is almost always shorter to paraphrase people's remarks.

Let's try an experiment: Without looking back at the Demjanjuk story, turn to someone (or the wall if you're alone) and just tell it out loud in whatever words come to you.

(I'm waiting.)

(Still waiting.)

(This *is* important. You should get in the habit of telling news stories aloud . . . and then reading aloud what you've written. It's the only way to judge how a story will sound on the air.)

Okay. Chances are you didn't try to utter any long-winded sentences, go into much history, or try to quote anyone's exact words. In short, what you ad-libbed to a friend, classmate, roommate, or the wall was probably very close to the way you should put the words on paper or in the computer.

In coming chapters we will examine these and many other matters in detail. Whenever possible, we will use actual news stories as our models. But before digging into the meat and potatoes of broadcast newswriting, we must spend some time setting the journalistic table.

EXERCISES

1. To give you and your instructor an idea of your raw talent, use the foregoing Demjanjuk story as source material and write a 20-second story for broadcast on radio

or television. Don't worry about the rules of style and copy appearance that we'll examine later in this book. Just try to tell the story simply and in short sentences.

2. Now write a second version, this one running 30 seconds. Use *different words* from your first version, especially in your lead (the way you begin the story). Assume that many in your audience have never heard of John Demjanjuk or the Treblinka death camp.

2

Preparing for Work

The so-called media explosion—brought about by new technologies derived from the space and defense programs—has yielded a concurrent explosion in news broadcasting, especially on television.

Despite some cost-cutting and staff layoffs in the mid-1980s, broadcast news has been a growth industry since the 1960s, and ever-increasing numbers of young people have decided to make careers in the field. Newcomers are attracted for many reasons in addition to the traditional desire to witness history in the making. Some of these are high pay in the major cities and at networks; the chance to meet people and see places generally off-limits to nonjournalists; the chance to influence the governmental process; and, not least, the "glamor" attached to membership in a high-visibility profession. (It is not unusual for young people to try to enter broadcast news because they want to be "stars.")

In other words, as in many fields, the motives of newcomers are mixed, and no one can predict with absolute certainty who will succeed. However, there is no doubt about what it takes to prepare oneself for a fighting chance in such a competitive environment.

READING HABITS

First, you must become an avid *reader*. Specifically, you must get in the daily habit of reading at least one newspaper, but preferably two—either your local morning and afternoon papers, or a combination of one local paper plus a paper of national standing such as *The New York Times* or *The Wall Street Journal*. You should also read weekly magazines of fact (*Time, Newsweek, U.S. News and World Report,* etc.) and opinion (*The New Republic, National Review, The Nation, The New Yorker,* to name just a few). You should read monthly publications that treat issues in depth (*Harpers, Atlantic Monthly, Commentary, Mother Jones, Texas Monthly,* etc.). And you should read nonfiction books dealing with subjects that recur in the news: race relations, economics, the space and defense programs, international affairs, issues in journalism, popular culture—the list is endless.

The point of all this reading is not to become an "instant expert" (although that is sometimes required in the news business), but rather to build up, over time, a solid foundation of knowledge on which to draw in assessing and writing the news of the day. You must develop a trained mind.

LISTENING AND VIEWING HABITS

Second, you must become an avid viewer and listener. You should get in the habit of listening to radio news in the morning (which is radio's "prime time") and watching TV news in the evening—on not just one but several competing stations. Mentally, you should compare different stations' handling of the day's news. And you should constantly be asking yourself, How would *I* handle each story? How would *I* tell it? What is really important about it? What does the audience want and need to know?

You should check the weekly TV schedule for documentaries and news-feature programs such as "Nightline" on ABC, "60 Minutes" on CBS, and "Frontline" on PBS. If it is inconvenient to watch such programs at their scheduled times, make arrangements to tape them for later viewing. You should also check the Sunday lineup of local and network interview shows ("Face the Nation," "Meet the Press," etc.); these programs frequently make news, in addition to providing background on current events.

I cannot overstress the importance of forming lifelong reading, listening, and viewing habits that are far in excess of the general public's. Because a journalist's work consists of selecting which facts and assertions to include in news stories, then writing these stories clearly and succinctly, it should be obvious that a journalist's foundation of knowledge must be greater than the average reader's or viewer's. A radio or TV newscast is supposed to be "authoritative," a test that can be met only if it is prepared by knowledgeable professionals.

PROFESSIONAL GOALS AND RESPONSIBILITIES

Although Chapter 1 stressed the differences between print and broadcast writing styles, attention must also be paid to things that unite journalists in all media.

Most broadcast writing is either original, as in the case of a reporter covering events at the scene, or is based on writing meant for print, as from wire service copy, government or industry handouts, and so on. A basic job of the broadcast newswriter is to translate this eye-oriented writing into ear-oriented writing.

However, the *content* of the writing, as opposed to its *form,* must meet the same *journalistic* criteria in broadcasting as in print. Journalists in all media share certain aims:

To inform and enlighten
To dig for the truth
To witness and chronicle events great and small
To render understandable a complex reality
To expose wrongdoing harmful to society at large
To scoop the competition wherever possible

Since the goals are the same and only the methods differ, broadcast journalists and their print colleagues also share the same professional responsibilities:

To be accurate
To be fair
To be first

Because broadcast news is ruled by time rather than space, deadlines occur much more frequently than at newspapers. In the case of all-news radio and TV, deadlines occur literally by the minute. The pressure for speed is relentless. A frequent result is that broadcasters are often preoccupied with being first, at the expense of being accurate. However that may be, they, like their print colleagues, are under an obligation to spare no effort to check the facts for accuracy and to use words and grammar correctly. All broadcast news executives agree: Much as they love to scoop their competitors, in the last analysis it is far more important to be right than to be first.

READY-REFERENCE MATERIALS

Broadcast newsrooms usually contain essential reference materials—dictionaries, atlases, telephone books, government directories, maps, street guides, ward and precinct diagrams, and so on. However, many of these materials are often nowhere to be found when you need them in a hurry. (Staffers borrow them and neglect to return them to their proper place.) Thus, many career journalists are careful to assemble their own reference materials on a shelf or in their desks.

Most such reference materials serve equally well for print or broadcast use. However, broadcasters require certain "extras" not contained in many standard reference books.

Dictionaries

Because the words will be spoken aloud, a broadcast writer's dictionary should contain easy-to-read pronunciations. This can be a two-edged sword, because some dictionaries list more than one pronunciation (look up the word "controversial," for example). Some grammarians insist the first pronunciation listed is the "preferred" and therefore correct one. Others contend that alternative pronunciations carry equal weight. Whatever the case, the total number of disputed pronunciations is very small, and the important thing is that your dictionary contain pronunciations for each word, along with its definition, so that you don't have to flip to some other part of the book for guidance.

Ever since its publication in 1961, Merriam-Webster's *Third New International Dictionary* (unabridged) has been the standard reference dictionary in most U.S. newsrooms. However, in 1987 it got a worthy competitor in the *Random House Dictionary of the English Language* (unabridged, 2nd edition), which has quickly been adopted in many newsrooms. Both are excellent . . . but far too big, heavy, and expensive for personal use. For everyday, quick-reference use, you can choose from a number of inexpensive paperback abridged dictionaries, including the *Scribner-Bantam* and the *Oxford American.* (But do *not* throw money away on the type of cheap, big-print pocket dictionaries sold at some supermarket checkout counters; such dictionaries are for elementary schoolchildren.) Whatever dictionary you use, it should

> be up-to-date, containing words having entered common use in the preceding decade;
> contain clear pronunciations (as already noted);
> contain alphabetized historical names and places;
> contain brief usage guidelines, also alphabetized.

(For help in pronouncing tricky words, as well as foreign names and places frequently in the news, the *NBC Handbook of Pronunciation* [Harper & Row, 4th edition, 1984] is a trustworthy addition to your personal or professional bookshelf. Unfortunately, there is no low-cost paperback edition available.)

Grammar and Usage Guides

When may you split an infinitive? Does "presently" mean "soon" or "now"? Does one "flout" the law or "flaunt" it? Should you write "The man *who* was going" or "The man *that* was going"? A good writer needs to find the answers to those questions, and the answers are not always in dictionaries. That's where grammar and usage guides come in handy.

Until recently, the standard reference was H. W. Fowler's *A Dictionary of Modern English Usage* (revised 1983 by Sir Ernest Gowers, Oxford University Press), usually known just as "Fowler" for short. Although Fowler remains the standard in many parts of the English-speaking world, its advice, apart from being somewhat long-winded, is keyed to British standards, not American. All of which is fine if you are writing for the BBC. American audiences, however, prefer Americanisms because that's the way they speak. (It's been said that Britain and America are "two countries divided by a common language." For example, the statement "I'm mad about my flat" means in America, "I'm angry about my flat tire," whereas in Britain it means, "I just love my apartment.")

There are two American-oriented language guides in widespread use: Wilson Follett's *Modern American Usage* (paperback, Warner Books, 1966) and Theodore Bernstein's *The Careful Writer* (paperback, Atheneum, 1965). Both list things alphabetically (as other guides do not), enabling the broadcast writer to resolve language problems quickly. Of the two, Bernstein is the more complete and more entertaining.

Serious writers and students of language will, over time, refine their skills by reading works by authors such as William Safire, Edwin Newman, Richard Mitchell, and John Simon, to name but a few. They will also follow magazine columns such as William Safire's "On Language" in the Sunday *New York Times Magazine.*

Atlases and Almanacs

Where is Maracaibo? What is the capitol of Angola? Who won the heavyweight boxing crown in 1947? What movie won the Oscar for Best Picture in 1933? What does the U.S Constitution say about the private ownership of firearms? Is a train from Prague to Budapest going east or west? Who was Speaker of the House before the present one?

These are the kinds of questions, ranging from the important to the trivial, that pop up every day in the news business. If you're like most of us, your first impulse will be to shout around the newsroom in hopes that someone will know the answer. The answer you usually get is, "The train would be going east—*I think.*" So you end up looking up the information anyway, which is what you should have done in the first place. For some reason, that short trip across the newsroom to the reference shelf seems like a major undertaking.

Save yourself the trip by buying a world almanac. There are several published each year. The publishers change frequently; past almanacs have been issued by CBS News, *The New York Times,* the *Washington Post,* and the Associated Press, among others. They all provide the same basic facts and figures. Just be sure the one you buy includes world maps of sufficient detail to enable you to tell listeners which way that train was going.

Computer Data Systems

Computers are now part of the newsroom landscape. Even if a broadcast news department is not entirely "computerized" (and many are not), you are still likely to find a computer workstation nearby that will enable you to do research without going to the library. The terminal may be linked to "Compu-Serve," "Nexis," or other commercial database services. Obviously, you must know how to use the system. If accessing computer systems is still a mystery to you, you must become "computer literate" as soon as possible, or you will be at a disadvantage in today's professional marketplace.

ASKING FOR HELP

Although your personal and shared reference works will answer your questions in most cases, the nature of the news business is such that sooner or later (probably sooner) you will be stumped by something or other. It won't be long before you come upon a story you don't quite understand and be expected to rewrite it in broadcast style. Well, don't fret. No journalist, no matter how long his or her experience, can be expected to understand every bit of information flooding the newsroom. The world is too complex. And yet the job requires explaining and simplifying that complexity for a mass audience. So what to do?

The solution lies in teamwork. The newsroom, like the classroom, is a shared experience. If you can't solve a problem by looking things up in reference books or accessing the "help" menu in the computer, ask a fellow student or your instructor. It is not stupid not to know something. It is stupid not to seek help.

Possibly, that help may be slow in coming. If so, be patient. And above all, *do not write a story you do not understand!* That's because if *you* don't understand it, chances are the *audience* won't understand it either. It is far, far better to make the audience wait than to pass along false information.

EXERCISES

1. Get to know what's on the radio! "Prime Time" on radio is in the morning, weekdays from 5 A.M. to 9 A.M. (Professionals refer to this period as "Morning Drive," because of the large number of car radios in use then. A secondary high-listening period on radio is from 4 P.M. to 7 P.M.—called "Evening Drive," again because of the large numbers of commuters driving home from work.) Scan the AM and FM bands to familiarize yourself with the local stations in your area that carry network newscasts (from ABC, CBS, "Morning Edition" on NPR, etc.) and/or locally produced newscasts, including all-news stations (if available in your area). Once you know the various radio news sources at your command, choose two or three that appeal to you, and listen to them every morning.

   (You may be in the habit of tuning your television to one of the network morning programs. If so, switch to morning radio for the time being.)

2. Pay attention to the opening words of each story, making mental notes of the different approaches used by different news organizations. At the same time, pay attention to the rhythm of the words and sentences. This may be difficult at first, because the art of good broadcast newswriting is to make listeners unaware that deliberate techniques are being used to compel their attention.

3. Read a morning newspaper thoroughly. Every day. You'll soon find that much of what you read is already "old news"—you already heard later information on the radio. However, the newspaper stories will be longer. They will include details omitted from the broadcast stories. They will probably also include analysis and interpretation for which there was no time on radio. Even though you may never have time to include this kind of material in stories you write for broadcast, it is important to know it; it forms part of your foundation of knowledge and helps you develop good news judgment.

4. Try to listen to radio newscasts periodically throughout the day, both on commercial radio and on NPR's "All Things Considered." If you carry a Walkman-type radio, so much the better. By late afternoon you should have an excellent idea of the day's major news stories.

5. Reserve time to watch at least two network evening TV newscasts—"NBC Nightly News," "CBS Evening News," "ABC World News Tonight," "CNN Prime News," or "The MacNeil/Lehrer NewsHour" on PBS. *Prepare* to watch them by predicting (1) the lead story and (2) which stories will be included. Were you right about the lead and the

story selection? In your opinion, did the network news producers make the right choices? (You may wish to substitute competing local TV newscasts for the network ones; however, as models of good writing and experienced news judgment, the network programs, as a rule, are far superior.)

6. Try to predict which of the stories you've just watched will appear on the front page of the next morning's newspaper. And try to think of good follow-up stories for the next day: What elements are still hanging unresolved? What things are interesting and vital enough to learn more about and possibly include in the following day's news? In short, if you were running a news department, what coverage decisions would you make?

3

Sources of News

A few explanations are necessary about the raw materials this book uses as models for examining the elements of broadcast style. Like biologists, we shall be dissecting laboratory specimens in order to fully understand the organism and its mutation into another form.

Radio and television stations get their news from the same primary sources as do newspapers, but the media utilize these sources quite differently. Broadcast news departments produce their newscasts from a combination of editorial and visual material gathered by their own personnel and that furnished by news agencies (also called "wire services," even though modern technology has done away with most of the "wires") and other suppliers.

The economics of "electronic" journalism makes the mix of these primary sources quite different in broadcasting from print. As a percentage of overall investment, broadcasters spend more on hardware than do newspapers. By and large, they thus spend relatively less on editorial personnel. A big-city radio or TV station typically has far fewer reporters and writers than does the same city's major newspaper. It takes a single newspaper or radio reporter to cover a routine story; a TV reporter is accompanied by a camera crew lugging thousands of dollars worth of sensitive equipment. The newspaper or radio reporter can call in the story over the nearest telephone; the TV crew requires a van equipped with editing and transmitting gear worth many more thousands of dollars.

Because they must cover the same territory, the result is that, like small-town newspapers, radio and TV stations rely to an enormous extent on news agencies to provide them with the basic stories that they will "repackage" for broadcast.

This book makes widespread use of such news agency copy—for the simple and practical reason that it represents by far the largest single type of basic material with which broadcast newswriters, editors, and producers must work. News agency copy is the clay from which broadcasters mold what we have been calling "broadcast style."

NEWS AGENCIES

News agencies began in the nineteenth century as cooperative efforts by newspapers to help fill the enormous gaps in news they could not cover by their own separate efforts. The first major news agencies were European: Havas (French), founded in 1835; Wolff (German), founded in 1849; and Reuters (British), in 1851. Of the three, only Reuters survives today as a major international news service.

In the United States, two major news agencies date from that early period: the Associated Press (AP), begun in the 1870s, and United Press (UP), founded in 1882. In somewhat different form, these two agencies are with us today. The Associated Press is a nonprofit cooperative financed by its many thousands of subscribers in print, broadcasting, and industry. By contrast, UPI (United Press International), as it now calls itself, is a for-profit agency whose services are sold to compete with those of AP. (UPI has often been on the brink of bankruptcy; in the 1980s, it underwent a series of cutbacks, reorganizations, and ownership changes.)

Perhaps nowhere in journalism is the competition to report the news more fierce than between AP and UPI. Part of that fierceness evolved as the result of the growth of broadcast news. Newspapers have deadlines, to be sure, but broadcasters have far more of them, requiring a relentless stream of updates, rewrites, and "exclusive" angles. In order to keep their competitive edge—and give broadcasters what they wanted—AP and UPI underwent two major operational changes: First, they expanded their services to offer broadcast-oriented material; and second, they entered the space age by transmitting their material "the modern way"—by satellite, computer, laser, and high-speed printer.

Today both AP and UPI offer a vast array of services, including audio and video material, in addition to the written news itself. Some services are devoted entirely to sports news, others entirely to financial news. Further, many of the services are tailored for local and regional use. Thus, the types of news agency services you encounter at one radio or TV station may be quite different from those at another station. Obviously, space does not permit us to review all these services, but we will include examples of many of them, including sports and financial news. We will introduce the basic services at length, because they are the ones you are most likely to encounter in your school or first professional newsroom.

Print-Style Agency Services

All radio and TV networks, as well as most stations located in major metropolitan areas, subscribe to the so-called newspaper wire of each agency. This used to be called the "A wire" because it was the agency's main transmission service for the most important world and national news. (Features and less important news were carried on other wires designated "B," "C," and so forth.) Previous broadcast subscribers to the A wire are now likely to receive a wire such as the Associated Press's "APTV," a high-speed service combining the major news written in print style and local/regional inserts often written in broadcast style.

These agency services are organized, edited, and transmitted in AM and PM cycles geared to newspaper deadlines (the AM cycle is aimed at morning newspapers and thus transmitted during the afternoon and evening hours; the PM cycle is for afternoon papers and thus transmitted during the morning hours). The stories tend to be long and full of detail. For radio and TV, they must be rewritten in broadcast style and, as we've seen, condensed radically. Networks and major local stations want a newspaper wire precisely because the color and detail offer their newswriters the opportunity to tailor their rewrites for their own audiences—in effect, to make them sound "original."

Let's take a look at a lengthy chunk of recent AP newspaper-wire material as it moved over a printer:

```
A233
     U 1 BYLZYVZYV A0588
AM--Turkey--Quake, 1st Ld, a222, 230
Eds: Death toll climbs to 509. Survivors endangered by cold.
By Ismail Kovaci
Associated Press Writer
     ISTANBUL, Turkey (AP)--A major earthquake struck eastern
Turkey early Sunday and officials said at least 509 people
were killed. Newspapers said 50 villages were leveled, and the
death toll was expected to climb.
     About three hours earlier a quake rolled through the
Hindu Kush mountain range, 1,400 miles to the east on the
border between Afghanistan and Pakistan, shaking Islamabad and
reaching as far as India's Kashmir state. There were no
immediate reports of casualties or damage. More than 12 hours
later, a strong quake shook southwestern Japan, but no
casualties were reported.
     The devastating quake struck Turkey at 7:12 A.M. (11:12
P.M. EST Saturday) and was felt in mountainous provinces
bordering Iran, Syria and Iraq.
     Nightfall and intermittent snowfall in several areas
hampered rescue efforts. A local army corps mobilized all its
soldiers to help survivors and clear debris in communities
reached earlier in the day.
     Dropping temperatures threatened thousands of homeless
survivors in remote towns, local officials said. Temperatures
of 35 degrees Fahrenheit were expected.
     Authorities said the quake was believed to be centered in
Erzurum and Kars provinces, where most of the damage was done,
but it also shook the provinces of Bitlis, Mus, Dyarbakir,
Bingol, Van and Malatya, according to the martial law command
of the eastern region.
     Journalists in: 6th graf
ap-ny-10-30 1738EST

A235
     U 1 BYLZYVWYF A0568
```

AM--Grenada--Press, Bjt, 560
American Commander Battling Snipers, Reporters
      By Kernan Turner
Associated Press Writer
      BRIDGETOWN, Barbados (AP)--The U.S. military commander of
the Grenada Task Force is f
Bust It
ap-ny-10-30 1757EST

A236
      B A BYLZYVVYX A0615
AM--Obit--Lillian Carter, 30
Bulletin
      AMERICUS, Ga. (AP)--Lillian Carter, the mother of former
President Jimmy Carter, died Sunday in Americus-Sumter County
Hospital at age 85, officials said.
      More
ap-ny-10-30 1758EST

A237
      U 1 BYLZYVEEV A0572
AM--Missing Ship, 340
No Sign of Missing Oil Drilling Ship
      PEKING (AP)--Searchers turned up no further signs Sunday
of an American oil drilling ship or its 81 crewmen, missing
since a typhoon five days ago in the South China Sea.
      "Unfortunately, these searches are sometimes a long and
hard job," said U.S. Air Force Senior Master Sgt. Bill Barclay
at the West Pacific rescue coordination center on Okinawa.
      Early Sunday, four ships searched an area where a plane
had spotted what might have been survivors, but found nothing,
said Air Force Lt. Col. Jack Gregory of the rescue center.
      "It doesn't mean they aren't there: but we haven't found
them," he said.
      Barclay said two U.S. Navy P-3 planes continued to take
turns searching for the 5,926-ton Glomar Java Sea, which had
been drilling for oil south of China's Hainan Island before
Typhoon Lex hit it with 75 mph winds.
      The ship, carrying 42 Americans, 35 Chinese, two
Singaporeans, an Australian and a Filipino, was doing the
exploration for Arco China Inc., a U.S. company working under
contract with China.
      The ship's Houston-based owner, Global Marine Inc., said
in Hong Kong that the sighting of what might have been two or
three survivors was made about 60 miles northwest of the
drilling location.
      Gregory said three Chinese ships and a vessel belonging
to Global Marine, the Salvanquish, went to the area.
      Earlier, China's official Xinhua news agency said China
had sent four ships to find a life raft flashing distress
signals in the area.
      There was no word from Chinese officials Sunday on any
findings. There also was no report on a Chinese ship that went
to investigate a large undersea object with sonar equipment
and underwater television apparatus.
      The object, discovered near the drilling site with sonar
equipment, was reportedly about 328 feet long, 164 feet wide
and 66 feet high, about the size of the missing ship.

So far, searchers have reported finding two fenders from
the missing ship, more than 10 life jackets and an empty life
raft.
ap-ny-10-30 1805EST

A238
        U 1 BYLZYVRYR A0235
AM--Grenada--Press, Bjt, 560
American Commander Battling Snipers, Reporters
        By Kernan Turner
Associated Press Writer
        BRIDGETOWN, Barbados (AP)--The U.S. military commander of
the Grenada Task Force is fighting two battles--one with the
resistance on the island and another with the frustrated
international press trying to cover the invasion.
        Vice Adm. Joseph Metcalf III says he has ordered naval
patrol boats to shoot at unauthorized small craft attempting
to land reporters and photographers on Grenada. Journal
Bust It
ap-ny-10-30 1807EST

A239
        U A BYLZYVQYV A0617
AM--Obit--Lillian Carter, 1st Add, a236
,110
Urgent
        AMERICUS, Ga.: Officials said.
        Mrs. Carter had been at the hospital for about a week.
The former president and his wife, Rosalynn, had been at the
hospital for the day.
        "Miss Lillian," as her neighbors in Plains, Ga., called
her, lived on the fringes of politics for most of her life.
        Her father, Jim Jack Gordy, a postmaster, never ran for
office. But she recalled during an interview in 1976 that he
"was the best, biggest politician in this part of the world.
He kept up with politics so closely that he could tell
you--almost within five votes--what the people who were
running would get in the next election."
        More
af-ny-10-30 1810EST

A240
        R 1 BYLUIVCZC A0614
AM--Grenada--Press, 560
American Commander Battling Snipers, Reporters
        By Kernan Turner
Associated Press Writer
        BRIDGETOWN, Barbados (AP)--The U.S. military commander of
the Grenada Task Force is fighting two battles--one with the
resistance on the island and another with the frustrated
international press trying to cover the invasion.
        Vice Adm. Joseph Metcalf III says he has ordered naval
patrol boats to shoot at unauthorized small craft attempting
to land reporters and photographers on Grenada. Journalists
presume he is joking.
        Metcalf, commander of the 15,000-member invasion force,
also has rejected complaints from the press about

restrictions, saying he is protecting reporters' lives by not granting them free access to the island.

Dressed in a beribboned white uniform, Metcalf told reporters at a news conference Saturday to stop trying to take their complaints to a higher authority.

"The buck stops with me. If you want to argue with somebody about it, you've got to argue with me, not the D.O.D. (Department of Defense), not anybody else but me," he said.

Earlier in the day, when he was wearing a jumpsuit and visored cap, Metcalf greeted a pool of reporters in Grenada on a closely guarded visit to the embattled island.

"Any of you guys coming in on press boats?" Metcalf asked. "Well, I know how to stop those press boats. We've been shooting at them. We haven't sunk any yet, but how are we to know who's on them?"

A number of tired correspondents have returned to Bridgetown after hiring boats that were turned away off the coast of Grenada by Navy warships, but there have been no reports of journalists ducking U.S. bullets.

Metcalf, a native of Holyoke, Mass., is a 1951 graduate of the U.S. Naval Academy. He is commander of the 2nd Fleet.

The commander's encounters with journalists have revealed a tough yet good-natured personality. He greets those on the pool tours at planeside, shaking hands and asking their names.

But when pressed for specific information, he often says, "I haven't the foggiest idea." He told one pack of perplexed reporters, "I love that quote."

On some occasions, he has misled reporters. When asked about the capture Saturday of Bernard Coard, the politician believed to have provoked the events leading to the slaying of Prime Minister Maurice Bishop, Metcalf at first told a news conference that Grenadians had detained Coard.

Told that a Marine officer had described to the press pool how Coard had been surrounded by Marines in a hideout and ordered to come out of the house or get blown up, Metcalf said, "Ok, let's be technical, Ok?"

Pressed further by the reporters, Metcalf acknowledged that he was at a Marine command post when Coard was brought in and was aware that the Marines had captured him.

Despite his restrictions, Metcalf insists he wants "the news media to get on with the legitimate business of public information."

Metcalf accepted full responsibility for keeping reporters out of Grenada despite "enormous pressure from Washington to get reporters in there" and called himself the journalists' "best friend."

"I want to get you there, but by golly: I'm going to insist that you can be supported when you get there," Metcalf said,

"I'm not a dog in the manger," he said. "You may think I am, but I'm really not."
ap-ny-10-30 1820EST

A241
    U A BYLUIVZVT A0619
AM--Obit--Lillian Carter, 2nd Add, a239 ,a236,170
Urgent
AMERICUS, Ga.: next election.

Mrs. Carter was offered her husband's seat in the Georgia Legislature when he died during his first term in 1953, but she declined.

"I was too shocked by his death," she said later. "But I think if later they offered the legislature seat to me again, I would have taken it."

A graveside service for Mrs. Carter will be at 3 P.M. Tuesday at the Lebanon Cemetery in Plains.

Mrs. Carter had 15 grandchildren and eight great-grandchildren.

She campaigned actively for her son when he ran for governor of Georgia in 1970, but her role in his 1976 presidential campaign, when he lost to Ronald Reagan, was more sedate. Her job was to care for granddaughter Amy, then 8, the only Carter child left at home.

It was the second death in the family in just over a month. Evangelist Ruth Carter Stapleton, Carter's sister, died Sept. 26 at age 54 after a months-long struggle with pancreatic cancer.

        More
ap-ny-10-30 1824EST

A242
        U A BYLUIVBYL A0622
AM--Obit--Lillian Carter, 3rd Add, A241, A239, A236, 200
Urgent
AMERICUS, Ga.: Pancreatic cancer.

In 1964, Mrs. Carter was a delegate to the Democratic National Convention and was asked to serve as co-chairman of Lyndon B. Johnson's local campaign headquarters.

"At that time, people around here didn't like Johnson because he was for blacks," she once said. "Anyway, I was delighted to do it, took the job and the blacks had access to the office over at the hotel just like the whites."

Mrs. Carter was known for being liberal about race in an era when most of her neighbors were exactly the opposite.

A registered nurse, she used her knowledge of medicine to help many poor blacks in Plains.

Carter recalled that his mother "taught us by her daily example to help the weak and handicapped even when it wasn't the comfortable or socially acceptable thing to do."

Born Aug. 15, 1898, in Richland, Ga., about 20 miles from Plains, Mrs. Carter attended public schools there and studied nursing at the now-defunct Wise Clinic in Plains. She earned her nursing degree at Grady Memorial Hospital in Atlanta.

She married James Earl Carter Sr., a peanut farmer and businessman, in 1923.
ap-ny-10-30 1828EST

Allowing for one lengthy story that has been omitted here, that's approximately 40 minutes' worth. The copy has been reproduced at length to give you a feel for this kind of basic raw material and to demonstrate some of the things that broadcast newswriters have to watch out for.

First, let's make sure you understand what you are seeing, going back to the start of the series, numbered "A233." Each story, you will have noticed, begins with a number. That is how this particular version of the wire story will be referred to in any upcoming additions, revisions, or corrections.

Just underneath is "U 1 BYLZYVZYV A0588." It's an internal AP code.

Next, "AM—Turkey—Quake, 1st Ld." "AM" means the wire is sending its stories for next morning's newspapers. "Turkey—Quake" is the slug, and "1st Ld" (short for "First Lead") means the story contains the latest information that the agency could find. This may be updated by later stories for the AM cycle; if so, they will be denoted "2nd Ld," "3rd Ld," and so on.

Next, on the same line, see "A222, 230." The first number, A222, is the number of the previous story on the Turkey Quake, which A233 updates. The second number, 230, is the number of words in A233, rounded off to the nearest 10.

The next line, beginning "Eds: Death toll climbs . . . ," calls writers' and editors' attention to the specific information making this story newsworthy.

Underneath this is the AP writer's byline. Then follows the story proper.

Skip now to the end of the story, where you find the words "Journalists in: 6th graf." This tells you that you will find the rest of the story by going back to the sixth paragraph of A222, which begins "Journalists in," and picking up the copy from there.

Now the final line: "ap-ny-10-30 1738EST." "ap" is obvious. "ny" is the identification of the AP bureau from which the story was edited and transmitted, in this case New York. "10-30" is the date, October 30. And "1738EST" is the exact time, based on a 24-hour clock, that the story was "timed off," the time transmission of that story ended, including the time zone: 5:38 P.M. Eastern Standard Time.

With minor variations, the organization of UPI's wire resembles AP's. Each gives specific directions, in highly abbreviated form, to guide editors and re-writers to find things quickly.

Now while this may be "old hat" to those of you who have worked or interned on newspapers, for most of you it is new and perhaps a bit complicated. So take a few moments and go back over the material provided. If you ever hope to reach the higher echelons of the broadcast news business (networks and major markets) where such wire service material is common, you will have to learn how to read it quickly. A professional radio or TV journalist would be expected to be able to scan all the foregoing material, and know what to save for broadcast rewrite, in just a minute or two.

Broadcast-Style Services

If you decide to enter broadcast news, chances are you will begin at a small station that does not buy a newspaper-style agency service. With its limited budget, the station cannot afford (or doesn't want to spend the money) to hire enough staff to rewrite it for broadcast. Instead, the station opts to buy one or two news agency services offering material already rewritten in broadcast style. This permits staffers to concentrate on gathering and writing local news while airing the agency-written versions of world and national stories.

Before examining the advantages and disadvantages of broadcast-wire material, let's look at some of it. The following AP "Newswatch" (an hourly summary) utilizes material from the foregoing newspaper-wire copy:

```
V2307
R D
AP-19th Newswatch
```

Here is the latest news from the associated press:

Officials in Americus, Georgia say that Lillian Carter--mother of former President Jimmy Carter--has died at the age of 85. Mrs. Carter had been in the hospital for about a week--although there's no immediate word on the cause of her death. It's the second death in the Carter family in just over a month. The former president's sister--Evangelist Ruth Carter Stapleton--died of cancer on September 26th.

It looks like one of the administration's main stated reasons for invading Grenada (Gruh-nay'-duh) wasn't much of a reason at all. All along: officials have been saying they were afraid the U-S citizens on the island were in danger of being taken hostage, but U-S intelligence sources are now saying there was no clear evidence that such a turn of events was likely.

According to a top U-S official, the U-S forces in Grenada have uncovered some secret documents about Grenada's relations with other communist nations. Deputy Secretary of State Kenneth Dam says the papers show Grenada entered into military supply agreements with Cuba, North Korea and the Soviet Union. He made the comment on the C-B-S program "Face the Nation."

Authorities in Turkey report more than 500 deaths as a result of a major earthquake that struck early today. Newspapers say 50 of Turkey's villages were leveled. According to officials, cold and snow in many areas are hampering rescue efforts and are likely to cause more deaths.

A scientist with the government's Hawaiian volcano observatory says Hawaii's Kilauea (Kih-luh-way'-uh) volcano is ready to erupt again. Kilauea's last eruption ended on October seventh. The geologist says molten rock continues to collect at the volcano's summit--and the next wave of volcanic activity could come at any time.

```
V2309
R D
AP-19TH Newswatch-Take 2
```

Last week, the citizen-labor energy coalition was telling natural gas customers that they can look for their bills to rise an average of 21 percent this winter. Today, the consumer and labor organization says the study that produced the figure was wrong. The coalition says there were errors involving 20 of the 80 cities studied.

```
     Hospital officials in Fort Lee, New Jersey report the
death of pioneer animator Otto Messmer. He was 91. Messmer was
the creator of "Felix the Cat"--although it was the studio he
worked for and not Messmer who got the credit.

     The tiny village of Lijar in Southern Spain has
apparently decided to let bygones be bygones. The villagers
have signed a peace treaty with France--ending what was
officially 100 years of war between the small town and the
neighboring country. The whole thing started in 1883 when the
king of Spain was insulted and hit with stones in Paris. The
war was declared to defend the king's honor--and ended today
with a festive ceremony.

APTV-10-30 1841EST
```

A staffer at a small radio or TV station can simply rip that copy off the printer (or command a computer printout) and read it on the air as is, bypassing the rewriting process. But this is a mixed blessing, especially in a competitive environment.

The advantages of broadcast-style wire services:

1. The station saves money by not having to hire writers.
2. Staffers save time; they are able to assemble newscasts quickly.
3. The copy is easy to read at a glance—no complicated editorial directions to follow.
4. Staffers can devote full attention to covering and writing local news.

The disadvantages:

1. Every station airing the copy unedited sounds identical. You can switch to another station and hear the news told in exactly the same words.
2. Each story tends to have the same length. The news delivery thus sounds static and without variety. Many broadcasters believe this fails to hold the audience's interest.
3. Broadcast wires fail to exploit immediacy (broadcasting's inherent speed) because they are *slower* to move major-breaking stories. Go back to the initial newspaper-wire bulletin (A236) slugged "Obit—Lillian Carter." Note that it was timed off at 5:58 P.M. Now look at how it moved on the broadcast wire:

```
V2295
U A
AP-U r g e n t

Lillian Carter
     (Americus, Georgia)--Officials say Lillian Carter, the
mother of former President Jimmy Carter, died today in
Americus-Sumter County Hospital in Georgia at age 85.
APTV-10-30 1802EST
```

Note that that version was timed off at 6:02 P.M.—four minutes *later* than the newspaper-wire version. In radio news, those four minutes constitute the difference between getting the story on the 6 P.M. news and having to wait until the next newscast. And in TV news, the station with the newspaper wire can get the story on the air four minutes sooner than the station with only the broadcast wire. In competitive broadcast journalism, those four minutes count.

4. Staffers at stations with only the broadcast wires find it next to impossible to be creative or original because they lack the color and detail with which to be inventive. For example, no further details on the Lillian Carter obit moved on the broadcast wire until 6:41 P.M.—39 minutes after its first report. But the newspaper wire moved sufficient details at 6:10 P.M. (in A239) to support the following rewrite:

```
Miss Lillian Carter died a short time ago in Americus, Georgia.  Her

son, former President Jimmy Carter, was at her bedside.
```

The writer was able to lift out this latter detail and thus make his or her station's version sound different and original—and do it half an hour before a staffer at a station without the newspaper wire.

The reason for the transmission delay of the broadcast wire is that its writers and editors must usually wait to see the newspaper wire version before they can set to work. Truly competitive news departments can't afford to wait. They want to beat the competition, and thus they rely on their own staffers to do it.

In sum: You can't learn to write effectively in broadcast style unless your source material is rich in detail. In broadcast news departments, your source material will be of two basic types: stories you cover yourself, either in person or by phone, and then write for broadcast; or stories from news agencies to be rewritten for broadcast. Because only print-style wires carry enough detail to stimulate the creative writing juices, this book relies heavily on print-style models. From these and other sources, we shall go step by step through journalism's Who, What, When, Where, and Why, showing how to transform stodgy print style into easygoing broadcast style.

Local Agency Services

Many large metropolitan areas have home-grown news agencies usually called City News or City News Bureau. These began as cooperatives among local newspapers and are now supported as well by radio and TV stations. Again, their purpose is to provide reliable coverage of local and regional events beyond the personnel limitations of any single news organization.

As a rule, extreme care must be taken in handling copy from such local agencies. Most of them operate on a shoestring. Typically, they serve as training grounds for print journalists who are just out of school and still wet behind the ears. The copy tends to be poorly written, unclear, inexact, and convoluted to the extreme.

That said, such city wires are also extremely valuable. They provide coverage of the nitty-gritty news stories that many big newspapers and broadcasters tend to neglect, sometimes to their dismay and regret: the "routine" homicide that turns out to be a VIP, the "routine" political campaign speech that turns out to be a bombshell, the "routine" court trial that reveals the appearance of a surprise witness, and so on.

In addition, city wires serve as conduits for the scheduling of events, from news conferences to rallies and marches. A single call to a city wire from a newsmaker or would-be newsmaker ensures that word of the upcoming event will get to just about every newsroom in town, enabling coverage to be planned ahead of time.

Handling Agency Copy

In writing news stories in broadcast style, you may often become frustrated by broadcasting's time constraints. The requirement to boil down a story to its essence to be able to tell it in 20, 30, or 40 seconds means that you will often have to omit details that are merely interesting in favor of those that are vital. But consider this: in broadcasting, you will be required to write many different versions of the same story; in TV you will write at least two or three (for the Early News and then for the Late News), and in radio perhaps as many as six or eight versions. By striving to make each version different, you can include some details in one that you left out of another, and so on down the line. By the end of your workday, you can have the feeling that, taken as a whole, your efforts did justice to that day's news. On the other hand, sometimes you'll just have to shrug and say, "I did what I could, under the circumstances."

Broadcast newswriters, reporters, and producers can easily fall into a dangerous trap. They can become so used to the requirement for brevity that they get in the bad habit of reading only the first few paragraphs of a news agency story. They come to think, "Well, since I haven't got time to tell this story fully, why should I bother to fill my head with details I won't have time to include?" That's a bad work habit because news agency copy often contains buried details that can provide you with a fresh lead, an arresting detail, or a local angle. Such buried information may reveal just the right peg on which to hang your own version of the story. Therefore, it is important to read news agency copy *all the way through;* only then are you properly ready to start writing.

You must also learn to regard news agency copy with a wary eye. Remember, such copy is often written in haste, because the agency is in competition with other agencies and news providers. Like you, agency writers are only human and subject to error. In particular, you should watch out for the following:

1. *Casualty figures.* Do they add up? Do the numbers of dead and injured reported in the lead correspond to the numbers given in the body of the story?
2. *Names, titles, and identifications.* Is an official or politician's title, party, or state given correctly?

3. *Unsubstantiated leads.* Do the facts of a story, as reported in its body, support the lead sentence or paragraph? Is there a quote or substantial paraphrase to back up the writer's interpretation of someone's remarks?

4. *Buried leads.* Did the agency writer pick the newsiest story element for the lead, or, in your opinion, did he or she "bury" it somewhere in the body of the story?

5. *Buried sources.* What is the real source of the news agency story? Is the reporting original, or is it based on a secondary source (such as a publication or independent study) identified somewhere in the body of the story? (The broadcast version should identify the true source.)

6. *Unnamed sources.* Are there tipoff phrases such as "It was learned today" or "According to congressional sources"? In other words, do you think the story is trustworthy? (If there is doubt, you should identify the news agency as the source: "AP reports that . . ." or "Sources quoted by the Associated Press say . . . ," etc.)

EXERCISES

1. Arrange to visit the news departments of at least one local radio station and one local TV station. (If you call ahead and explain you are a journalism student, you will most likely be welcomed.) In addition to observing (unobtrusively, please) how staffers go about their various tasks, familiarize yourself with each station's sources of news. Which services do they buy? Which would they add? Which would they drop?

2. If neither of the stations has a computerized newsroom, try also to visit one that has "gone electronic." Ask to see the mix of news agency services available for call-up on-screen, and compare it with the mix of services in the nonelectronic newsroom.

Copy Preparation

Now we are ready to examine the first set of rules governing broadcast style: how the words should be arranged on copy paper or computer screen.

Although most broadcast newsrooms are "electronic playgrounds" with the latest gadgets to record, edit, and transmit sounds and pictures, many have been slow to computerize the word processing functions of newscast preparation. A modern newspaper relies on powerful mainframe computers and networked workstations to receive news agency copy, write and edit copy from reporters and copyeditors, and to format page layout. In recent years, a growing number of broadcast news departments have installed similar mainframes, customized for the requirements of newscast preparation. However, many broadcast newsrooms still rely on the older method of preparing newscast scripts on 8½-by-11 inch copy paper with manual or electric typewriters.

At the college level where broadcast journalism is taught, only a handful of universities have had the resources to install professional-style computer systems. Many schools do have personal computers (PCs), some of them networked, enabling students to write and edit stories on the screen and to print out clean copies. But most rely on the older typewriter-and-copy-paper method.

The older method is not a disadvantage for learning. For, whether by computer or on paper, the finished product looks essentially the same. The rules regarding copy appearance are virtually identical. It is, of course, much easier to rewrite (that is, edit and correct) a story by computer. And the final printout is always clean—free of messy and distracting corrections. Students and professionals using paper and typewriters spend a lot of time on clerical tasks (mainly retyping) that the computer eliminates. To save themselves from clerical drudgery, they are thus forced to weigh their words carefully before committing them to paper. And that is a good habit to get into, regardless of the system you use.

A few words of warning: If you don't know how to type, you are in big trouble. You *must* be able to type—or forget about working in journalism. It doesn't matter whether you are a touch typist or a two-finger "hunt-and-peck" typist. Without typing ability, you are a journalistic illiterate, and no one will ever hire you for any kind of editorial position. (You may, however, become a video-tape photographer or tape editor.)

USING TYPEWRITER AND COPY PAPER

Although there are minor variations in copy appearance in different news organizations, the following rules are standard throughout the profession:

1. Use plain, unruled 8½-by-11-inch white, ivory, or buff-colored paper.
2. Type only one story per page.
3. Use only one side of the paper, leaving the reverse side blank.
4. Use 10-pitch (pica) typeface. (Elite, or 12-pitch, is too small to sight-read.)
5. Use a 70-space line for radio; 35-space line for television.
   (For radio, set left margin at 10; right margin at 80.)
   (For TV scripting, set the left margin at 42; the right margin at 80.)
6. Double- or triple-space. This leaves adequate room to type or write in minor corrections. (Many standard typewriters do not have settings for triple-space; in this case use the maximum allowable, which is very often the "2½" setting.)
7. Leave a top margin of at least 1½ inches. This allows room for the writer's name, the date, and the air time of the newscast (which go in the extreme upper left), the slug (a one- or two-word identification of the story), and the running time of the story.
8. Type all copy in upper/lower case—*not* all caps or all lowercase. As we will see, this permits maximum flexibility in providing eye-oriented punctuation, pronunciation help, and technical instructions.
9. Do *not* split or hyphenate words between lines. Split words are difficult for the anchor's eyes to follow, thus causing announcing errors.
10. Do *not* split sentences between pages. Do not force the anchor to switch pages with the end of a sentence still hanging, which also leads to announcing errors.
11. Do *not* use print copyediting symbols. Correct errors by striking out the entire erroneous word, then retype or print the correct word just above the strikeout. Make corrections with a dark-leaded copy pencil or medium-point blue or black ballpoint pen (not a felt-tip or fountain pen). Do not use colored inks, crayons, or any pen or pencil with a fine point. Corrections should be bold and easy to read. If handwritten, use block lettering, *not* longhand.

No: The brown quick fox jumped over the lazy dog.

Yes: The ~~brown quick~~ *quick brown* fox jumped ~~over~~ *over* the lazy ~~dig~~ *dog.*

No: The quick ~~black~~ *brown* fox jumped over the lazy ~~cat~~ *Dog.*

Yes: The quick ~~black~~ *brown* fox jumped over the lazy ~~cat~~ *dog.*

Yes: The quick brown fox jumped over the lazy dog.
             ~~The brown quick fox jumped over the lazy dig.~~

12. If a sentence or page contains enough corrections to make sight-reading difficult, retype the *entire* sentence or, if necessary, the *entire* page.

13. If a story is so long that it must be continued onto a second page, indicate "more" by drawing a bold arrow toward the lower right corner of the first page. That is broadcasting's way of saying "more" or "continued."

          Once again today, Demjanjuk proclaimed his innocence.   The
     death sentence now goes before the Israeli High Court of Appeals.

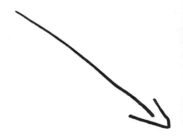

14. It is *not* necessary to type "30" (or "-0-," "#," or any word or symbol) to indicate the end of a story. If there is no arrow, the anchor knows the next page will contain a new story.

15. Do not clip, staple, tape, or paste pages together. Script pages must remain freely interchangeable and be of uniform size.

16. For the most accurate timing of your completed story, read it aloud briskly, using a stopwatch or the chronograph function of a digital wrist watch. Enter the timing, rounded off to the nearest :05 seconds, in the upper right corner of the page, and circle it.

As a rough guide, figure that each regulation line of radio copy equals :03 seconds, and that each two lines of TV copy equals :03 seconds. Thus, a one-minute (:60) story will require about 18 to 20 lines of radio copy, and 35 to 40 lines of TV copy.

Your completed typewritten radio copy should resemble the following model:

Bard, 5/13, 1p

(:35)

DEMJANJUK

    An Israeli court today sentenced John Demjanjuk (Dem-YAHN-yook) to death by hanging for crimes at a World War Two concentration camp. The court said Demjanjuk's crimes were so horrible they can never be forgotten or forgiven.

    Demjanjuk, now 68, is a native of the Ukraine. He spent more than 30 years in the Cleveland area before being deported for trial in Israel. Witnesses identified him as a camp guard known as "Ivan the Terrible" because of his savage cruelty to prisoners. They testified he ran the gas chambers at Treblinka, Poland, where more than 800-thousand people were murdered, most of them Jews.

    Once again today, Demjanjuk proclaimed his innocence. The death sentence now goes before the Israeli High Court of Appeals.

USING COMPUTERS

Except for rule 8, typing in upper/lower case, which remains a choice for the individual writer, all the foregoing rules are programmed into newsroom computers. Thus, it is only if you want your copy to look different on the final printout that you must give a specific command to override the preset form; for example, if you want the printout single-spaced or in boldface.

In addition, the computer is programmed to time your copy cumulatively as you write it; you will not have to time your story afterwards by counting lines or reading aloud (although reading it aloud is definitely advisable to judge how it will sound on the air). At the press of a specified key, usually designated "New Story," the screen will show a template similar to this one:

```
 PG_____    _____    #_____VO_____SND_____CUME__0:00_____

  SHOW_____  COPY__0:00_ WTR_Bard____ KT_____ ANC_____ DATE__May_21_09:31
================================================================================
```

Note that the template already contains the date, the hour (based on a 24-hour clock) and, because you have logged in under a personal access code, your name (in this case "Bard"). It remains for you to fill in the page number (which may or may not be known as you write), the slug, the identification of any taped material you will be incorporating into your story, the internal time of such material, the scheduled air time of the newscast your story is for, and the name of the anchor who will be reading the story on the air.

In short, the computer does most of the clerical work for you, saving time and effort. It even times your copy to the exact second (instead of rounded off to the nearest 5 seconds), at the reading speed of the anchor whose name you have entered. If no anchor's name is entered, the computer will time your copy at a "normal" delivery speed of about 180 words per minute. All your corrections, revisions, and rewriting are done on the screen, and when you "Save" the finished story, the computer stores it along with other stories destined for the same newscast, until the "Print" command is given shortly before air time. The printed script thus produced is always clean. Its only drawbacks (both minor) are that computerized newsrooms use high-speed dot matrix printers with continuous-feed paper; the resulting printout is less sharp than the letter-quality print produced by a manual, electric, or electronic typewriter, and the script pages must be separated manually.

The computer printout will resemble this one:

```
PG_____    _DEMJANJUK_____    #_____VO_____SND_____CUME__0:33_____

SHOW_1p____ COPY__0:33_ WTR_Bard____ KT_____ ANC_____ DATE__May 21 09:39
==============================================================================



          An Israeli court today sentenced John Demjanjuk (Dem-YAHN-yook)

     to death by hanging for crimes at a World War Two concentration

     camp.

          Demjanjuk, now 68, is a native of the Ukraine.  He spent more

     than 30 years in the Cleveland area before being deported for trial

     in Israel.  Witnesses identified him as a camp guard known as "Ivan

     the Terrible" because of his savage cruelty to prisoners.  They

     testified he ran the gas chambers at Treblinka, Poland, where more

     than 800-thousand people were murdered, most of them Jews.

          Once again today, Demjanjuk proclaimed his innocence.  The

     death sentence now goes before the Israeli High Court of Appeals.
```

PUNCTUATION

Whether on paper or by computer, broadcast news copy requires eye-oriented punctuation to help the anchor's phrasing, stress, and inflection. Of course, writing short sentences helps enormously (as we shall see in coming chapters). Even so, broadcast copy profits from the liberal use of commas (,), hyphens (-), dashes (--), ellipses (. . .), and, to a lesser extent, colons (:)—all of which help the anchor's eye by breaking up long clusters of words. (On the other hand, a semicolon (;), while very useful in newspapers, magazines, and books, is virtually useless in broadcast copy.)

Here's an exmaple of the use of ellipses as visual punctuation for a story:

```
Mayor Tom Smith said today...he will not seek re-election to a third

term. The mayor...who was considered a shoo-in...said he is...in his

words..."growing tired and stale."
```

Another way to visually punctuate broadcast copy is to <u>underline</u> words you want the anchor to stress. The underlining may be done ahead of time in the typewriter or computer, or afterward by hand:

```
     Mayor Tom Smith said today he will not seek re-election to a

third term.  The mayor, who was considered a shoo-in, said he is, in

his words, "growing tired and stale."
```

PARAGRAPH STRUCTURE

In print, the start of a new paragraph usually means the start of a new thought or subject matter. But in broadcast news, listeners and viewers can't see the paragraphs; all they hear is the anchor's voice. Thus, paragraph structure is important only insofar as it helps the anchor's delivery. Some writers neglect paragraph structure entirely. Others begin a new paragraph after every sentence. The best writers use paragraphing to help anchors shorten stories at a glance; they put the essential material in the first few paragraphs, then write a final paragraph or two, enclosed in parentheses, which the anchor may delete on the air without sabotaging the story as a whole.

SPELLING

By now you may be thinking that, because listeners can't see the punctuation and paragraph structure, they also can't see the spelling, and therefore spelling doesn't matter. If listeners can't see spelling errors, who cares if you write "sow" for "sew," "there" instead of "their," or "Jon" instead of "John"?

If you want to write news for television, it matters a great deal. That's because TV news staffers write more than just the copy read aloud by anchors; they also write the copy that appears on-screen in electronic graphics and titles. That's where any spelling errors stick out like the proverbial sore thumb and can make the news department look stupid. And, just as in newspapers, it is extremely important to spell people's names right—not least because people are offended when you spell their names wrong. So even if you work in radio, it is an excellent idea to pay close attention to proper spelling. You never know when you'll suddenly find yourself working in television.

PRONUNCIATION AND PHONETICS

As we've seen, pronunciation is a key aspect of a broadcast news script. Once or twice a day, news agency radio wires send a Pronunciation Guide to names and places currently in the news. Here's a sample from UPI:

World-Prono-Guide 0597

　　AL-WAZIR, Khalil (Kah-lihl Ahl-vah-ZEER'), Palestine
Liberation Organization Number Two man assassinated in a
Tunis, Tunisia, suburb; also know as Abu Jihad (Ah-BOO'
Zhee-HAHD')
　　AQUINO, Corazon (KOH'-rah-zohn Ah-KEE'-noh), president of
the Philippines.
　　ARAFAT, Yasser (YAH'-sehr Ahr-ah-FAHT'), head of the
Palestine Liberation Organization
　　Chernobyl (Chihr-NAW'-bihl) nuclear power complex in
Soviet Ukraine
　　CICIPPIO (Chih-SEE'-pee-oh), Joseph, American hostage in
Lebanon
　　CUOMO (KWOH'-moh), Mario, New York Democratic governor
　　Daedalus (DEHD'-ehl-ehs), U-S-designed human-powered
aircraft
　　DE MITA, Ciriaco (Chee-ree-AH'-koh Day MEE'-tah), new
Italian prime minister
　　DELVALLE, Eric Arturo (Ahr-TOO'-roh Dehl-VAH'-yeh),
ousted Panamanian president
　　DEMJANJUK (DEHM'-yahn-yook) John, retired American auto
worker convicted in Israel on charges of committing Nazi war
crimes while a death camp guard
　　DUKAKIS (Doo-KAH'-kihs), Governor Michael, Massachusetts
Democrat
　　GORBACHEV, Mikhail (MEEK'-high-yehl GOHRB'-ah-chawf),
Soviet leader
　　Hezbollah (Hehz-BOH'-lah), Islamic party in Lebanon, also
known as "Party of God"
　　Hormuz (HOHR'-mooz), Strait of, channel connecting the
Persian Gulf with the Gulf of Oman
　　Jihad (Zhee-HAHD'), Islamic, a pro-Khomeini terrorist
group
　　Kabul (KAH'-buhl) capital of Afghanistan
　　Kharg (Kakrk), Iranian island in Persian Gulf, site of
key oil terminal
　　Kuwait (Koo-WAYT'), Persian Gulf oil state
　　NIDAL, Abu (Ah-BOO' Nee-DAHL'), leader of Libyan-backed
P-L-O splinter group
　　NORIEGA (Nohr-ee-EH'-gah), Manuel Antonio, Panamanian
military strongman
　　Noumea (Noo-MAY'-uh), New Caledonia, French territory
east of Australia
　　ORTEGA (Ohr-TAY'-gah), Daniel, Nicaraguan president
　　PERES, Shimon (Shee-MOHN' PEH'-rehs), Israeli foreign
minister
　　RABIN, Yitzhak (YIHTS'-hahk Rah-BEEN'), Israeli defense
minister
　　Sapoa (Sahp-WAH'), Nicaragua
　　SHAMIR, Yitzhak (YIHTS'-hahk Shah-MEER'), Israeli prime
minister
　　SHEVARDNADZE (Shyeh-vahr-nahd-sheh), Eduard, Soviet
foreign minister
　　Shiite (SHEE'-ight), Moslem sect
　　Sikh (Seek), religious sect
　　Sunni (SOO'-nee), Moslem sect
　　Tbilisi (Tuh-bihl-YEE'-see), capital of Soviet Georgia

Notice that the guide makes full use of upper/lower case typing and simple phonetics (that is, without diacritical marks such as are often found in dictionaries):

1. Unstressed syllables are written lower case (except for the first letter in the first syllable of proper nouns). Stressed syllables are typed entirely upper case. (Stressed syllables can also be indicated by underlining. However, using all caps saves several steps both on a computer and on a standard typewriter.)

2. Simple phonetics such as these utilize various combinations of English alphabet letters to approximate foreign pronunciation for which there is really no English-language equivalent. English does not contain the nasal sounds typical of French and Portuguese, the guttural sounds of Dutch and German, or the harsh sybillants of Russian and other Slavic tongues. Nevertheless, these sounds may be approximated by picking appropriate combinations of letters.

Of course, you have to know the right pronunciation before typing a phonetic spelling. If your dictionary offers no help with a foreign name or location, you will have to turn elsewhere, perhaps to a colleague or classmate. Or, if it's really important, call the nearest language school (such as Berlitz), embassy, consulate, trade mission, or business enterprise staffed by native speakers of the language in question. (At a university, you may find help with a quick call to the appropriate foreign-language instructor.)

Remember, it's not always necessary to render exact pronunciations of foreign names and places. If it were, we'd be saying "Pa-REE" instead of "Paris." What is necessary is to avoid the kind of mispronunciation that gives the impression that we haven't the foggiest idea what we're talking about.

Phonetic Placement

In a radio/TV news script, the proper place for a phonetic rendering is *immediately following* the actual spelling, *in parentheses:*

```
Polish Labor Leader Lech Walesa (Lek Vah-WEN-sa) . . .


                             -0-


French President Francois Mitterand (FRAWNH-swah MEE-ter-awnh) . . .
```

Phonetic Table

Unfortunately, there is no standardized phonetic pronunciation guide. While everyone agrees the phonetic rendering of "tough" is "tuff," no one can agree if "cough" should be rendered as "coff," "koff," or "cawf." (For example, is it "Gorb-ah-CHAWF" or "Gorb-ah-CHOFF"? Both seem equally clear.) The Phonetic Table reproduced below is designed as a simple guide to the phonetic rendering in broadcast news copy of English- and foreign-language names and places. It is by no means the last word on the subject, but it should prove useful much of the time.

PHONETIC TABLE

Letter(s)	As in	Phonetic rendering
a	fat, glad, cap	a
a	late, great, race	ay
a	father, car	ah
a	(unstressed syllable) lull*a*by, *a*ffect	uh
an	*banc, sang, Le Mans* (French)	awnh (nasal)
ao	*Macao, gabao* (Portuguese)	onh (nasal)
au	*braun, kauen* (German)	ow (as "now")
au(x)	*faux, chapeau* (French)	oh
b	boy, build, drub	b
c	cede, citizen	s
c, ch	cord, chemical	k
ch; c,cc	cheap, beach, *citta, bacci* (Italian)	ch
ch	*cher* (French)	sh
ch,gh	loch (Scottish), Bach (German), Gogh (Dutch)	kh (guttural)
d	dog, stud	d
e	neck, edge	e
e,ee	cede, seek	ee
é,er	*éclair, passé, diner,* (French)	ay
è	*grève, cèpe* (French)	e (as "get")
eu	*Heute, Kreuz* (German)	oy (as "boy")
eu,ö,ü	*feu* (French), *schön, kühn* (German)	ooh (as "foot")
f,ff	fix, offer	f or ff
g	(hard) get, go	g
g	(soft) gem, ledge	j
gn	*bagno* (Italian), *magnifique* (French)	n'y
gu	*Miguel* (Spanish), *gueppe* (French)	g (as in "go")
h,j	him, how; *joya* (Spanish)	h
h	*hirondelle* (French, unaspirated)	(silent)
i	bit, miss, sin	i
i,y	bite, sky	y (as vowel)
i	*mineur* (French), *si, mi* (Italian, Spanish)	ee
in	*vin, lapin* (French)	a (as "fat," nasalized)
j	justice, jerk	j
j	*Jahr, jung* (German)	y (consonant)
j	*je, juste* (French)	zh
k	kid, like	k
l,ll	lip, killer	l
ll	*llegar* (Spanish); *oreiller* (French)	y (consonant)
m	man, ember	m
n	not, knot	n
ñ	*niño, piña* (Spanish)	n'y

Letter(s)	As in	Phonetic rendering
o	note, toad	oh
o	not, body, closet	ah
o	dog, frog	aw
oo	room, shoot	oo
oi	*moi, trois* (French)	wah
ou	*pour, nous* (French)	oo
oy	boy, buoy	oy
p	pot, slip	p
ph	phone, lymph	f or ff
qu	quick, square	kw
qu	*chequier* (French); *quemar* (Spanish)	k
qu	*quer, Quatsch* (German)	kv
r	rude, rodeo, car	r
r,rr	*trois* (French); *perro* (Spanish)	rr (rolled)
s,ss	sit, risk, assess, kiss	s or ss
sh	shrug, sure, crush	sh
sch	*Schade* (German)	sh
shtch	*tovarishtch* (Russian)	sh'ch
t	ten, wait	t
th	thick, thin (hard) *and* this, the (soft)	th (for both)
u	but, upper	u
u	burn, curse	u
u	usual, sure, butte	yoo
v	vixen, novice	v
v	*Volk, vier* (German)	f
w,wh	wit, what	w
w	*warum, wo* (German)	v
x	extra, sex	x
y	sky, byline	y (vowel)
y	mainly, *Lyon* (French)	ee (vowel)
y	yes, yolk	y (consonant)
z	size, zoo	z
z	azure; *muzik* (Russian)	zh
z,zz	*Zigeuner* (German); *mezzo* (Italian)	ts

Almost insurmountable obstacles occur in attempts at phonetic rendering of languages based largely on tonal scales or click-sounds. Chinese, for example, is a tonal language that has been transliterated in so many ways over the years that, depending on date and origin of publication, you may see the capital city of China written as *Pekin, Peking, Beiping,* or *Beijing.* This last spelling, which has now been adopted by many news organizations, is the closest to the actual pronunciation: "Bay-ZHING." But so many Chinese and other tonal-language words come up in the news these days that, lacking a reliable source (such as a native speaker of the language), you will find yourself doing a lot of guesswork. This is especially true of African languages employing click-sounds.

Fortunately, such pronunciation headaches do not occur often.

EXERCISES

1. Using the following news agency story as raw material, write a maximum 30-second (10-line) radio story slugged COLLAPSE. Use your name, today's date, and make the story for a 7 P.M. newscast. Be careful to make your copy conform to the rules given in this chapter.

```
     BURNABY, British Columbia (AP)--A rooftop parking area
collapsed Saturday during the grand opening of a grocery
store: dropping automobiles and blocks of concrete onto store
displays and injuring 21 people, police said.
     It was not immediately known how many people were in the
Save-on-Foods store when the parking area, holding about 22
autos, collapsed, but Constable Lloyd Wall of the Royal
Canadian Mounted Police in Burnaby said estimates ran as high
as 900. Many were elderly people being given a preview tour.
     Three of the injured were admitted to hospitals, with one
in serious condition.
     Police used cranes to remove huge blocks of concrete and
cars that fell about 40 feet from the parking area to the
floor of the store, in the Metrotown shopping center, Mounted
Police Constable Dave Muir said.
     It took several hours for searchers, who used police
dogs, to get through the rubble. Officials believed everyone
was accounted for, Wall said.
     "We're being optimistic there won't be any deaths," said
Mounted Police Sgt. Gary Schauer. "But we're still going
through the rubble."
     Some cars were piled on each other on the supermarket
floor amid soda and produce displays, while above, other autos
teetered on the edge of a hole about half the size of a
football field.
     "I heard a crack and I looked up and saw the center beam
wobble and saw the floor from the parking garage come down so
1 immediately told people to get outside," said one witness,
George Sanderson.
     "As soon as the first crack came (in the beam), they
started getting people out," Heppell said.
     The collapse was preceded by the sound of a buckling beam
and spray from a bursting water pipe, officials said. There
were three warnings over the store's loudspeaker system to
clear the area.
     Clarence Heppell, president of Overwaitea Foods, which
operates the store chain, said a structural failure caused the
cave-in.
     Eight people were taken to a hospital by ambulance, and
others went to emergency wards on their own.
```

2. Is your copy clean?

Did you time it by counting lines or by reading it aloud against a stopwatch?

Did you make an attempt at "visual punctuation" of any sort?

Did you use any phonetic renderings, and did they resemble the following?

Burnaby (BURN-uh-bee)

Gary Bauer (BOW-er)

Clarence Heppell (HEP-el)

5

"What": Short Sentences, Short Leads

BARE-BONES SENTENCES

Most of us speak in short sentences. Often, when we try to utter a short sentence, we lose the thread, get hopelessly confused, and have to start over.

Listeners, too, are accustomed to receiving information that way—in short bursts. Thus, because we want listeners to understand the news, it makes sense to write in short sentences.

Although many daily newspapers and the major news agencies have now adopted a style favoring shorter sentences, the traditional print journalism sentence, especially the lead sentence, is too long to *say* comfortably. A case in point:

WASHINGTON—Supreme Court nominee Douglas H. Ginsburg issued a statement Thursday admitting that he smoked marijuana on a number of occasions, apparently including the period when he was a member of the Harvard University Law School faculty—an announcement that raises questions about his continued viability as a candidate for the nation's highest court.

"It was a mistake, and I regret it," he said.

(David Lauter and Melissa Healy, © 1988 *Los Angeles Times*, reprinted with permission)

Counting the dateline, the lead sentence in that story is 54 words long. If you say it aloud (go ahead, try it!), you will run out of breath long before you reach the period. It is a fine *newspaper* lead; it is comprehensive, contains all five W's, and summarizes the important points of the story as a whole.

But as a *broadcast* lead, it is entirely unacceptable. Not only is saying it fluently a virtual impossibility, but it contains *too much* information for listeners to swallow in one gulp. The sentence is complex in structure and uses long words and locutions ("issued a statement" instead of "said," "occasions" instead of "times," and "continued viability" instead of "chances" or "prospects"). So the first step is to cast it aside in favor of shorter, simpler, more direct sentences.

```
Supreme Court nominee Douglas Ginsburg admitted today that he smoked

marijuana when he was a law school professor.

    The admission raises serious doubts about his chances for

confirmation.
```

The first sentence in that broadcast version is 18 words long, the second 10 words long, for a total of 28 words—about half the number in the print version's single lead sentence. Both sentences are direct and to the point—no wasted verbiage. Most important, they tell the essence of the story (the bare facts and their significance). They do not get bogged down by long words and unwieldy grammar.

Using the same approach, let's try a few other versions:

```
A potentially damaging admission today from Supreme Court nominee

Douglas Ginsburg...

    Ginsburg says he smoked marijuana several times while on the faculty

of Harvard Law School.

                            -0-

    Douglas Ginsburg says he smoked marijuana many years ago.

    The admission raises doubt that the president's latest Supreme Court

nominee can win confirmation.

                            -0-
```

And, using information from the print version's second sentence:

```
    Calling it a regrettable mistake, Supreme Court nominee Douglas

Ginsburg admitted today that he has smoked marijuana.

    Ginsburg said it happened a number of times while he was a law

professor at Harvard.
```

–0–

```
    "It was a mistake, and I regret it."  Those were the words of

Supreme Court nominee Douglas Ginsburg today as he admitted to having

smoked marijuana.

    The admission threw doubt on Ginsburg's prospects for confirmation.
```

As you can see, the English language provides a wide variety of options even when you must keep words and sentences short and simple. There's no hard-and-fast rule about the maximum number of words, but, generally speaking, if you find yourself writing a sentence longer than 22 words (about two lines of radio news copy or four lines TV news copy), start over and make a deliberate effort to write two sentences instead of one. Say goodbye to long, complex sentences. Don't use them even in direct quotes; paraphrase instead, using short sentences.

STORY STRUCTURE

Another important element of broadcast newswriting is the overall structure, or organization, of a story.

In print journalism, it is normal to write a "roundup" that groups a number of related developments into the same news story. The roundup typically begins with a so-called umbrella lead mentioning two or more of the developments in the first sentence; following paragraphs then skip back and forth from development to development, filling in a few details here and a few there. Readers are not bothered by this hopscotch approach because they can always go back and reread an earlier paragraph.

But as we've seen, listeners and viewers have no such luxury. They get one chance only. So broadcast newswriters must take what's called a "linear" (or "straight-line") approach toward storytelling; that is, they must deal with one story element at a time, finish it off, and only then go on to the next element.

Here's a typical "roundup" story meant for print:

```
    TEL AVIV (AP)--Hundreds more Arab policemen in the
occupied West Bank and Gaza Strip resigned Saturday to protest
Israeli treatment of Palestinians in the territories, while in
Tel Aviv, about 100,000 Israelis rallied on the eve of Prime
Minister Yitzhak Shamir's trip to the United States to urge
him to support the American peace initiative.
    Israel Radio said about 450 of the 800 to 1,000 Arab
police officers in the occupied territories have quit their
jobs in the past two days. About 20,000 Palestinians work for
the government in the territories.
    The resignations began Friday, one day after the
self-styled Unified National Leadership for the Uprising in
```

the Occupied Territories issued a statement reiterating its
call for the Arab policemen to retire immediately.
      Israeli warplanes, meanwhile, struck five Palestinian
guerrilla targets east of the port town of Sidon in southern
Lebanon, the army said. Police said one guerrilla was killed
and at least eight others were wounded. It was Israel's second
raid this year in the region.
      A palestinian military leader said on Saturday that Arabs
will continue to protest in Israeli-occupied territories
despite the air raids.
      Scattered violence was reported in the West Bank and Gaza
Strip on Saturday.
      Near Tulkarm, a 50-year-old woman was wounded when prison
service employees opened fire after their bus was stoned.
      On Friday night, Israeli soldiers shot and seriously
wounded a Palestinian from Bani Naim, near Hebron, after he
threw a hand grenade at them, the army command said. The
grenade did not explode.
      At least 89 Palestinians have been killed since the
uprising began Dec. 9.
      In the Tel Aviv demonstration, the group Peace Now urged
Shamir to support a U.S. peace initiative.
      Tzaly Reshef, one of the Peace Now activists who
organized the demonstration, told the crowd, "One hundred
thousand people tonight in this square send a clear message to
Prime Minister Shamir: You can't say no to peace plans in our
name."

In case you weren't counting, there were four developments in that
roundup story:

  1. More Arab policemen resigned.
  2. More Palestinians were shot and wounded.
  3. Israeli planes attacked suspected guerrilla bases in Lebanon.
  4. An estimated 100,000 Israelis staged a peace rally.

In other words, there are four *separate* stories. The print writer has been able
to interweave them and sometimes not refer back to a development until many
paragraphs later. For example, the Peace Now demonstration is included in the
lead sentence, but then is not mentioned again until the final two paragraphs.

In linear broadcast writing, you can*not* do that. You are dealing in time, not
space, and because time will have elapsed between your first mention of the
Peace Now rally and your later mention of the details, many listeners will have
forgotten what is being spoken about.

Thus, in addition to shortening the sentences and simplifying the details,
you must reorganize the entire structure. You must tell one development first,
then another, then another. No jumping forward, no going back:

Bard, 11/27, 5p

ISRAEL

An estimated 100,000 Israelis rallied in Tel Aviv tonight...in
support of the latest U-S peace plan. They urged Prime Minister
Shamir to accept the U-S formula for ending the Palestinian uprising
in the West Bank and Gaza Strip. Shamir leaves tomorrow for talks
in Washington.

The uprising gained momentum today with the resignations of
hundreds more Arab policemen. Israel Radio says about 450 Arab
police have quit in the past two days. That's roughly half the
entire force.

Israeli forces shot and wounded at least two more Palestinians
in the past 24 hours. Near Hebron, soldiers shot one man they said
threw a hand grenade. At least 89 Palestinians have been killed
since the uprising began in December.

Also today, Israeli warplanes attacked suspected guerrilla
targets in Southern Lebanon. Lebanese police said one guerrilla was
killed and eight wounded.

Notice how the writer has told each development separately. That version
led with the Tel Aviv rally because it was the latest of the day's events, then went
on to relate what happened earlier. However, the technique of telling develop-

ments separately facilitates the rearrangement of the story and enables the writer to lead with whichever element he or she desires:

Bard, 11/27, 6p

ISRAEL

    Hundreds of Arab policemen in Israel's occupied territories resigned today at the request of Palestinian leaders. According to Israeli Radio, a total of 450 Arab policemen in the West Bank and Gaza Strip have quit since yesterday. That's about half the force.

    Israeli forces wounded at least two more Palestinians today...as the anti-occupation uprising continued. In one incident, soldiers shot a man they said threw a hand grenade at them.

    In Tel Aviv tonight, about 100,000 Israelis rallied in support of the latest U-S peace plan. They called on Prime Minister Yitzhak Shamir to accept the plan during his upcoming talks in Washington.

If it troubles you that the choice of words for the broadcast versions is sometimes very different from the print model, rest assured. You are *supposed* to use different words. Broadcast editors and producers *want* you to use your own words. It's what you're being paid for.

LEADS

By and large, a print lead seeks to cram a wealth of information into a single opening sentence. The result is a mini-story that stands on its own.

    By and large, a broadcast lead seeks to impart only as much information as can be grasped easily. It can stand on its own—but just as often it can't.

    Except for the word "tonight," the following lead could serve either print or broadcast:

    A bullet-proof vest saved a policeman's life in the Kenmore District tonight, stopping a handgun bullet fired by a teenage assailant.

But the following leads lend themselves only to broadcasting:

```
There's a lucky cop in the Kenmore District tonight...
```

```
                              -0-
```

```
A Kenmore District patrolman is alive and well tonight, thanks to
```

```
his bullet-proof vest...
```

Such leads, which require follow-up sentences to complete the essential information, serve the double function of piquing the listener's interest while setting up the rest of the story.

Immediacy

Although most of the time your lead sentence will reflect the most important development of a story, frequently it will reflect merely the *latest* development.

Radio and TV news have a built-in advantage over newspapers: They transmit the news instantaneously, either as it happens (live coverage) or as quickly as possible thereafter. Broadcast news of an event reaches people many hours before the newspaper version. This time advantage is called *immediacy*, and broadcasters exploit it whenever possible. Although immediacy can be expressed through proper phrasing of the "When" element (see Chapter 8), it can also be implicit in the choice of a lead. For example:

```
Democratic contender Jesse Jackson brought his presidential hopes to

North Carolina tonight after campaigning all day in California.

    In Fresno, Jackson strongly denied reports he will soon drop out of

the race in the face of a seemingly insurmountable lead by Michael

Dukakis.  Jackson vowed he's in the race...in his words..."through the

convention and into the White House."
```

Undoubtedly, what Jackson said in California was more newsworthy than the mere fact of his flying to another state. Still, his change of location happened much later in the day and is thus an effective, immediate way to begin a broadcast story airing at night (when much of the audience has already heard the earlier news of the day). In other words, it's okay to begin a story with a less newsworthy fact as long as the story as a whole reports the more newsworthy facts.

Leading with a Quote

Earlier in this chapter we saw an example of leading a story with a quote:

```
"It was a mistake, and I regret it."  Those were the words of

Supreme Court nominee Douglas Ginsburg today...
```

A pithy, colorful quote, or even a paraphrase of one, is an especially attention-grabbing way to begin. The audience is forced to continue listening to find out who said it and why. The technique works even with the Demjanjuk story that began this book:

```
"I am innocent...innocent...innocent."  The plea of John Demjanjuk

(Dem-YAHN-yook) today in an Israeli court --*a court that sentenced him

to death for war crimes.
```

As with many techniques in broadcast newswriting, the effectiveness of leading with a quote depends on not doing it too often. And it is vital to follow up a quote *immediately* by telling who said it and in what context.

Another consideration is the ability of the news anchor or on-air reporter to deliver the quote effectively and without appearing foolish. Delivering the quote properly requires an expressive voice, an expressive face, or both. A deadpan, flat delivery is death to a choice quote.

Incomplete Sentences

Although it is ungrammatical to use incomplete sentences, such constructions can occasionally be useful in a broadcast lead. Again the Demjanjuk story:

```
A death sentence for "Ivan the Terrible."  An Israeli court today

sentenced John Demjanjuk (Dem-YAHN-yook), the ex-concentration camp guard

known as Ivan the Terrible, to death by hanging.
```

In this chapter's Ginsburg story, an opening sentence fragment might go like this:

```
Trouble for the Ginsburg nomination:  Supreme Court nominee Douglas

Ginsburg admitted today he smoked pot while a professor at Harvard Law

School.  The admission raised doubts about...etc.
```

Of the lead techniques examined so far, this one is the least likely to be overused. Don't be afraid to experiment with it.

The Chronological Lead

From time to time, it is very effective to tell a story chronologically, saving the most important development for later. In other words, you lead with old information (background) as a means of setting the stage for new information (the news):

```
After years of calling them a nuisance, beat cops last month began

wearing those new-model bullet-proof vests.  Well, tonight, one of those

"nuisances" saved a cop's life.
```

Will this technique work with the Demjanjuk story? Let's see:

```
Last week, an Israeli court found retired Cleveland autoworker John

Demjanjuk (Dem-YAHN-yook) guilty of war crimes at a concentration camp in

Poland.

Today, the court sentenced him to death by hanging...
```

Yes, it works. But again the trick is to use the technique sparingly.

The "What's-next" Lead

Sometimes it's better to start a story with what is *going* to happen rather than with what has already happened. For example, newscasts airing at night contain a preponderance of past-tense stories telling what happened that day. By that time, many listeners and viewers will already have heard much of the day's news and will be more interested in later angles, such as what will happen next.

Let's go back to a story we used briefly in Chapter 1:

```
      WASHINGTON (AP)--Higher postage rates, including a
25-cent charge for first-class mail, will begin April 3, the
Postal Service announced Tuesday.
      The 25-cent rate is for the first ounce of a first-class
item. For each additional ounce, the rate will rise to 20
cents from 17 cents.
      The postcard rate will increase to 15 cents from 14
cents.
      First-class mail will cost 14.7% more under the new
rates, compared with increases of 18.1% for newspapers and
magazines and 24.9% for advertising materials.
```

The AP carried that story on March 22. The new rates would not take effect until nearly two weeks later. Although the amount of the postage increases, which were announced "today," is the heart of the story, the effective date is in the future. This enables the broadcast writer to start a story this way:

```
Starting next month, you'll be paying a quarter to mail a letter.
```

or

```
You'll soon be paying a quarter to mail a letter.
```

This is known as leading with a next-day angle and can be applied to many types of stories. Let's say your station has spent the entire day reporting the final day of a murder trial. Although what occurred in court forms the substance of the story, you can begin nighttime stories with what will happen next:

```
A verdict is expected tomorrow in the murder trial of...
```

or

```
There may be a verdict tomorrow in the trial of...
```

or

```
The jury may deliver a verdict tomorrow in the murder trial of...
```

The flexibility of lead-writing in broadcast news takes some getting used to for people whose previous journalistic training has been in print. Their tendency is to write a comprehensive, self-sufficient lead sentence for every story. But that is a poor practice in radio and television. It's important to remember that in broadcast news, stories are presented in a series (formally known as a newscast). If each story has the same kind of lead, the result is a lack of variety and pacing, leading to boredom among the audience—which, unfortunately, can lead to a premature switching-off of the program. Obviously, that's just the opposite of what station owners want.

It will help if you learn to think of a broadcast lead in non-newspaper terms. A broadcast lead is nothing more than a *beginning,* a way of introducing the story. It need not be a capsule version of the entire story, but rather just an attention-grabber—like saying, "Stay tuned, folks—wait till you hear this!"

EXERCISES

1. Using the following truncated newspaper story as raw material, write a maximum 25-second (8-line) radio story slugged INTERNEES. Make sure that no single sentence is longer than two lines (about :06 seconds). In other words, your story should contain *at least* four sentences.

WASHINGTON—The Senate, moving to close a controversial chapter in American history, overwhelmingly passed legislation Wednesday that would make $20,000 payments to about 60,000 Americans of Japanese descent who were ordered from homes in California and other West Coast states during World War II and put in detention camps.

Under the historic bill, which was approved 69 to 27, the federal government also would issue a formal apology to these people, most of whom were American citizens at the time of their incarceration. The estimated $1.3 billion in payments would be spread out over five years.

The detention policy began in 1942, when the nation experienced a wave of anti-Japanese sentiment after the attack on Pearl Harbor. Amid mounting fears of an invasion on the West Coast, the federal government required the mandatory evacuation from the area of all individuals of Japanese ancestry, saying they might be security risks.

Eventually, more than 120,000 people, mostly in California, were sent from their homes. Many had to sell all their belongings, often on 72 hours' notice. More than 77,000 of the evacuees were American citizens, according to a U.S. Senate report.

Although most of these people spent the war in the camps, about 35,000 were allowed to leave the camps after taking loyalty oaths, by joining the U.S. Army, or by taking jobs or attending college away from the West Coast. The internment policy ended in December, 1944.

(Josh Getlin, © 1988 *Los Angeles Times,* reprinted with permission)

2. If you did not do so on the first try, rewrite your story to lead with an incomplete sentence.

3. The following news agency roundup is slugged DISASTERS. Reorganize and rewrite it in broadcast style. Maximum length: 40 seconds (12 lines).

(Remember what we've been saying about broadcast structure and linear writing. Be careful not to hopscotch back and forth from one development to another.)

```
AM--Disasters Rdp, 2d Ld--Writethru,0872
Search Continues For Last Body In Wake Of Three Disasters
By The Associated Press
        Tangled wreckage hampered the search for a worker still
missing Saturday in the wake of an explosion and fire at a
Louisiana oil refinery, while fire officials said California's
tallest building would remain closed indefinitely following a
deadly fire.
        An official of a rocket fuel company whose plant exploded
on the edge of a Nevada town said a replacement plant would be
built at a more remote location.
        Six bodies had been recovered at the refinery. Two people
died in the Nevada blast, and the California disaster killed
one person.
        Two crews worked through a maze of wrecked equipment
Saturday at the refinery at Norco, La., skirting small fires
in the search for the missing man.
        Shell Oil Co. spokesman Bill Gibson said company
engineers and safety and environmental experts were trying to
find out what caused the explosion.
        "They've gotten out right into the area, as close as they
safely could," he said Saturday.
        The causes of the three conflagrations, all of which
```

began during a 14-hour period Wednesday and Thursday, have not been determined.

In Los Angeles, fire officials were joined by state legislators and local politicians in calling for a tough new law requiring sprinklers in hundreds of older high-rises in the wake of the fire late Wednesday and early Thursday that destroyed 4-1/2 floors of the 62-story First Interstate Bank tower.

The building was built in 1973, one year before a law was passed requiring sprinklers in all new buildings over 75 feet tall.

The building was ordered closed indefinitely Friday, said Russell E. Lane, the city's chief building inspector. He said repair work cannot begin until the steel superstructure is extensively tested.

In advance of that testing, "We had the original architects and engineers go in and they were very pleased with the shape of the building," said bank vice president Simon Barker-Benfield. He said a few people had been allowed into the building "to begin the process of salvaging files and that kind of thing."

Operators of the demolished Pacific Engineering & Production Co. rocket fuel plant at Henderson, Nev., were fined four times in the last five years for safety violations, but state officials defended the plant Friday as having a "good, moderate record" overall.

Keith Rooker, counsel for the company, said locations in more remote regions of Nevada, Texas and Utah were being considered for a replacement for the plant destroyed Wednesday.

The plant had been given 10 citations from 11 state inspections since 1983 but the problems were "mostly minor," said Jim Barnes, state industrial relations director.

The company produced ammonium perchlorate, a component of the solid rocket fuel used in some military missiles and the space shuttle's booster rockets.

Kerr-McGee Corp. makes the same chemical in a plant about a mile closer to most of Henderson's residential area. That plant was shut down voluntarily Thursday, and some worried residents want to keep it closed.

The blast damaged homes and businesses in Henderson and 326 people were treated for injuries.

The explosion at a Shell Oil Co. refinery at Norco, La., shattered hundreds of windows in homes and stores in the area and shook buildings in New Orleans, 30 miles to the east.

"The area is very much in disarray," plant manager Fred Foster said Friday. "There are large pieces of equipment off of foundations and down around the cat cracker."

The catalytic cracker is used to break crude oil into usable products.

"We still have a few small flames burning and so we have not gotten into the unit," company spokeswoman Wendy Jacobs said Saturday.

The body of one Shell employee was found shortly after the blast and five others were found Friday. One person was missing.

The cause of the Los Angeles high-rise fire may never be known because of the extreme heat of the blaze, said Fire Department Battalion Chief Gary R. Bowie.

The chief spokesman for First Interstate Bancorp discounted arson speculation prompted by news that the company's capital markets group, which employs 100 people on the floor where the fire apparently broke out, was sold in a deal that closed Wednesday night.

"I firmly believe that at this stage it's random chance," said spokesman John Popovich. "If the idea is that there is a disgruntled employee, that would have been six months ago," when the decision to sell was announced.

A sprinkler system was being installed in the building but was not yet complete. Los Angeles City Councilman Nate Holden introduced a motion Friday to require owners of all high-rises to install sprinkler systems.

About 200 members of the California Fire Chiefs Association, attending an annual convention, urged that sprinklers be required in all buildings more than 75 feet tall.

State Sen. Art Torres said Friday he will introduce a bill in the state Legislature this week to require sprinklers in all commercial high-rise structures in California.

AP-NY-1757EDT--

6

"Who" (Part One)—Names and Numbers

In this chapter and the next, we'll look at how broadcast journalists identify and describe people, organizations, and numbers. Grammatically speaking, we'll be dealing with substantives (nouns) and modifiers (adjectives) in common newsroom usage.

NAMES AND TITLES

By and large, broadcast journalists identify and describe people in the news by combining respect for their accomplishments (or misdeeds) with the American penchant for informality. More specifically, they tell

1. *on first mention* a person's title, first name, and last name

```
Los Angeles Mayor Tom Bradley (or Mayor Tom Bradley of Los Angeles)

Senator Edward (not "Ted" or "Teddie") Kennedy of Massachusetts

Soviet Party Leader Mikhail Gorbachev (Meek-hah-EEL Gorb-ah-CHAWF)
```

(Broadcasters do *not* give a person's middle name or middle initial unless it is part of how the person is known professionally: Economist John Kenneth Galbraith; Actor Michael J. Fox, et al. Do *not* use nicknames.)

2. on second and all subsequent mentions, a person's *last name only*

```
Bradley also said...

Later, Kennedy visited...

Gorbachev escorted his wife, Raisa (Rah-EE-suh)...
```

In many newsrooms, there are four exceptions to those two rules:

1. The president of the United States is usually shown respect by being referred to as "Mr." or "President" on *every* mention. The same respect is usually *not* shown toward foreign leaders.

2. Members of the clergy are reidentified by title on every mention.

```
Archbishop John Mahoney (1st); Archbishop Mahoney (2nd)

Rabbi Arnold Gold (1st); Rabbi Gold (2nd)

(The) Reverend Jerry Falwell (1st); Reverend Falwell (2nd)
```

(This practice of showing respect for the clergy has been on the decline. It is now common to hear some clergymen identified by last name only.)

3. A few news organizations insist that women be identified as "Miss," "Mrs.," or "Ms."

```
British Prime Minister Margaret Thatcher (1st); Mrs. Thatcher (2nd)

Actress Faye Dunaway (1st); Miss Dunaway (2nd)
```

However, most newsrooms now give men and women equal treatment. On second mention, the above women become simply "Thatcher" and "Dunaway."

4. In obituaries, the deceased is identified by full name on both first *and last* mention.

```
Earl Tupper, who made his name a household word by popularizing

plastic containerware, died today in Costa Rica. Tupper marketed his

"Tupperware" line after World War Two, became wealthy, and retired a

decade ago. Earl Tupper was 76.
```

The Title or the Name?

Fully identifying a newsmaker can sometimes require a mouthful of words.

```
Republican Senator David Durenberger of Minnesota...

Nicaraguan Sandinista Leader and President Daniel Ortega...
```

In such cases it is better not to use a full identification on first mention. Instead, use a part-identification on first mention, and complete the identification on second mention. Thus,

```
Senator David Durenberger today proposed a sweeping revision of U-S

trade policy with Japan. The Minnesota Republican said...


                              -0-


Nicaraguan President Daniel Ortega today rejected the latest U-S

formula for a permanent truce with the Contra rebels. The Sandinista

leader said...
```

Frequently in the news, the title or role of a newsmaker is more important to immediate understanding of a story than his or her name. Thus, first mention can be of title or role only, leaving the name itself to a follow-up sentence.

```
print:      FAIRWAY, Kan. (UPI)--"Doonesbury" creator Garry Trudeau
       will take a leave of absence early next year and temporarily
       cease production of his Pulitzer Prize-winning comic strip in
       more than 700 newspapers, Universal Press Syndicate officials
       said Wednesday.
            "I need a breather," Trudeau, 34, told Universal Press
       Syndicate officials in a telephone conversation from his home
       in New York City.

b'cast:    Doonesbury is going on extended vacation -- or, more exactly, his

       creator is. Garry Trudeau, whose "Doonesbury" comic strip appears in

       some 700 newspapers, says he needs a rest...
```

or

The creator of "Doonesbury" says he'll take a leave of absence next year -- and take his comic strip along with him. Cartoonist Garry Trudeau says...

Sometimes it is preferable in broadcasting to omit names altogether if they are obscure and not relevant to understanding the story:

print:

SINGAPORE (UPI)--Garlic, known to scare away vampires and members of the opposite sex, may soon do the same to mosquitoes, two Indian scientists say.
The pungent herb has been found to be an effective pesticide, New Delhi scientists A. Banerji and S. Amonkarby said in an article in the Singapore Scientist Tuesday.

b'cast:

Two Indian scientists have come up with what they say is a new and effective way to chase mosquitoes: squirt them with garlic. The scientists report...

or

Bothered by mosquitoes? Well, two Indian scientists say they've found a product that'll drive mosquitoes away. The product is garlic. Of course, it may drive your friends away, too...

(This last version is an example of a "kicker," a light item often used at the end of a radio or TV newscast. More about kickers in Chapter 11.)

AGES

In print journalism, a person's age is given after his or her name, set off by commas.

ST. LOUIS (UPI)--A couple said to be members of a white supremacist group were ordered held without bail Tuesday on charges they conspired to assassinate the Rev. Jesse Jackson.
Londell Williams, 30, and his wife, Tammy J. Williams, 27, of Washington, Mo., appeared Tuesday before U.S. Magistrate Carol Jackson. She determined that there was enough of a

threat to the Democratic presidential candidate to hold the
couple without bail pending grand jury action.
    The pair are charged with conspiring to kill Jackson and
with possession of illegal weapons. They were arrested Friday
in Franklin County, Mo., about 50 miles west of St. Louis.

In broadcast journalism, a person's age *precedes* his or her name. "Year-old"
is spelled out and hyphenated along with the age:

A Missouri couple accused of plotting to kill Democratic

presidential candidate Jesse Jackson has been ordered held without bail.

Thirty-year-old Londell Williams and his **27-year-old** wife, Tammy,

were arrested last week about 50 miles west of St. Louis. They are said

to be members of a white supremacist group.

Unlike print journalists, broadcasters do not automatically include people's
ages in their stories. There's no hard-and-fast rule about when to include ages
and when not—except that ages should be included whenever they are essential
to the nature of a story. For example:

A grandmother won today's seven-mile run in Chesterton.

Forty-four-year-old Elise Harvey was met at the finish line by her

daughter, **22-year-old** Cornelia, and her granddaughter, **18-month-old**

Elaine.

Sometimes an age may be given and a name omitted entirely, depending on
the nature of the story and its distance from the immediate audience.

print: NAPLES, Italy (UPI)--Two young muggers stripped their
victim of his trousers Tuesday when he refused to hand over
$4,100 in his pockets, police said. Enrico Barcella, 48,
appeared at police headquarters in his underwear to report the
robbery in Piazza Bovio in the center of Naples.

b'cast: In Naples, Italy, a pair of muggers took more than **a man**'s money

today. They also took **his** pants.

Police say the muggers forced the **48-year-old** man to strip when he

refused to hand over the 41-hundred dollars stashed in his pockets.

NUMBERS

Many news stories deal in some fashion with numbers, not just in people's ages and amounts of money, but also in the form of statistics issued by companies, government agencies, researchers, or international organizations. Journalists come upon an unending stream of statistics to measure the economy, law enforcement, defense procurement, government appropriations, crop production, and so on. Broadcasters (who also rely on statistics to measure audiences—the ratings) treat numbers very differently from print journalists, chiefly by using *fewer* of them.

Numbers on paper can be reread. Numbers on the air are heard just once. A steady barrage of them can lead to audience confusion. Here's a typical example of the sort of statistics-laden copy streaming into broadcast newsrooms:

```
     DETROIT (AP)--Domestic automakers wrapped up their best
model year in two years as late September car sales surged 7.9
percent ahead of year-ago figures, U.S. carmakers said
Tuesday.
     Imported cars sold at a near-record pace in the model
year but fell 9.1 percent in September from a year ago because
of low inventories, the companies said.
     As a whole, estimated sales of 8.81 million foreign and
domestic cars in the model year that traditionally runs from
Oct. 1 to Sept. 30 were up 14.7 percent from 1982 and the best
since 1981's 8.95 million.
     The six major domestic automakers sold 6.48 million cars
in the model year, up 16.8 percent from 1982. The 1982 model
year was the worst since 1961, while the 1983 model year was
the best since 6.59 million cars were sold in 1981.
     In late September, domestic automakers delivered 241,198
cars compared with 223,512 a year earlier. The daily selling
rate of 26,800 was the highest since 33,756 were sold each day
in the period in 1978.
     General Motors Corp. said it sold 144,841 cars in late
September, a 7.9 percent boost. For the month, GM shipped
314,315 cars, a 4.2 percent gain. GM's model year tally was
3.88 million, a 14.4 percent gain over 1982 and the best since
4.03 million were delivered in 1981.
     Ford Motor Co.'s late September sales totaled 58,657, a
13.2 percent improvement over a year earlier. In the month,
Ford shipped 133,442 cars, up 21.2 percent. The model year
tally was 1.48 million, up 14.8 percent from 1982 and the best
since 1981's 1.49 million.
     Chrysler Corp. delivered 27,279 cars between Sept. 21-30,
a 2.6 percent increase over a year ago. In September, it sold
64,061 autos, up 16 percent. The model year count was 819,209,
a 24.4 percent boost over 1982 and the best since 1979's
986,647.
```

Broadcasters must translate this mesmerizing cascade of figures into a form the audience can readily follow and understand. They choose the most significant figures, then round them off whenever possible. Here's an idea of what we're striving for:

It's been a good year for the U-S car industry. Figures just released in Detroit show U-S carmakers sold **nearly six-and-a-half million** cars in the model year **1983**. That's up almost **17 percent** over the year before. The biggest gain was at Chrysler, which boosted sales by **nearly 25 percent**.

Although that story is somewhat dated, it clearly shows how radically statistics must be simplified for broadcast news storytelling. The rules are as follows:

1. Choose only a few numbers—the most important ones.
2. Never report a statistic without telling its significance.
3. Round off numbers whenever possible.
4. Spell out the numbers one through nine. Use figures for all other numbers—*except* when a number occurs as the first word of a sentence; in that case, spell it out (Example: "**Thirty**-year-old Londell Williams . . .").
5. Spell out any numbers subject to error in pronunciation.
    For example, everyone knows how to say the year 1990. But what about the year 2017? Is it "twenty seventeen" or "two thousand seventeen"? You must decide which is correct, then script it that way.
    Street addresses pose a similar problem. Addresses are expressed differently in different cities, according to local custom. The address "3049 E. Main St." might be expressed "three-oh-four-nine East Main Street" in one locality and "thirty forty-nine East Main" in another. You must script your copy according to correct local usage.
6. To avoid confusing the person who reads your copy on the air (who is very likely to be yourself), *hyphenate* connected numbers ("six-and-a-half million," "11-thousand-648" or "11-thousand-six-hundred-48").
7. Try to avoid long numbers. A number scripted as "4,372,612" is destined to cause trouble. If it is vital to tell the exact number, make it "four million, 372-thousand-612." Otherwise, round it off ("nearly four-and-a-half million").
8. Spell out all signs, fractions, and decimals. "$600" becomes "six hundred dollars" or "600 dollars"; "18¼" becomes "18-and-a-quarter"; "20.7 million" becomes "20-point-seven million"; and so on.
9. Never use Roman numerals, mathematical symbols, or print-style abbreviations for weights and measures.
    Super Bowl XXIII should be written "Super Bowl Twenty-three." Pope John Paul II is "John Paul the Second." Shakespeare's *Henry V* is "Henry the Fifth."
    You will see an Einstein formula written as "$e=mc^2$." In broadcast news copy this becomes "E equals M-C squared." Always spell out "plus," "minus," "times," "divided by," and so on.
    If a college fullback stands 6'3" and weighs 220 lb., the radio or TV account of his performance in the big game will say he "stands six-three and weighs two-twenty" or he is "six feet, three inches tall and weighs 220 pounds."
10. Whenever possible, personalize numbers for your audience. Example:

```
print:        BIGTOWN (CNS)--The City Council voted on Thursday to
        raise $2.4 billion through a 1% retail sales surtax, effective
        next Monday, to finance construction of a crosstown
        expressway.
```

```
b'cast:       The City Council passed a surtax today that'll add a penny to each

        dollar you spend at the store.

               The retail surtax of one percent goes into effect next Monday.   It's

        designed to raise nearly two-and-a-half billion dollars for a new

        crosstown expressway.
```

The foregoing is a very effective way to relate numbers to a viewing and listening audience. It tells the effect of numbers on *them*. In other words, it puts the audience in the story.

ABBREVIATIONS AND ACRONYMS

By now you are sufficiently aware of the need to spell things out in broadcast news copy. So let's formalize it.

> *Rule:*
> ***Do not use abbreviations.***

That said, let's note a few exceptions. "Mr.," "Mrs.," and "Dr." are okay, as are military rank designations such as "Gen.," "Sgt.," "Lt.," etc. Among clerical titles, "Rev." is clear enough, but *not* "Msgr.," which should be written out ("Monsignor").

Among political designations, "Sen." and "Rep." are okay, but *not* "Cong." Why? Because an anchor seeing "Cong. Pat Schroeder" might say "Congress-*man*," realizing too late that it should have been "Congress*woman*." The same applies to all titles where English makes a distinction as to gender: Chair-man(woman), Spokesman(woman), etc.*

---

*The subject of gender in language has become rather touchy in recent years, largely because of the feminist movement and the major advances of women in the professions, including broadcast journalism (where women now number roughly half of the people entering the field). Unfortunately, the battle against "sexism" in language has led to certain excesses. Sometimes you will hear newly coined titles like "Chairperson" and "Spokesperson." Most broadcast news departments reject such designations as being uncolloquial.

In the effort to avoid "sexist" language, some writers lapse into grammatical errors, such as "The consumer gets *their* money's worth." Proper English requires the masculine pronoun (he, him, his) when the gender of the singular antecedent is unspecified. To be grammatically correct, the sentence should read "The consumer gets *his* money's worth."

Because broadcast newswriting should follow the rules of grammar, and because using nonsexist language is a good idea, the solution is to put such constructions in the *plural:* "Consumer*s* get *their* money's worth."

What about all those government agencies—FCC, FAA, FHA, SEC, and so on? They should be *hyphenated* in broadcast copy: F-C-C, F-A-A, S-E-C. However, if the agency is relatively obscure (that is, if most listeners wouldn't recognize it by its initials), then it should be *named* on first mention and its letters used only on subsequent mention:

```
The Securities and Exchange Commission filed suit against two Wall

Street firms today for alleged stock manipulation.  The S-E-C suit

charges that the two firms...
```

Once again, the practice is to write things the way they are to be said. Thus,

```
N-double-A-C-P leader Benjamin Hooks says...(not "NAACP" or

"N-A-A-C-P")
```

As for acronyms (initial letters pronounced as a word), the practice is to begin with a capital letter and put all remaining letters in lower-case. Thus,

```
Nato commanders met in Brussels today...
```

```
                              -0-
```

```
Senator Murphy said Nasa's budget should be increased drastically...
```

```
                              -0-
```

```
In Vienna, the Opec ministers ended their meeting without a decision

on oil prices...
```

Some initials and acronyms are so obscure that they require virtual translation to be comprehensible. For example, CINCPAC, which is pronounced "Sink-pak" and which is the Pentagon abbreviation for "Commander-in-Chief, Pacific," should be rendered as "The U.S. Pacific Command" or "U-S Naval headquarters in the Pacific." In other words, whenever you come upon an abbreviation or an acronym for an agency whose function you do not know, find out what that agency does and include that information, if pertinent, in your story:

```
The Government Accounting Office -- that's the agency that oversees

federal spending -- says the Commerce Department is overspending its
```

```
budget. The G-A-O says the Commerce Department spends 40 million dollars

a year just for paper...
```

LISTS

Like long series of numbers and long titles, long lists can bog down newscasters and listeners alike. An example of a "list story":

```
    WARSAW--Crowds of Poles jammed stores throughout the
country Tuesday to buy milk, eggs, bread, salt, sugar, frozen
meat, canned goods, and other food products affected by
drastic government austerity moves that will raise prices by
as much as 50 percent by Thursday.
```

If you tried to say all that on the air, you'd risk losing listeners well short of the checkout counter. For broadcast use, the shopping list must be shortened radically:

```
Poles rushed today to stock up on basic foodstuffs to beat huge

price increases set for later this week.  The Polish government has

decreed price hikes of as much as 50 percent on bread, sugar, and other

foods.
```

Another type of list story is an account of a newsmaker's spoken or written remarks beginning with "I would like to make four points. First . . ." or "The panel makes the following recommendations: 1 . . ." followed by a point-by-point list. Print journalists can retain the newsmaker's structure ("The President also made these points:"). But that won't work on radio or TV because of time constraints; it would simply eat up too much time to respect the newsmaker's organization. Therefore, broadcast newswriting requires the rejection of the "list of points" structure and the substitution of straightforward wording: ·

```
...The President also said he has asked the Commerce Secretary to

work up a new trade policy with Eastern Europe.  On still another matter,

the President said he will ask Congress to increase the budget of the

Drug Enforcement Agency.
```

Getting rid of the list structure enables you to pick and choose among the points, according to your news judgment, and to keep your sentences short.

EXERCISES

1. The following news agency story combines the pitfalls of statistics and lists. Using the guidelines detailed in this chapter, write a maximum 40-second story slugged DRUG DEATHS.

```
bc-drugdeaths   5-22 0532
Study: L.A. most drug deaths, S.F. most per capita
     DETROIT (UPI)--Cocaine-related deaths in tri-county
metropolitan Detroit skyrocketed by 1,350 percent from 1983 to
1987 and all drug-related deaths increased by 68 percent
during that period, a new federal study indicates.
     The five-year study also found that Los Angeles had the
largest number of drug-related deaths in the country, although
the number has declined in recent years. San Francisco led in
terms of per-capita drug-related deaths.
     The study, conducted by the National Institute of Drug
Abuse in Rockville, Md., and published Sunday in the Detroit
Free Press, also found that last year, cocaine contributed to
145 deaths in Wayne, Oakland, and Macomb counties, compared
with 10 in 1983.
     Nationwide, cocaine contributed to 1,207 deaths in 1987,
surpassing heroin for the first time as the country's leading
killer drug, the study shows.
     The institute tracked drug-related deaths and emergency
room visits in about two dozen metro areas, focusing on the
most frequently cited illegal drugs, such as heroin, cocaine,
PCP, marijuana and LSD.
     Among the findings:
     --Of the cities surveyed, the most drug-related deaths in
1987 were reported in Los Angeles, which had 1,488. However:
that number was down from 1,693 in 1983 and 2,878 in 1986.
Philadelphia was third with 869 deaths and San Diego was
fourth with 412.
     --Calculations by the Free Press from the institute's
figures found Detroit had 92.59 drug-related deaths per
100,000 people in 1987. San Francisco led all major cities
with 115.29 deaths per 100,000. Philadelphia ranked third with
52.82 deaths per 100,000.
     --In Detroit, drug-related deaths increased from 595 in
1983 to 999 in 1987 when the city's drug-related death rate
ranked second out of the 10 largest cities surveyed by the
institute.
     --Detroit-area deaths involving the mixture of heroin and
cocaine known as a "speedball" rose from eight in 1983 to 71
in 1987--the highest among the cities surveyed. Los Angeles
had the second highest number of speedball-related deaths (61)
followed by Philadelphia with 48.
-------------------
upi 01:52 ped
```

2. Slug the following obituary DAVIS OBIT and write a version running no longer than 20 seconds.

bc-davis-obit 1stld-writethru 5-21 0403
     BEVERLY HILLS, Calif. (UPI)--Sammy Davis Sr., a
vaudeville dancer whose career spanned 40 years and launched
his popular entertainer son into show business, died Saturday
at his home, a family spokesman said. He was 87.
     Davis, the grandson of slaves who was born in 1900 in
Wilmington, N.C., died at his Beverly Hills home of natural
causes, said Arnold Lipsman, a family spokesman.
     Davis began his career before World War I in New York
City where he won a series of dance contests.
     When his son was born in 1925, Davis was a dancer in Will
Mastin's Holiday of Dixieland vaudeville revue. His wife,
Elvira, was a chorus girl.
     Sammy Jr. first toddled onto a stage in Columbus, Ohio,
when he was 18 months old. His surprise walk-on fouled up his
parent's dance number, but brought down the house.
     The youngster soon joined Mastin's family revue and by
the time he was 4, was performing with his father on the
Orpheum Circuit, where skimpy finances often forced the pair
to share a hotel bed.
     After World War II, "The Will Mastin Trio"--Davis, his
son and Mastin--became a box-office draw in nightclubs in Los
Angeles, New York and Las Vegas and also appeared on the Ed
Sullivan, Jackie Gleason and Eddie Cantor television shows,
with the younger Davis emerging as the star.
     The elder Davis also portrayed jazz musician Fletcher
Henderson in the 1955 film, "The Benny Goodman Story."
     After several years of touring together, Sammy Sr.
retired but Sammy continued, still billed as "The Will Mastin
Trio starring Sammy Davis Jr." The younger Davis last appeared
with his father in a 1973 General Electric Television special.
----
upi 09:13 ped

7

"Who" (Part Two)—
Libel and Attribution

We come now to the more difficult aspects of handling the "Who" element—more difficult not just for broadcast journalists but for writers and editors in all media. On the one hand, journalists have a duty to tell the audience where they get their information (the source, the attribution). On the other hand, they also have a duty to protect sources who supply important information at great personal risk.

At the same time, unless they weigh their words carefully, journalists risk committing libel, the penalties for which can be extremely severe.

AVOIDING LIBEL

In the broadcast news business, you may be committing libel when you as a writer, reporter, anchor, editor, or producer broadcast false information about someone's activities or character, the effect of which is to harm that person's reputation and/or livelihood. In effect, if *you* convict someone before a court does, the result may be a libel suit against you and your employer; if you lose, you both may be sentenced to pay an enormous sum of money in actual and punitive damages.

In short, libel is to be strenuously avoided. The matter is so serious that many news departments have a policy of clearing potentially libelous stories with a company lawyer before putting them on the air.

However, it is in the nature of broadcast news to work fast, to report breaking developments as quickly as technically possible—indeed, even transmit them live. Thus, in the everyday course of writing and airing newscasts, there will seldom be time to consult a lawyer. Broadcast journalists must understand both the law and the *language* that will protect them.

So let's be precise on how to avoid libel. If you as a journalist go on the air and say

> John Doe robbed a bank today,

and John Doe did not rob a bank, you have committed a libel, and Mr. Doe's lawyer may come after you. But if you say

> *Police say* John Doe robbed a bank today,

you have not committed a libel—as long as the police did say it. The police may be wrong, and if so, Mr. Doe can sue them for false arrest. Mr. Doe's lawyer may think he can sue you for libel because you broadcast a false charge and possibly harmed his client's reputation—but unless you knew the charge was false and aired it anyway, Mr. Doe's lawyer will not be successful.

What you have done is to follow routine journalistic practice by placing responsibility for the charge with an established authority, also known as an "official source." You have attributed the accusation to an executive agency. You have, in effect, put the charge in someone else's mouth.

Rule 1:
Always attribute. Tell what you know and how you know it.

But wait. Suppose you had said,

> Bank manager Richard Roe said his bank was robbed today by John Doe.

Matters have suddenly become tricky. Is bank manager Roe right or wrong? Did John Doe do it or didn't he? Roe has made the accusation, but are you as a journalist correct in reporting it?

The answer is *no*—especially if all you have is Roe's accusation. Bank manager Roe is not an official source. His charge against John Doe is not an official one. Only law enforcement agencies (police, prosecutors, grand juries, etc.) can make official charges.

Suppose, however, that you have not only Roe's accusation but also John Doe's denial. May you broadcast both the accusation and the denial? Again the answer is *no*. If Doe is innocent, he may sue both Roe, for raising a false charge, and you, for propagating (spreading) a libel.

Realistically speaking, there will be times when you will be writing news stories containing unofficial charges against private citizens. The stories may be a result of your own investigation, or the result of a tip from a source you cannot name on the air. Either way, you must *not* air the story without giving accused persons the chance to tell their side. And if you were unable to reach such accused persons, you must be prepared to prove that you made diligent, repeated efforts to contact them in person or by phone.

Rule 2:
You must make every effort to give accused parties
a chance to defend themselves.

Although your station's attorney may contend that your repeated efforts to get the other side of the story demonstrate your fairness and good intentions, the safest course is *not* to report Roe's accusation, even with Doe's denial. It is better to wait until the authorities take legal action—in other words, until you have an official source—than to air a potentially libelous story.

Why so much caution? Because John Doe is a private citizen, fully entitled to the presumption of innocence and full legal process. Private citizens have the right to be left just that—private. Only when established public agencies name them, or when news organizations have compiled convincing documentary evidence, may private citizens be named as alleged wrongdoers.

Now suppose the story goes like this:

Bank manager Richard Roe said today his bank was robbed by Mayor Jones.

May you legally say that on the air even before you get Mayor Jones's reaction? Yes, you may—because Mayor Jones is a *public official,* not a "private citizen." (However, if you *know* Roe's charge to be false, but you broadcast it anyway because of its "human interest" value, you may be opening yourself up to a libel charge.)

You see, current U.S. law makes a distinction between how the news media may treat public officials as opposed to private citizens. The Supreme Court, in the landmark Sullivan decision (*The New York Times Co.* vs. *Sullivan,* 1963), ruled that public officials may not successfully sue for libel even if the reporting is wrong, unless the news media act out of *actual malice,* showing a *reckless disregard* for the truth. In other words, to wage a successful libel suit, a public official must prove that a news organization deliberately printed or aired falsehoods in full knowledge of their falsity, or without taking steps to substantiate the information. The Court held that granting public officials the same absolute protection as private citizens would tend to inhibit and discourage reporting on important public issues.

In subsequent decisions, the Court broadened the definition of public officials to include public *figures,* anyone voluntarily in the public eye—such as performers, professional athletes, etc.

To summarize:

1. The best defense against libel is truth—to report only what is ascertainable or can be clearly attributed to official sources.
2. The next best defense against libel is to report both (or all) sides of an accusation—to diligently seek out an accused party and report his or her reaction to the charge.

This may sound complicated to some of you. Although I've tried to simplify matters, libel is in fact a complicated facet of American jurisprudence. Libel laws are different in each state. Ideally, you should familiarize yourself with the libel laws in each state where you find employment. At the very least, you must adhere to the two rules given in this chapter. In a professional broadcast newsroom, you will be expected to follow them routinely as you write and air the day's news.

There is also a commonsense way to approach these matters once you start working in a radio or TV newsroom. As you gather information on a story, and then as you write it, ask yourself, Am I being fair to all parties mentioned in my story? Have I done everything possible to reach all sides? Have I made every effort to double-check the facts as I know them? What can I do to follow up any loose ends after the broadcast?

And then, just for good measure, put yourself in the shoes of the accused and imagine how they fit. If they pinch your toes, perhaps you better do some more checking.

PROTECTIVE LANGUAGE

Those of you with experience in print journalism probably know most of the words commonly used in connection with potentially libelous stories. Chief among the verbs are

> say
> allege
> charge
> accuse

and past participles used as adjectives:

> alleged
> accused
> reputed

Chief among the nouns are

> allegations
> charges
> accusations

All these words, especially the verb "say" or "said" put in the mouth of police or other official sources, serve to protect the rights of accused persons even as they protect you and your employer against libel charges. They signify "What I'm reporting is an official charge or accusation. I cannot vouch for its ultimate truth, which, in time, will be decided by the proper authorities."

The trouble with such protective words is that, except for "say" or "said," they are seldom used in informal speech and therefore tend to sound stilted on the air. Unfortunately, there is really no adequate solution to the problem. The matter of legal rights and duties is too important to risk avoiding occasional stodginess in favor of everyday speech. So this is one area where the phrasing you must use in broadcast news is very close to the phrasing of newspapers and news agencies.

However, you can often rely heavily on "say" and "said"—provided you mention the source of an allegation in *every sentence*. For example:

```
Police have arrested a suspect in this morning's First National Bank

robbery.  They identified him as 41-year-old John Doe.  Police say Doe

was caught three blocks from the bank with the stolen money in a laundry

bag slung over his shoulder.  They say he was identified by bank

employees.
```

That sort of language is simple, the storytelling style informal, and the wording nonlibelous (even if it turns out that suspect Doe is innocent and merely picked up the bag dropped by the real culprit; police accounts are often inaccurate and demolished in court by defense attorneys. And the bank employees could be mistaken).

Indictments

Indictments are a bit trickier. An indictment is merely an *accusation* of wrongdoing, not proof. Anyone under indictment has a right to a trial in a courtroom, not in the news media. But since public perception of this elementary legal point is somewhat shaky (to say the least), broadcasters are better advised to use the more stilted wording:

```
A Nelson County grand jury today indicted two Ridgewood building

contractors in an alleged bid-rigging scheme.  Contractors John Doe and

Richard Roe are accused of conspiring to drive up the price of county

garage-building projects.  The indictment charges that Doe and Roe

overbilled county taxpayers to the tune of nearly four million dollars.
```

In reporting charges and indictments, you should be aware of nuances in wording that can endanger the legal protection of your story. If you say

Police are seeking 18-year-old John Doe **for** the kidnapping and murder of (or **for** kidnapping and murdering) an 8-year-old girl . . .

you are in effect saying that Doe did it; you have convicted him, when in fact he merely has the status of suspect. If he is innocent, your story is potentially libelous.

However, if you say

Police are seeking 18-year-old John Doe **in** (or **in connection with**) the kidnapping and murder of . . .

you are on safe ground. "In connection with" is a loose term connoting Doe's suspect status; it indicates that police think he may have done it. At this point they want to arrest him for questioning, and formal charges may or may not follow. Such wording is nonlibelous.

Safeguarding Nonlibelous Attribution

If you are writing a story based on original reporting—if, for example, you are covering a police beat either on the scene or by phone—it will be up to you to use the proper nonlibelous language; you will have no print model to work from. But much of the time you will be writing a broadcast version of a story you have received from a news agency—perhaps a story like the following:

```
     SAN ANTONIO (AP)--A former Libertarian congressional
candidate was accused Tuesday of trying to hire a "patriot" to
kill Mayor Henry G. Cisneros, authorities said.
     Parker E. Abell, 74, a tax protestor who claims to head a
political extremist group called the American Patriots, was
held without bail in the Bexar County jail on charges of
solicitation of capital murder.
     Abell, who had been under surveillance for about a month,
was arrested after agreeing to pay an undercover officer
$5,000 to kill Cisneros, Dist. Atty. Fred Rodriguez said.
     "He didn't want just anybody. He wanted a patriot to
carry out the execution," Rodriguez said.
     Cisneros, 40, a four-term mayor and former president of
the National League of Cities, said he was not getting
additional protection and joked that he was insulted he was
worth only $5,000.
     Abell, a resident of Natalia, 18 miles east of San
Antonio, mentioned other possible targets, including State
Comptroller Bob Bullock, before deciding on Cisneros, the
prosecutor said.
     Officers arrested Abell at a supermarket pay phone. In
his car were a .22 caliber rifle and "executive warrants"
issued by the "Sovereign Court of the People," police said.
     "The above-named traitor or traitors are to be executed
on sight," the warrants read. "Each accused has given public
proof of guilt beyond reasonable doubt that he or she is a
traitor to the people of the United States and the United
States Constitution."
     Abell was a Libertarian candidate for the 23rd
Congressional District seat in 1982. Gary Johnson, secretary
of the Libertarian Party of Texas, said Abell's affiliation
with the party ended in 1985.
```

As with virtually all news agency copy, the writer and editor were extremely careful to give the specific source of each specific allegation before transmitting that story to newspapers and broadcast news departments. The radio or TV newswriter's job is to transform the story into broadcast style, without compromising its nonlibelous nature. For the broadcaster, the freedom to choose a lead remains. So does the freedom to shorten sentences. So does the freedom to use informal language. But there is *no* freedom to omit the specific source of a specific allegation. Thus, a 20-second story might go this way:

```
San Antonio police have arrested a man for allegedly plotting to

kill Mayor Henry Cisneros.

A prosecutor identified the man as 74-year-old Parker Abell, a one-

time congressional candidate on the Libertarian ticket.

The prosecutor said Abell was arrested after offering an undercover

cop posing as a hit man 5,000 dollars for Cisneros's murder.  Abell is

being held without bail.
```

That is a bare-bones version. Longer versions (30 or 40 seconds) can detail the right-wing extremist background of the detainee, and perhaps mention Cisneros's reaction. But notice how the lead contains the modifier "allegedly" and how every sentence containing an allegation also contains an official source. It was not necessary to identify "District Attorney Fred Rodriguez" by name or title (unless your station is in San Antonio), but it was necessary to specify his official role, that is, prosecutor or prosecuting attorney. No matter what your personal feelings or opinions, you are obliged as a matter of journalistic fairness to "play it straight"—to tell *who* is making an accusation.

ATTRIBUTION (SOURCING)

Naming the source of potentially libelous statements is just one part of the larger matter of attribution. Journalists in all media attribute (give the source of) all events and remarks they have not witnessed personally. Because journalists cannot be everywhere, that means accounts of most events are attributed to other people. The purpose of attribution is to give readers, listeners, and viewers a guide by which to judge the accuracy of the reporting.

To put it another way: What you see with your own eyes is firsthand information and needs no attribution; the attribution is implicitly yourself. What other people tell you is secondhand information and does need attribution because it cannot always be confirmed quickly.

The difference between attributing in print style and attributing in broadcast style is more of form than of substance. Each medium must attribute, but not in the same way. By and large, print journalism requires the writer to attribute in the lead and followup sentences. But as we've seen, this can result in longwinded, convoluted language. An illustration:

WASHINGTON—Because of better food distribution and improved health care, the world's population has reached 5 billion— more than triple the level at the turn of the 19th century—and is likely to grow by another billion by the end of this century, **the Population Crisis Committee** reported today.

Growth rates are highest in Third World countries, where more than 75% of the world's population lives and nine out of 10 infants are born, **according to a study by the committee, a Washington-based group that works to slow population growth.** At current rates, *it said,* populations will double in Africa, Latin America, and Asia in 24, 31, and 37 years, respectively.

(Don Irwin, © 1988 *Los Angeles Times,* reprinted with permission)

Broadcasters are faced with their customary task of turning this into conversational language. At the same time, they must specify the source of the information. Part of the technique, as we've seen in earlier chapters, is to attribute at the start of sentences instead of at the end:

A research group predicts world population will reach six billion by the end of this century.

The Washington-based Population Crisis Committee says a billion people will be born between now and the year 2000. **It** says 90 percent of them will be in the less-developed nations in Asia, Africa, and Latin America.

However, in the effort to find an attention-getting lead, broadcasters may *delay* the attribution until a followup sentence:

World population will reach six billion by the end of the century. That's the prediction from **the Population Crisis Committee, a Washington- based group that favors slow population growth.**

The group says one billion people will be born...etc.

or

If you think the world's crowded now, just wait until the year 2000. **According to a Washington-based research group,** that's when world

```
population will reach six billion.  The Population Crisis Committee says

a billion people...etc.
```

Get the idea?

Raising Doubt

Another reason for attributing carefully is to raise doubt about the reliability of the information you are reporting. You may well ask, If information isn't reliable, why report it at all? Well, ideally, you wouldn't. But the job of newsgathering and reporting does not operate under ideal conditions. Without the benefit of first-hand experience—in other words, most of the time—journalists are forced to rely on information supplied by others. Most of the time, such secondhand information is accurate and trustworthy. Very often, however, it is not. It ranges from the honest mistake (a wrong date, a wrong time, a wrong name), to the misperception (John Doe didn't knock the man down; he was trying to help him up), to the outright lie ("We are not negotiating a hostage deal with Iran"; "I am not a crook").

Despite repeated efforts to check and verify what they are told, journalists are often at the mercy of their sources of information, and it sometimes happens that mistakes, misperceptions, and lies are reported as fact. Broadcast news is especially susceptible to reporting inaccuracies because of its very speed. Broadcasting's advantage of immediacy becomes a disadvantage in the editorial process of checking information. In an environment of never-ending competition, the temptation to broadcast *now*, this very minute, is almost irresistible.

Therefore, the doubt-raising nature of clear attribution is often the only help listeners or viewers will get in deciding whether to believe what they hear.

As you gain experience in journalism, you will develop a sense for which sources are generally trustworthy and which are not. But as a matter of writing technique, you should always include an attribution. In the case of news agency copy, this means retaining the attribution given by the agency. Sometimes that attribution is buried deep within the text:

```
     WARSAW (UPI)--Communist Party bosses Monday told Poles,
struggling with the worst financial crisis since World War II,
that they face 30 percent to 40 percent increases in food
prices and reported hoarding already has begun.
     In the past, such increases have sparked riots and the
downfall of party leaders.
     A senior party official, Manfred Gorywoda, told a meeting
of economic experts at a Central Committee headquarters in
Warsaw that workers face a drop in living standards of 4
percent when the food price increases take effect in January,
1984, the official PAP news agency reported.
     Gorywoda described the economic plight of the debt-ridden
nation as "very complicated," the agency said.
     He then confirmed reports that panic buying and hoarding
of basic foods already had started in some Polish provinces as
a result of persistent rumors that increases would be
dramatic.
     "We are getting signals from the provinces about the
```

```
buying up of some foodstuffs," Gorywoda said. "Common sense
and avoidance of the madness of hoarding lie in the interest
of all of us."
```

You have to read to the end of paragraph 3 to learn the source of this story: PAP, short for the Polish words for "Polish Press Agency." The writer of this print-style story was not present to hear the reported remarks and thus attributed to identify the source.

PAP, like its Soviet counterpart TASS (an acronym for the Russian words for "Telegraph Agency of the Soviet Union"), is a government-run agency. It is not independent as are most Western news agencies. Being an agency of a Communist government, it rarely, if ever, reports anything unfavorable to the government or to Communism anywhere. It is therefore not very trustworthy, and its accuracy is suspect. Thus, it *must* be identified as the source in any print or broadcast story for U.S. news media.*

UPI's writer has taken some justifiable liberties in interpreting the significance of PAP's account in order to put the story in context. For instance, it's hardly likely that PAP would have mentioned that past food price increases led to "riots and the downfall of party leaders." No, that was the UPI reporter calling upon his knowledge of his beat.

Broadcasters are entitled to the same freedom of responsible, informed interpretation, at the same time as they make the story more "speakable":

```
Poles, already struggling to make ends meet, may soon find the going

even tougher.  A high Polish Communist official says Poles can expect

food prices to go up by 30 or 40 percent next January.  The official, as

quoted by the official Polish news agency P-A-P, said people have already

begun to hoard food.  He said such hoarding will only make matters worse.
```

The broadcast version credits PAP only once. As a general rule, it is necessary to credit a source only one time during a story (except, as we have seen, when the story is potentially libelous; then the source is given in every sentence containing an accusation).

Giving Credit

Proper attribution includes giving credit to other, possibly competing, news organizations, whether print or broadcast. Every journalist wants a "scoop," an exclusive story. Scoops are sometimes a matter of luck, but mostly they are a journal-

---

*Under the *glasnost* liberalization, many Soviet and Eastern European news media began to report on matters they previously ignored: crime, corruption, shortages of consumer goods, religion, human rights, and so forth. Despite such "openness," they remain government-controlled and must therefore be named as sources in Western news media stories.

ist's reward for hard investigative work or personal contact with newsmakers and their organizational staff. Just as journalists are elated to get scoops, they are miffed (to say the least) when competitors get them. Part of their annoyance is because they know credit must be given where credit is due. Here's an example of a minor scoop:

NEW YORK—Sen. Albert Gore Jr., who ran a distant and disappointing third in Tuesday's New York primary, will bow out of the presidential race today, sources in his campaign said.

The sources, who spoke on condition of anonymity, said Gore was still struggling to decide between two options: officially suspending his campaign—which would allow his 421 delegates to attend this summer's Democratic convention—or taking the less expensive and cleaner route of simply pulling out of the race.

(Karen Tumulty, © 1988 Los Angeles Times, reprinted with permission)

An exclusive story such as this eventually reaches broadcast newsrooms via the AP or UPI, which will write their own versions and credit the originating news organization. (In Los Angeles, local radio and TV stations would see this story at the same time as the local AP and UPI bureaus, and would write broadcast versions directly from their copies of the newspaper.) The broadcast versions thus amount to a rewrite of a rewrite, but transformed into broadcast style:

The Los Angeles Times reports that Senator Albert Gore will drop out of the presidential race today.

The paper, quoting Gore campaign sources, says the Tennessee Democrat is still deciding whether to quit his campaign outright...or merely to suspend it. Suspending it would allow him to keep the 421 convention delegates he's won so far.

or

A newspaper reports this morning that Senator Albert Gore is about to throw in the towel.

The Los Angeles Times quotes Gore campaign sources as saying the Tennessee Democrat will announce later today his withdrawal from the presidential primaries...etc.

Note that the credit goes to the news organization, not to the individual reporter. Individual newsgatherers are named only in the case of well-known syndicated columnists (Jack Andersen, Evans and Novak, etc.).

Note also that the same sort of credit must go to a competing broadcast news organization, whether local or network. The station with the scoop may turn out to be one with which your own station is engaged in hot competition; fairness requires you to credit your competitors, just as they are required to credit you when the scoop is yours.

(In the real world, stations would scramble either to confirm the story or find their own angles. Once they do, they may report the story as their own, without crediting the competition.)

Unnamed Sources

So far we've looked at how broadcasters rewrite material compiled by other news organizations. But how do they handle their own original material which, for one reason or another, cannot be attributed to an official source?

Unfortunately, there's no simple rule that applies throughout the profession. Some news organizations permit very loose attribution ("Sources say. . ." or "Sources tell W-W-X-X News . . ."). Some require slightly more precise, but still loose attribution ("City Hall sources say . . ." or "W-W-X-X News learned at City Hall this morning . . ."). And some require a still higher degree of precision ("Sources in the Mayor's office say . . ." or "Sources on Mayor Smith's staff tell W-W-X-X News that . . .").

To complicate matters, different news departments have different policies on the sort of "bargain" you may enter into with your sources. Typically, a source will agree to tell you something "off the record" in return for a guarantee of anonymity. However, some news departments forbid the reporting of "off the record" remarks under any circumstances. Others grant staffers wide leeway in using material from unnamed sources.

There is also a legal dilemma facing reporters and editors. There are risks in reporting unsourced information because a judge may order a reporter to reveal the name of his or her sources or be cited for contempt of court, and even go to jail. Although most news organizations fully back the presumed right of reporters and editors to guard the privacy of their news sources, the "right" is not absolute; in the meantime it is the reporter who may go to jail.

In short, this is a very thorny issue abounding with legal and professional traps.

That said, here are some guidelines to serve in most situations:

1. Make sure you thoroughly understand the policy of your news department regarding the gathering, writing, and reporting of information from unnamed sources.
2. Always be as precise as you can. For the sake of credibility, it is important to establish as close a link as possible between the subject matter and its source.
3. Some editors and producers will ask you to divulge the identity of your sources—not for broadcast, but rather as a means of judging your story's

credibility. Whether you decide to share the names of your sources with your superiors is up to you, but *in no case* should you reveal the names to other people, not even to your colleagues, family, or friends. You must allow them the legal privilege, in case they are asked, of honestly being able to say, "I don't know."

QUOTATION AND PARAPHRASING

Quoting someone's words is, of course, the most direct form of attribution. Much of the time, broadcast journalists quote people by means of recorded excerpts of their remarks; the excerpts are integrated into the written news stories. Called "actualities" or "voice cuts" in radio and "sound bites" or "talking heads" in television, these recorded excerpts employ writing techniques so specialized that they require lengthy consideration in later chapters. For now, we'll limit ourselves to quotation in broadcast style without the use of audio- or videotape.

As you read the following print-style story, remember that while *you* can see the quotation marks, your eventual viewers and listeners cannot:

```
        WASHINGTON (UPI)--Dick Gregory, a comedian who used
prolonged fasts to draw attention to civil rights and other
issues, came to Capitol Hill on Wednesday to ask Congress to
help Americans who are so overweight that their health is in
danger.
        Gregory, who appeared at a news conference with several
patients he is now treating, said: "The crisis of obesity in
America, which threatens the lives of more than 11 million of
our citizens who are dangerously overweight, is a public
nightmare that demands immediate federal attention."
        Referring to a Hempstead, N.Y., man he helped to lose
about 400 pounds, Gregory said: "Thanks to Walter Hudson and
the press, thousands of obese folks decided to come out of the
closet. I got thousands of calls."
        The comedian said he became aware of Hudson's case after
newspaper reports described how a rescue team had to free him
when he got stuck in a doorway. Hudson, who had remained in
his bedroom for 17 years and remains homebound, once weighed
1,200 pounds.
        Gregory urged Congress to establish a hot line, to set up
an institute for obesity at the National Institutes of Health,
and to conduct hearings on the problem.
```

Suppose, in rewriting this story for broadcast, we said,

```
Comedian Dick Gregory called on Congress today to help end "the

crisis of obesity in America."  Gregory said "Eleven million of our
```

```
citizens are dangerously overweight" -- "a public nightmare that demands

immediate federal attention."
```

Please read that paragraph *aloud*.

Do you *hear* the effect of listeners not being able to see the quotation marks? In case you retain any doubts, the effect is to give the impression that Gregory's *opinions* are factual. Unless we make crystal clear that a newsmaker is stating opinions rather than facts, we risk giving listeners inaccurate information.

Is there a "crisis of obesity" in the United States? Although Gregory says so, we have only his word for it. Are "Eleven million of our citizens dangerously overweight?" Where did Gregory get that statistic? Is it accurate and reliable? And in what sense is being overweight "dangerous" for 11 million people? The story doesn't say. So again we have only Gregory's word for it. Is the matter of obesity really a "public nightmare"? Does obesity demand "immediate federal attention"? Again, these are Dick Gregory's opinions, not facts. He may be right, but he may also be wrong, in whole or in part. As journalists, it is not up to us to decide if his opinions are right or wrong—but it *is* up to us to write a *clearly labeled* account of them.

In sum, Gregory's words are so laden with value judgments and questionable assertions that we must make clear that the remarks are his alone and that we, the transmitters of his assertions to a wider audience, do not necessarily accept or share them. We do this by using certain verbs and locutions to enable listeners to identify quotes whose punctuation they cannot see. The most commonly used verbs and locutions are:

> call
> term
> claim
> what he (she, it, they) called
> what he (she, it, they) termed
> calling it
> terming it
> in his (her, its, their) words
> as he (she, they) put it
> —and these are his (her, their) words—
> in the words of
> according to

By careful paraphrasing and by using one or more locutions, we can clearly label opinions in broadcast style. (Frequently, the verbs "say" and "said" will suffice to identify an opinion, usually a noncontroversial one. But if that opinion is to be quoted exactly, it is better to use a locution.)

Examples:

Comedian Dick Gregory urged Congress today to take action on **what he called** the "public nightmare" of obesity in America. **In Gregory's words,** 11 million Americans are "dangerously overweight" and need public assistance.

Gregory called on Congress to set up an obesity hot line...and an institute for obesity at the National Institutes of Health.

–0–

In Washington today, a call for help for the overweight and obese: Comedian Dick Gregory urged Congress to set up an obesity hot line...and an obesity section at the National Institutes of Health.

According to Gregory, 11 million Americans are "dangerously overweight" —— a situation **he called** "a public nightmare that demands immediate federal attention."

–0–

Claiming that 11 million Americans are "dangerously overweight," the comedian and political activist Dick Gregory called today for aid to the obese.

As Gregory put it, obesity is "a public nightmare that demands immediate federal attention." He said Congress should create an obesity hot line...and an obesity division at the National Institutes of Health.

Notice that in each of the above broadcast rewrites, it is possible to delete the quotation marks without misleading the audience. However, the quotation marks are left in as a sort of visual punctuation for the anchor. With or without the quotation marks, the combination of paraphrasing and locutions makes clear to the audience that it is hearing opinions rather than facts.

Paraphrasing can be a delicate matter. After all, many newsmakers choose certain words because they think they're the right ones. For newswriters to reject those words in favor of other ones that lend themselves to broadcast style can be viewed as unfaithful to the real meaning, or even arrogant. Using your words to report someone else's ideas and opinions does indeed hold that risk. However, most of the time a careful newswriter can use clearer words, and *fewer* words, to convey accurately the sense of a newsmaker's remarks.

But there are times when broadcast newswriters must closely adhere to the exact words of a newsmaker, even though the result might sound stilted and unwieldy on the air. A case in point:

WASHINGTON—Ultraconservative Sen. Jesse Helms (R-N.C.) bitterly attacked the late Dr. Martin Luther King, Jr., in a speech Monday on the Senate floor, calling him unworthy of a holiday in his honor and denouncing him as a communist sympathizer.

"Dr. King's action-oriented Marxism . . . is not compatible with the concepts of this country," Helms said as he launched a filibuster to prevent the Senate from voting on a bill to make the third Monday in January a paid federal holiday in honor of the assassinated civil rights leader's Jan. 15 birthday.

"The legacy of Dr. King was really division, not love," Helms said many people in this country believe.

Helms' Senate remarks seemed almost temperate compared with a report prepared by his office and released Monday that accuses King of "hostility to and hatred for America" and speculates:

"King may have had an explicit but clandestine relationship with the Communist Party or its agents to promote, through his own stature, not the civil rights of blacks or social justice and progress, but the totalitarian goals and ideology of communism."

Evidence "strongly suggest(s) that King harbored a strong sympathy for the Communist Party and its goals," said the report, which concluded, nonetheless, that "there is no evidence that King was a member of the Communist Party."

(Ellen Warren, © *Chicago Sun-Times*, reprinted with permission)

The racial and political overtones of that story make it pretty strong stuff: a U.S. senator describing as a crypto-communist a man perceived by millions of Americans as a hero. The senator's words are potentially offensive, and the standard locutions may not suffice, especially if the story runs longer than 20 seconds on the air. So here are the more formal locutions that serve for this kind of story:

quote
unquote
end quote
quoting him (her, them) directly
and these are his (her, their) exact words

Thus, broadcasters might render the foregoing story this way:

```
The senator leading the fight against a national holiday for the
late Dr. Martin Luther King Junior today called Dr. King a communist
sympathizer. In a speech on the Senate floor and in a report released by
his office, Senator Jesse Helms of North Carolina denounced Dr. King in
very strong terms. Helms said, and these are his words, "Dr. King's
```

action-oriented Marxism is not compatible with the concepts of this

country." Helms said many Americans--**again quoting him directly**--believe

"the legacy of Dr. King was really division, not love." The report from

Helms' office said there's evidence, **quote,** "that King harbored a strong

sympathy for the Communist Party and its goals," **end quote.** Helms'

remarks came at the start of a filibuster against a bill to make the

third Monday in January a federal holiday in Dr. King's honor.

Yes, that's a mouthful, and yes, it sounds stilted. But this is a case where the nature of the material overrides the customary informality of broadcast newswriting. The material cries out for quotation at length: You can't have a U.S. senator calling someone a communist and let it go at that.

So, in cases where you want to (or must) quote at length, it is fine to use the words "quote . . . end quote" (or "unquote"). But try not to overdo it. Rely whenever possible on the more informal phrasing.

To sum up,

1. If *you* can say something more clearly and directly than the original speaker, then *paraphrase.*
2. If the original speaker's words are clear, colorful, biased, or controversial, then *quote directly,* either formally or informally, as the story dictates.

EXERCISES

1. The following story demonstrates many of the pitfalls of quotation and attribution. Slug it SNYDER and write *two* versions of it, each 40 seconds long. Following the guidelines in this chapter, do your best in the first version to paraphrase in broadcast style, and, in the second version, to quote directly.

NEW YORK (AP/UPI)--CBS Sports commentator Jimmy "the Greek" Snyder said Friday that if blacks "take over coaching jobs like everybody wants them to, there's not going to be anything left for the white people."

Snyder, known for his predictions on sporting events, later apologized to anyone he said he may have offended by the remark and others in an interview with WRC-TV in Washington. He has worked for CBS for 12 years.

Snyder was interviewed at Duke Zeibert's, a Washington restaurant. WRC reporter Ed Hotaling went there on Friday, the Rev. Martin Luther King Jr.'s birthday, to ask people about the progress blacks have made in society.

"I'm truly sorry for my remarks earlier today, and I offer a full, heartfelt apology to all I may have offended," Snyder said in a statement released by CBS Sports.

The network had made no decision Friday on whether Snyder would work Sunday's NFL broadcast, CBS spokeswoman Susan Kerr said.

Irv Cross, a black who is one of Snyder's colleagues on "NFL Today," said he was shocked by the remarks.

"They don't reflect the Jimmy the Greek I know, and I've known him for about 13 years," Cross, a former defensive back with the Philadelphia Eagles, said in a telephone interview from his Virginia home.

In the WRC interview, Snyder said blacks had been bred to be better athletes since the Civil War, when "the slave owner would breed his big black with his big woman so that he would have a big black kid. That's where it all started."

Snyder, 70, also said that if blacks "take over coaching jobs like everybody wants them to, there's not going to be anything left for the white people. I mean all the players are blacks. The only thing that the whites control is the coaching jobs.

"Now, I'm not being derogatory about it, but that's all that's left for them. Black talent is beautiful, it's great, it's out there. The only thing left for the whites is a couple of coaching jobs."

Pluria Marshall, head of the Washington-based National Black Media Coalition, said Snyder's comments made him sound like "some plantation master."

Marshall said professional sports remains an area of segregation where "everything is white except for the athletes that draw people to the stadiums."

Snyder said one of the reasons blacks were better athletes is that whites were lazy.

"There's 10 players on a basketball court. If you find two whites you're lucky. Four out of five or nine out of 10 are black. Now that's because they practice and they play and practice and play. They're not lazy like the white athlete is."

In addition to Snyder's apology, CBS Sports issued a statement saying that it "deeply regrets the remarks made earlier today to a news reporter by Jimmy (The Greek) Snyder. We find them to be reprehensible. In no way do they reflect the views of CBS Sports."

8

"When"

By now you must have noticed that we've been saying "today" in all broadcast versions of news agency and newspaper copy, instead of naming the day of the week. As we noted in our preliminary discussion of "immediacy," broadcasting's advantage over print is speed, the ability to transmit the news many hours ahead of newspapers. In broadcasting, today's news happens *today*, not "Monday" or "Thursday." And increasingly, as all-news radio and television continue to grow in popularity, the news happens *now*, this very minute. There used to be a deadline every hour. Now's there's a deadline every minute. The expression "This just in . . ." has become part of the national vocabulary.

Rule:
Always use wording that shows immediacy.

Here's a list of "When" words and locutions broadcasters commonly use to exploit the immediacy of radio and TV news:

today
tonight
this morning
this afternoon
this evening
yesterday

tomorrow
last night
the day before yesterday
the day after tomorrow
last week
next week
in a few days
a few days ago
next Sunday (Thursday, Friday, etc.)
a week from Thursday (Sunday, Friday, etc.)
by next week
this (last, next) month
"This just in . . ."
moments ago
at this hour
within the hour
a short time ago

I may have missed some, but you get the idea. In broadcast news, the "When" element is expressed in relation to *now,* the moment the story is on the air.

We don't want listeners and viewers to lose the thread of the story by having to recalculate the When element in their heads. If the date is April 14 and tax returns are due on April 15, we do not want to go on the air and say "The tax filing deadline is April 15th . . ." because people might pause to think, "Well, let's see, today is April 14th, and tax returns are due April—Hey, that's tomorrow!" We do the calculating for them. On the air we say, "The tax filing deadline is tomorrow."

Exploiting broadcasting's immediacy requires far more than just throwing in a "today" or a "moments ago." It requires keeping on top of the news in order to be able to air the latest angles of stories and to be prepared for what happens next. Depending on which fresh story elements are available at air time, the wording broadcasters use at 6 P.M. is different from the wording at 3 P.M.; it changes again at 10 P.M., again after midnight, again in mid-morning, again at noon, and again in mid-afternoon.

Proper use of the When element in broadcast newswriting also depends on understanding the heart of the broadcast-style sentence—the verb and its attendant voice, person, and tense.

VERBS

Broadcast verbs should be short and active. "Short" is easy enough to understand: *buy* instead of "purchase," *say* instead of "declare," and so on. But "active" gives newcomers (and some veterans) a lot of trouble. So let's take a few minutes to revisit English 101.

Voice

The "voice" of a verb is either active or passive. When a verb shows the subject of a sentence to be doing the action,

> He **sees** the ball

the verb is in the *active* voice. When the verb shows that the subject is being acted upon,

> The ball **is seen** by him

the verb is in the *passive* voice.

So when we say broadcast verbs should be active, we mean they should be written in the active voice; the subject of the sentence should be acting upon the object of the sentence. Whenever possible, a print-style news agency story written in the passive voice should be rewritten in the active voice.

Before this gets to sound too much like grammatical jargon, let's cite a typical example:

```
     TAMPA, Fla. (AP)--More than four tons of cocaine were
discovered in hollowed-out Brazilian lumber bound for U.S.
cities, federal authorities announced Wednesday.
```

The verb in that sentence—"were discovered"—is in the passive voice. And "discover" is a long word compared to "find." So putting the verb in broadcast style requires both a change of word and a change of voice. To do that, you must rearrange the sentence:

```
Federal agents have found more than four tons of cocaine hidden in

Brazilian lumber bound for U-S cities.
```

By now your eyes should be growing accustomed to the form of broadcast-style sentences. But in case they are not, please read both the print and broadcast versions aloud. Perhaps your ears will tell you what your eyes may have missed— namely, that the broadcast version is easier to say and easier for the listener to follow. And see what a change of voice does for the following:

```
The Supreme Court today handed down a ruling on civil rights...
```

(instead of: A ruling on civil rights was handed down today by the Supreme Court . . .)

–0–

Governor Clements **has announced** his stand on the proposed highway

tax...

(instead of: A stand on the highway tax was announced today by Governor Clements . . .)

–0–

Observers **saw** the action as a thinly veiled response to...

(instead of: The action was seen by observers as a thinly veiled response to . . .)

Why the active voice? Because most of the time it is

1. Clearer
2. More concise
3. More natural to the rhythms of spoken English

That said, using the active voice is not an ironclad rule. There are exceptions. Most of the time, it is better to say "Police arrested so-and-so" rather than "So-and-so was arrested by police." However, in the case of a well-known person, a "name in the news," opening the story with the name works as an attention-getter, even though the verb winds up in the passive voice. Thus,

Comic Richard Pryor **was released** from the hospital today...

(instead of: The hospital released comic Richard Pryor . . .)

–0–

A New Jersey senator **was indicted** today on charges of...

(instead of: A grand jury indicted a New Jersey senator today on charges of . . .)

Please remember that by using conversational language, you can avoid the active/passive dilemma altogether:

```
Comic Richard Pryor went home today.  Pryor left the hospital nearly

two months after critically burning himself while free-basing cocaine...


                              -0-


A New Jersey senator is in legal trouble this evening, following his

indictment on influence-peddling charges...
```

Person

Okay, back to English 101. Grammatically, "person" refers to the relationship between an action (expressed by a verb) and the person being addressed. The distinguishing pronouns are:

First Person:	I, we
Second Person:	you
Third Person:	he, she, it, they

In broadcast journalism, just as in print journalism, the expression of the verb/person relationship is overwhelmingly in the third person. A reporter may occasionally write a first-person "eyewitness" story saying "I saw this" or "I'm told that," and a writer may have occasion to use a phrase like "As we reported earlier." But as narrative, broadcast storytelling usually assumes the detached viewpoint inherent in the third person.

Where print and broadcast journalism differ markedly is in the use of the second person—*you*. As we've noted repeatedly, broadcast newswriting favors the informality of everyday speech, and when people converse, they throw in a lot of "yous." Even though the anchor/listener "conversation" is one-sided, the reality of one person talking to another should be exploited. A "you" may refer to viewers and listeners directly, or it may be impersonal, the equivalent of the French *on* or the German *man*. Either way, the effect of "you" is to personalize the anchor/listener relationship, making broadcast newswriting even more like traditional storytelling.

We used some examples of the second person in earlier chapters:

```
If you think the world's crowded now, just wait till the year

2000...


                              -0-
```

```
    The City Council passed a surtax today that'll add a penny to each

dollar you spend at the store...
```

In broadcast news, there is also a special use of the third person plural
"they." "They" may be used like the impersonal "you" as a substitute for "people"
or "observers," or, in a limited way, for official sources. For example, people
normally say something on the order of "They say it'll rain tomorrow." "They"
may refer to an official weather forecast heard on radio or TV, or merely to an
idle remark overheard at the supermarket. Broadcasters have the freedom to use
"they" informally from time to time—provided that they go on to specify who
"they" are:

```
    They came from all over the Southwest -- young people packing a fair

grounds near San Bernardino for what's being billed as the largest rock

music festival since Woodstock...


                              -0-


    They're calling it the largest stock swindle in U-S history.  The

Justice Department has charged two Wall Street firms with bilking

thousands of retired people of their life savings...
```

After a while you will begin to recognize the kind of news agency copy that
lends itself to "you" and/or "they" rewriting. Typically, it will be a feature story
where the action itself (the What element) is more compelling than the specific
person(s) who did it (the Who element). For example:

```
    NEW YORK (AP)--The first bales of the nation's best-known
garbage collection were unloaded, inspected and burned Tuesday
after being towed 6,000 miles on a barge, rejected by six
states and three nations, challenged in court and lampooned on
television.
    "Good riddance," city Sanitation Commissioner Brendan
Sexton said as he oversaw the work at the Southwest Brooklyn
Incinerator.
    It was the beginning of the end of the five-month saga of
the garbage barge. Incineration of the 3,186 tons of trash is
expected to take about two weeks, and the ashes will be
trucked away to be buried at a landfill at Islip, on Long
Island.
    The barge set out on March 22 from a private dock in
Queens. The barge was turned away from a North Carolina
landfill for lack of proper permits. That started the
6,000-mile trip, on which the cargo met with angry rejections
```

```
from Alabama, Mississippi, Louisiana, Texas, Florida, Mexico,
Belize and the Bahamas.
```

Some broadcast versions will retain the third person (but will nevertheless put the story in the active voice):

```
In New York, sanitation workers have at last begun destroying that

bargeload of garbage nobody wanted...
```

However, by using "you" and "they," a broadcast writer can do a more arresting job of storytelling:

```
You remember that bargeload of garbage nobody wanted?  Well, today

they finally started to burn it.

    Sanitation workers destroyed the first bales of the more than 3,000

tons of garbage at an incinerator in Brooklyn, New York.  The trash had

gone on a barge ride that covered 6,000 miles in five months.  Six states

and three foreign countries refused to accept it.

    Are they happy the odyssey is over?  Well, in the words of the New

York Sanitation Commissioner, "Good riddance."
```

Viewers and listeners are going to remember a story written that way. It is storytelling as only radio and television can do, relying on the informality and inflections of spoken English.

But a word of caution: The trick to using "you" or "they" effectively is not to overdo it. Most news stories involve serious matters and thus require a serious approach. So save "you" and "they" for stories where they do not detract from the seriousness of the subject matter.

Tenses

We've seen that the When element in broadcast news is expressed according to two factors:

1. The time an event occurs
2. The air time of the newscast

Grammatically, this entails choosing the verb tense that best demonstrates immediacy. Thus, our last stop at English 101 requires a review of verb tenses. We'll use "say," which is by far the most frequently written verb in broadcast news.

	infinitive:	to say
	present participle:	saying
	past participle:	said
	present gerund:	saying
X	present tense:	say, says; is (are) saying
X	past tense:	said
	past imperfect tense:	was (were) saying
X	present perfect tense:	has (have) said
	past (plu)perfect tense:	had said
X	future tense:	will say; will be saying
	future perfect tense:	will have said
	conditional future tense*:	would say; would be saying
	conditional future perfect*:	would have said

The four tenses marked by *X*—present, past, present perfect, and future—are the ones used overwhelmingly in broadcast news copy. Context and shades of meaning may occasionally require use of other tenses, but such cases are rare. Much of the time, you will be changing the verb tenses you see in print-style news copy. Because the present—the here-and-now—is broadcasting's trump card, to be played whenever possible, you will often be changing a print-style past tense into a broadcast-style present tense. And in compound sentences, you will be changing the past/conditional to the present/future.

Now let's translate all this grammar into detailed guidelines and examples:

1. Use the present tense whenever possible, especially for events that are occurring at air time (known as "breaking news").

```
The school board is meeting (at this hour) on the teachers' request

for a pay raise...
```

-0-

```
A fifth hook-and-ladder company is on its way (or is en route) to a

three-alarm fire on the South Side...
```

-0-

---

*Some grammarians identify what I here call "conditional" as the "past future tense," the "subordinate future tense," or the "past subjunctive." We could quibble endlessly. For the purposes of newswriting, the help word "would" indicates a preexisting condition: Something might happen *if* something else does. As this chapter attempts to explain, "conditional" tenses are avoided in broadcast news copy, unless it is important to make a distinction indicating doubt about a future occurrence.

Senator Danforth **is** the guest speaker tonight at a downtown
fundraiser...

2. Use the present tense for statements or conditions that, although having
occurred earlier, are still true at air time.

Three Ridgewood businessmen **are** under indictment (**this evening**) for
alleged bid rigging at Westwood Mall...

-0-

The District Attorney **is lodging** fraud charges against the Widget
Corporation...

-0-

Building Commissioner Rex Danforth **is announcing** his retirement...

3. Because statements by newsmakers and allegations from official sources
usually require you to write compound sentences, use the broadcast-style
present/future or present/past tenses in place of the print-style past/past or
past/conditional.

The White House **says** President Jones **will veto** the new trade
bill...(present/future)

-0-

Senator Smith **says** he **will not** (or **won't**) **run** for a third
term...(present/future)

-0-

Police **say** the suspect **fired** twice before escaping...(present/past)

-0-

The indictment **alleges** the businessmen **conspired** to rig construction
bids on the Westwood Mall...(present/past)

4. Use the simple past tense for one-time events that took place shortly before air time.

```
Fire destroyed a warehouse this morning on West Eighth Street.
```

-0-

```
A bridge over the Lackawanna River collapsed a short time ago.
First reports say no one was hurt.
```

5. Switch to the present perfect tense as the time lag widens between event and air time.

```
Fire has destroyed a warehouse on West Eighth Street.
```

-0-

```
A bridge has collapsed over the Lackawanna River.
```

-0-

```
Three Ridgewood businessmen have been indicted on bid-rigging
charges.
```

Many fledgling newswriters get confused on the wording of past tense and present perfect tense sentences. Here's a guideline: *include* the specific When element with the simple past tense, and *omit* the specific "when" with the present perfect.

```
A one-armed man swam the English Channel today, in both directions.
(past)
```

-0-

```
A one-armed man has swum the English Channel, in both directions.
(present perfect)
```

-0-

Peru **this morning warned** foreign fishermen to stay out of its
territorial waters. (past)

-0-

Peru **has warned** foreign fishermen to stay out of its territorial
waters. (present perfect)

or

Peru **is warning** foreign fishermen...(present)

Again, consider the flexibility of *spoken* English, allowing broadcasters to
break the grammatical constraints of written English:

It's never been done before –– a one-armed man swimming round-trip
across the English Channel...

-0-

A warning from Peru to foreign fishermen: Stay out!

Using the foregoing guidelines, let's take a typical local news story and see
how the broadcast-style When element works in practice. Situation: A fire breaks
out at a warehouse at 10 A.M. and is put out by 10:30 A.M. Only between 10 and
10:30 may we use the present tense on the air·

Firefighters **are battling** a warehouse fire on West Eighth Street...

or

Firefighters **at this hour are** at the scene of a burning warehouse on
West Eighth Street...

By 11 A.M., the fire having been extinguished, we must switch (obviously) to
the past tense for the 11 A.M. News and the Noon News. But we can still show
immediacy by saying "this morning."

A fire **destroyed** a warehouse on West Eighth Street **this morning.**

or

A fire **destroyed** a warehouse on West Eighth Street **a little while**

ago.

For the 1 P.M. and 2 P.M. News, we can still say "this morning." After all, it happened only a few hours ago. We will still sound fresh and immediate.

But by 9:00 P.M., we risk sounding stale if we retain "this morning." (In the news business, staleness sets in *very* quickly.) We have two options. We can switch to "today":

Fire **today destroyed** a warehouse on West Eighth Street.

or

Fire **destroyed** a warehouse **today** on West Eighth Street.

or we can switch to the *present perfect* tense:

Fire **has destroyed** a warehouse on West Eighth Street.

What we have done in each case is to slightly de-emphasize the time lag between the event and our reporting of it. And in so doing, we have preserved our *sound* (or "image") of immediacy.

To show you how far this goes, let's continue with the present example. The word "today" or use of the present perfect tense will carry us through the Evening News (radio or TV). But by the Late News (10:00 P.M. or 11:00 P.M.), not only will the story be stale but it will also be very close to ancient history. (In broadcasting, ancient history is hot on the heels of staleness.) So once again, we must find a way to preserve our immediacy. By Late News time, we want very much to be able to say "tonight." So we must find a legitimate way, both in news gathering and in language, to remain on top of the news.

Investigators **tonight are ruling out** arson in a fire that **destroyed**

a warehouse on West Eighth Street.

or

Fire investigators **tonight are probing** the cause of the blaze that

leveled a warehouse on West Eighth Street **today**.

This way, we have not only found a way to get "tonight" into the lead, we have been able to return to the present tense as well.

And to push the example a step farther, let's say it's now the next morning—nearly 24 hours after the event (which, for the record, is fast receding into prehistoric times). If we report the story at all, it must only be in terms of a fresh and immediate angle.

```
Fire investigators are still puzzled this morning over the cause of

that warehouse fire on West Eighth Street.
```

Okay, I grant you, that's not all that fresh. The point is, that's the kind of wording and approach you must use if you decide to use the story at all. It emphasizes what is happening *now* and treats what happened yesterday as common knowledge.

Contractions and "Not"

Contractions may be forbidden in most print journalism, but they are very useful in broadcast journalism because they are characteristic of informal speech. We've used lots of examples in our model stories—and you should use them, too.

However, be careful in using *negative* contractions and the word "not." In news stories, "not" is often used to stress something important and out of the ordinary. If you write (for example),

```
President Jones says he won't visit the Philippines next month...
```

the meaning may in fact be clear enough. But if the development was unexpected (that is, if the visit had been on the president's schedule), you should consider avoiding the contraction in order to stress the change in plans:

```
President Jones says he will not visit the Philippines next month...
```

In their scripts, many newswriters and anchors like to underline the word "not," just to make sure the word is not overlooked and the meaning of the story therefore reversed. Another way NOT to lose "not" is to capitalize it.

Still another method of avoiding the pitfalls of "not" is to choose completely alternative wording. For example,

```
President Jones has cancelled plans to visit the Philippines...
```

PLACEMENT OF "WHEN"

A few words about where to put the word "today," "tonight," and so on, in the sentence: Take the sentence "The White House announced President Jones will visit Mexico today." The meaning of such wording is that the *trip* begins today. That's probably not what the writer meant. If the meaning is the *announcement* came today, the sentence should read, "The White House announced today that President Jones will visit Mexico."

That was a rather obvious example. Even so, it illustrates the general rule that in broadcasting, *the "when" should be placed close to the verb it modifies.*

No: A bomb *exploded* at the El Al ticket office in Manhattan, wounding 12

people *this morning.*

–0–

Yes: A bomb **exploded this morning** at the El Al ticket office in

Manhattan, wounding 12 people.

–0–

No: *Today* a truck *collided* with a school bus on Interstate–80, injuring

six children and the bus driver.

–0–

Yes: A truck **collided today** with a school bus...

or

Yes: A truck **ran into** a school bus **today** on Interstate–80, injuring...

As with so many things concerning writing, there are exceptions, especially when we wish to maintain informality or to achieve stylistic effect:

Last month, President Jones **said** he did not intend to visit Mexico

in the near future. **Today** he **changed** his mind. The White House

announced the president **will** go to Mexico City and Cancun next Friday and

Saturday...

EXERCISES

1. The following story is slugged JUNK FOOD. Write a 30-second story utilizing the second person "you" or the third person "they" in your lead sentence.

```
        LONDON (UPI)--Teen-agers' consumption of junk food and
soft drinks is to blame for the rise in soccer hooliganism,
delinquency and weekend rural rowdiness, two leading
nutritionists said in a report published today.
        "You cannot hope for good behavior on a junk-food diet,
whatever social improvements are made. If only the government,
(soccer) authorities and schools realized this, we could start
to make progress," said Dr. Damian Downing, and Ian Stokes of
the British Society for Nutritional Medicine.
        "Unruly schoolchildren almost always turn into delinquent
teen-agers: and analysis of the diet of (soccer) hooligans
would show a huge amount of nutritional deficiencies," Downing
and Stokes wrote in Healthy Living.
        They want school shops to ban soft drinks, potato chips,
ice cream and chocolate, and instead serve fresh and dried
fruits, sandwiches and pure fruit juice.
        School cafeterias should quit selling french fries,
sausages and baked beans, and offer salads, fresh green
vegetables, meat and fish, they said.
```

2. Write two 30-second versions of the following story (slugged HEROIN ARRESTS), the first for a 6 P.M. air time, the second for an 11 P.M. air time. Lead your 11 P.M. version with the most immediate angle you can find in view of the fact that many in the audience have already heard your first version.

```
AM-Heroin Arrests, 1st Ld-Writethru
U.S., Italian Authorities Hit Sicilian Mafia Drug Ring
        WASHINGTON (AP)--The FBI and Italian authorities on
Thursday arrested more than 100 people, charged dozens more
and cracked a major Sicilian Mafia drug ring that used cocaine
from the United States to buy heroin in Italy for return to
U.S. markets, officials said.
        Attorney General Edwin Meese III called it "the largest
international drug case ever developed by the Department of
Justice." He said it would have a "significant impact on
heroin imports into this country from Italy," but he said he
could not say what volume of drugs has been affected.
        By evening, 38 people had been arrested in the United
States and 64 in Italy, the FBI said. An additional 14 were
already in U.S. jails. A total of 69 arrest warrants were
issued in the United States and 164 were to be issued in
Italy. Some people were being charged in both countries, the
FBI said.
        Meese said the investigation uncovered a Sicilian Mafia
plan in which cocaine was exported from different points in
the United States to Switzerland and Italy, where it would be
exchanged for southwest Asian heroin.
```

The heroin then would be smuggled back to the United States in a variety of ways, including body packs attached to female dancers, stuffed in furniture and inside rare books.

"This is one of the few situations in which there was an attempt to set up a barter economy in drugs," the attorney general said.

The exchange was profitable because cocaine is less expensive in the United States than in Italy, while heroin is cheaper in Italy than the United States. Two kilograms of cocaine can be exchanged for one kilogram of heroin in Italy, FBI spokesman Gregory Jones said. A kilogram equals about 2.2 pounds.

The 69 defendants in the United States include 38 charged in New York City, six in Los Angeles and Boston, 10 in Charlotte, N.C., eight in San Juan, Puerto Rico, two in Cleveland and five in Washington, D.C., the FBI said. In Italy, authorities intended to charge 164 people, the FBI said.

U.S. authorities seized 6 kilograms of heroin and 4 kilograms of cocaine along with cash, weapons, vehicles, fur coats, paintings and jewelry during the course of the investigation, the FBI said. Italian authorities said they seized 25 kilograms of heroin, 5 kilograms of cocaine, and arms, ammunition and counterfeit currency.

The investigation was continuing, Meese said.

According to a government affidavit filed in U.S. District Court in Manhattan, two of the defendants in New York City and one of those charged in Charlotte are fugitives from Italian drug convictions. Some of the other defendants are illegal aliens, according to the document.

Suspects arrested Thursday have been charged with conspiracies to import, possess and distribute drugs, the FBI said.

FBI Director William Sessions said Italian law enforcement officials had made 64 arrests and were pursuing fugitives in Italy, Sicily, Venezuela and several U.S. cities.

"The Sicilian Mafia that today's actions are directed against is one of the primary groups responsible for the importation of southwest Asian heroin into the United States," he said.

He said that three other primary groups bringing drugs into the United States are Mexicans, Colombians and Asians.

9

"Where"

Newspapers and newsmagazines sometimes print a map alongside a story to help readers visualize its location. Readers may pause at any point to study the map, then resume reading the story.

As we've noted, viewers and listeners do not have that option. They do not carry detailed maps in their heads or have time to consult an atlas while watching or hearing the news. If they become confused about a story's location, they may also become confused about the story itself. As journalists, we don't want that to happen. Thus, telling the Where element simply and clearly is an essential part of broadcast newswriting.

(TV journalists are able to use maps and other visual aids to show the Where element. This often makes it unnecessary to use extra words to pinpoint locations in the news copy itself. We will be looking at this in Chapter 15. For now, it is important to understand that the rules of broadcast style apply equally to radio and television. Thus, in order not to get bogged down in technical details, we shall stick for the moment to the radio newswriting format.)

As is our custom, we begin with a print-style model:

```
    PHOENIX (AP)--Hundreds of U.S. and Mexican firefighters
on Sunday battled fires that burned thousands of acres of
brush and timber on both sides of the border and raced across
an Apache Indian reservation, officials said.
    A forest fire that started in Mexico charred 6,000 acres,
about 3,500 on the U.S. side of the border near Nicksville,
```

```
and damaged two structures in a park picnic area, said U.S.
Forest Service spokesman Jim Payne in Phoenix.
      Payne called the blaze "a raging monster out of control"
and said it had threatened ranch homes in the Coronado
National Monument, about 50 miles south of Tucson, before they
were saved by crews who started backfires.
      Nearly 200 miles north, a second fire that was sparked by
lightning Friday on a reservation near Cibecue had burned more
than 500 acres of timber and brush by early Sunday, Payne
said.
```

Stylistically, that story offers all sorts of rewriting challenges for broadcast journalists. Especially appealing as a lead is the quote from the forest ranger (who called the forest fire "a raging monster out of control"—words that may be somewhat overdramatic but which certainly do provide a terrific opening). You are also familiar by now with many of the routine changes required to achieve broadcast style: changing "Sunday" to a more immediate "today" or "this morning," switching to the present tense, reorganizing the structure to tell each element separately (there are two fires, hundreds of miles apart), shortening the sentences, keeping the numbers to a minimum, moving attribution to the start of sentences, and so forth. That takes care of Who, What, When, and Why/How. But handling the Where element is somewhat tricky and requires closer examination.

The AP datelined the story "Phoenix" because that is where the agency got its information (from the U.S. Forest Service). But the events themselves were taking place hundreds of miles away. That is often the case in the news business; reporters may be forced to rely on public or private agencies (which have their own internal communications systems) to provide information that might otherwise be inaccessible. So there are really two Where elements to consider:

1. In writing stories for radio and TV, the first priority is telling the location of the events themselves.
2. The second priority is telling the location of the source of information. But if that source is trustworthy, it is permissible to omit its location altogether.

Here, then, are some of the ways broadcasters might rewrite this story:

```
A forest fire is raging out of control along the Arizona-Mexico

border. The U-S Forest Service says the fire has destroyed 6,000 acres

so far, mostly on the Arizona side near Nicksville.

     Farther north, a brush fire charred more than 500 acres, including

an Apache Indian reservation near Cibecue.

     There are no reports of injuries in either fire.
```

−0−

"A raging monster out of control." That's how a U−S Forest Service spokesman describes a forest fire still burning **along the Arizona−Mexico border.** He says the fire has charred 6,000 acres so far, more than half of them **on the U−S side near Nicksville.**

About 200 miles north of that fire, a brush fire triggered by lightning swept across an Apache Indian reservation. There are no reports of injuries.

−0−

Hundreds of U−S and Mexican firefighters are battling a forest fire **along the Arizona−Mexico border.** A U−S Forest Service spokesman **in Phoenix** says the fire has destroyed 6,000 acres so far, mostly **on the Arizona side.** The spokesman calls the fire "a raging monster out of control."

In central Arizona, a brush fire raced across an Apache Indian reservation −− but there are no reports of injuries.

Each of these versions is short, running about 20 seconds. However, despite their brevity, each paints a clear mental image of the *geography* of the story. It is a judgment call whether or not to place the Forest Service spokesman in Phoenix. It is a judgment call whether or not to place the fires near Nicksville and Cibecue; both communities are so small they do not appear on many maps. But since virtually everyone knows where Arizona and Mexico are, it is vital to situate the action in geographical terms that the audience can understand. We can formulate this into a rule:

Rule:
Always state an unfamiliar location
in relation to a more familiar one.

That rule is worth closer consideration, because some news agency stories contain little help with geography (which is why we suggested many chapters ago that you provide yourself with an almanac or world atlas). Here's an example of how consulting a map can help you draw a geographical picture for your audience:

print
model:

TAYLORSVILLE, Ky−−A coal mine collapsed during the early

shift Monday morning, killing at least 11 miners and sending
at least 14 others to nearby hospitals, authorities said.

broadcast
rewrites:

A coal mine collapse killed at least 11 miners today in

Taylorsville, Kentucky, about 30 miles southeast of Louisville. At least

14 miners were injured.

–0–

At least 11 miners died in a coal mine collapse this morning **in the**

town of Taylorsville, southeast of Louisville, Kentucky.

–0–

A coal mine collapse **in Kentucky** today... At least 11 miners were

killed in **Taylorsville, midway between Louisville and Frankfort.**

–0–

In Taylorsville, Kentucky –– that's about 30 miles from Louisville –

– a coal mine collapsed this morning, killing 11 miners.

–0–

At least 11 miners are dead in a coal mine collapse **in north central**

Kentucky. It happened in Taylorsville, outside of Louisville.

However, if you happen to be working at a station in the Louisville-Taylorsville-
Frankfort region, where people *already know* the geography, you need only write,

A coal mine collapsed **in Taylorsville** this morning, killing at least

11 miners...

And if your station is *in* Taylorsville or a nearby community, you can come right
out and name the mine and its address:

```
     At least 11 coal miners died this morning in the Cardwell Number

Four mine on West Burnham Road.  The mine collapsed just after nine

A.M....
```

You see, just as stating the When elements depends on a combination of time of occurrence and time of broadcast, so stating the Where element depends on a combination of (1) the location of the event and (2) the location of your station.

ADDRESSING THE LOCAL AUDIENCE

It comes as no surprise that most people are more interested in what happens down the block than in what happens halfway around the world. People are more interested in events close to home or in places they have visited, or where they have friends and relatives, than in what to them may be obscure points on a map.

Unless you work at a network, where you must write for a widely scattered audience, you must tailor your copy to suit the needs of your specific local audience. Most of you will begin and end your broadcast news careers at local stations . . . for the simple reason that that's where most of the jobs are. At the same time, however, most of the news agency copy you receive is, like network news, aimed at a nationwide (or worldwide) audience. Part of your job will be to tailor copy like the following for local consumption:

```
     SOUTH CHARLESTON, W.Va. (AP)--A natural gas explosion
destroyed a crowded supermarket Monday, injuring at least 17
people, authorities said.
     All employees and customers were believed accounted for,
said a state police superintendent, but searchers continued to
use shovels to dig for more victims possibly trapped inside.
     "All those who were in the store have now been accounted
for. We no longer expect to find any bodies," said Supt. John
O'Rourke, but he said he could not rule out the possibility
that someone may be in the debris.
     The explosion occurred shortly after an employee lit a
cigarette in the supermarket, said State Trooper A. W.
Robinson, but he said it was not immediately known if the
cigarette caused the explosion.
     Also under suspicion was a major gas line about 40 feet
from the Foodland supermarket that was accidentally ruptured
about noon by construction crews working on an Appalachian
Corridor G highway project, said Bill Reed, district manager
for Colombia Gas of West Virginia. The line was leaking at the
time of the blast, he said.
```

If you were writing for a network or a local station *far away* from the scene, you might make it,

```
        At least 17 people have been hurt in a gas explosion at a

supermarket just outside (or near) Charleston, West Virginia...
```

If your station is closer to the scene, say, in the same state or a bordering state, you might make it,

```
        In South Charleston, just west of Charleston, a gas explosion today

injured at least 17 people at a supermarket...
```

And if your station is in the immediate area, you might make it,

```
        At least 17 people are hurt in a gas explosion at the Foodland

supermarket near the Appalachian Corridor G highway project...
```

Note that in the first example, only the larger, better-known place is named in the lead, and in the third example the exact location is named. As the audience grows more specific, so does the Where element grow more specific.

Do not be disturbed that spelling out the Where element causes you to write extra words and thus eat up precious air time. The extra words are normal and necessary in broadcast writing. Again, the objectives are clarity and immediate understanding.

RESTATING LOCATION

As for reinforcing the Where element, the wording can be much simpler. In fact, a single word will usually suffice, that word being the name of the location used as an adjective: "The *New York* Governor," "The *Taylorsville* mine," "The reaction of the *Roanoke* town council," and so on. In the case of the preceding South Charleston explosion story, "where" reinforcement might go this way:

```
        A natural gas explosion injured 17 people today at a supermarket

near Charleston, West Virginia.  The explosion leveled the store, but

rescuers who combed the debris say all shoppers and employees are now

accounted for.  The supermarket was near a gas line and highway project

in the town of South Charleston.  West Virginia state police speculate

the explosion was caused when a lighted cigarette touched off leaking gas
```

```
fumes.   A gas company official confirms the gas line was leaking at the

time of the blast.
```

The desirability of renaming the location in the body of the broadcast story is one major difference with print style. Another major difference is that sometimes you don't have to name the location geographically *at all*. In broadcasting, some "datelines" are superfluous:

```
The White House announced today in Washington...
```

—0—

```
In Paris, the French government said today its soldiers will stay in

Lebanon...
```

In these examples, naming the city was unnecessary. *Of course* the White House is in Washington and the French government is in Paris! It is only when events occur *outside* their accustomed place that it's necessary to tell where:

```
President Smith announced today at Camp David...
```

—0—

```
Governor Thompson, on a visit to Rockford, called today for a

massive highway repair project...
```

Normally, those two officials would be located, respectively, in Washington and Springfield. Had they made news in those locations, naming the cities would have been superfluous. But since they spoke elsewhere, the specific "where" had to be included.

While we're on the wording of the Where element, consider the following:

```
Prime Minister Margaret Thatcher of Britain warned today that that

country will not tolerate Argentinian occupation of the Falkland

Islands...
```

The wording "that country" is an example of a writer obeying the dictum, probably laid down by a high school English teacher, always to avoid repeating the same word and, conversely, always to find a different word. In broadcasting, this is not, repeat *not*, always desirable. It sounds stodgy, unclear, or both. The lead should read

```
    Prime Minister Margaret Thatcher warned today that Britain will not
tolerate...
```

Similarly,

```
    The mayor of Warsaw today told the people of that city that they
face serious food shortages this winter...
```

should read

```
    The mayor of Warsaw today told his city's people they may face
serious food shortages...
```

In short, if you've found the right word, don't stretch for another one.

LOCALIZING THE NEWS

In addition to expressing the Where element in terms relevant to the local audience, broadcast journalists also reshape the *substance* of news stories for the local audience. Whenever it is possible to find a local angle, a local reaction, or a local follow-up to a national or foreign news story, no matter where it occurs, the local elements are given prominence. The process is called *localizing*. It entails the careful, complete reading of news agency material to identify angles of interest to specific local audiences. For example:

```
    CLEVELAND (AP)--About 4,700 United Rubber Workers members
struck Firestone Inc. plants in six states Sunday, and another
15,000 union members are poised to strike Goodyear Tire &
Rubber Co. at noon Tuesday.
    The Firestone employees walked out after negotiators in
Cleveland failed to reach an agreement prior to a 12:01 a.m.
Sunday deadline.
    The disabled Firestone facilities are in Akron, Ohio;
Noblesville, Ind.; Des Moines, Iowa; Decatur, Ill.;
Russellville, Ark.; and Oklahoma City. The Des Moines,
Decatur, and Oklahoma City plants make tires, the Noblesville
plant makes molded rubber products, and the Russellville plant
makes inner tubes.
    In Des Moines, about 20 Firestone employees picketed the
plant's five gates Sunday afternoon, even though no work
```

shifts were scheduled until 11 p.m., said Bill Winslow, a
production worker and picket captain.

At Firestone's tire plant in Oklahoma City, about 10
workers were on a picket line, said Don Adams, vice president
of Local 998.

As the Firestone strike began, a vote Sunday by a local
in Danville, Va., threatened to produce an even larger
nationwide strike Tuesday against Goodyear.

The Goodyear pact was negotiated as an agreement to serve
as a pattern for the other rubber companies. But Goodyear's
15,000 URW members rejected the tentative contract by a 3-1
ratio two weeks ago.

Fewer than half of the 1,668 members of Local 831 turned
out for the secret ballot on Sunday on whether to take another
look at the proposal. The vote was 467-339 against
reconsidering, union officials said.

"If nothing changes, if the union and the company don't
get back together at 12 o'clock Tuesday, high noon, there will
be a strike," said Linwood Saunders, president of the local.

URW President Milan Stone said Firestone's latest
proposal did not match the pattern settlement.

Clearly, that story contains two developments of national (that is, network)
interest: a rubber workers' strike against Firestone, and a threatened strike
against Goodyear. However, the story names a total of eight cities where the story
has immediate *local* interest: Cleveland, where labor negotiations were held;
Akron, Noblesville, Des Moines, Decatur, Russellville, and Oklahoma City, the
sites of the struck Firestone plants; and Danville, site of a URW Local at
Goodyear. In those eight cities—and in all other cities where Goodyear plants are
located—local journalists will be giving prominence to developments in their
areas. They will reach deep into the news agency copy to "lift up" and stress those
angles affecting local listeners and viewers.

Thus, radio and TV stations in Oklahoma City might say

The Firestone rubber plant **here in Oklahoma City** is one of half a

dozen struck today by the United Rubber Workers.

or

The rubber workers' union struck Firestone plants across the country

today, including the tire plant **here in Oklahoma City**.

They might also come right out and give the plant's street address. They will also
get on the phone to local company and union officials, and they will dispatch
reporters and camera crews to the plant and local union headquarters. In short,
they will transform the story from a network one into a local one.

Meanwhile, local journalists in the other affected cities will be doing the same in their areas, shifting the emphasis to developments affecting their own local listeners. In Danville, Virginia, local radio and TV might say

Danville Local 8-3-1 of the United Rubber Workers today rejected a

new contract with Goodyear. The rejection raises the possibility of a

nationwide strike against Goodyear beginning Tuesday. The strike would

follow a strike that began today against Firestone.

As you can see, the original news agency copy is treated as raw material to be refashioned and rewritten to suit local needs and interests. To put it another way, the most desirable "where" is *here*.

Another example of what to watch for:

NORFOLK, Va. (AP)--Navy salvage workers found the bodies
of three missing sailors at their work stations aboard the
drifting submarine Bonefish on Wednesday, nearly three days
after explosions and fire forced the evacuation of the vessel.
Eighty-nine crew members evacuated the submarine, which
filled with smoke and toxic fumes from an explosion in a
forward battery compartment.
"Shortly after midnight, the salvage crew went aboard and
discovered the bodies," said Chief Petty Officer Terry D.
Borton, a spokesman at Atlantic Fleet headquarters here. "Two
of the victims were discovered in the control room and the
other in an administrative compartment."
The crewmen were identified as Lt. Ray Everts, 30, of
Naoma, W.Va.; Petty Officer 1st Class Robert W. Bordelon Jr.,
39, of Willis, Tex.; and Petty Officer 3rd Class Marshall T.
Lindgren, 21, of Pisgah Forest, N.C.

In the three localities named in the last paragraph, the hometowns of the dead sailors, there are people who knew the victims: family, friends, teachers, merchants, and so on. To these people, the victims are far more than cold statistics; they were flesh and blood, and there are strong emotional reactions. So in Naoma, West Virginia, Willis, Texas, and Pisgah Forest, North Carolina, listeners and viewers must be told more than "Salvage workers have found the bodies of three sailors on the derelict submarine Bonefish. . . ." In each town, the story should be localized to mention *in the lead* that a hometowner was involved:

(In Willis, Texas, and surrounding communities)

The U-S Navy says **Robert Bordelon, Junior, of Willis** was one of

three victims of the Bonefish submarine disaster. Salvage workers found

the 39-year-old Petty Officer First Class...and two other seamen...dead

at their workstations aboard the derelict sub. They were found three

```
days after explosions and fire forced the sub's evacuation at sea.

Eighty-nine crew members survived.
```

Meanwhile, in Naoma and Pisgah Forest and their surrounding communities, local broadcasters were giving similar prominence of place to the local victims.

Not every story can be localized; local journalists should not invent local angles where none exist. However, it's a rare story out of Washington or a state capital that doesn't have ramifications, or at least reaction, on the local level. Local journalists should constantly be asking, "What is the effect of this story on people in my listening area?"

If the defense budget is cut, do any of the cuts affect local defense contractors and their employees? If the president or the governor proposes a highway reconstruction bill, would local roads and traffic patterns be affected? How do local elected officials feel about it? What are their reactions and counterproposals? If the Supreme Court rules on abortion, what are the reactions of local pro- and antiabortion groups? And what are their next moves?

The examples are endless. And so must be your efforts to find local angles. You are broadcasting to neighbors and fellow residents who have an immediate interest in such things. You are also competing with newspapers and other local stations. You can bet that the competition won't be sitting back waiting for local angles to drop into their laps. They'll be out digging for them.

"WHERE" AS TRANSITION

In broadcast news, a "transition" refers to the words bridging the gap between two stories. We will examine transitions—also known as "links"—in a later chapter. But since we're in the midst of the Where element, it's worth noting that "where" serves extremely well as a simple transition, especially when you don't know in advance which stories will precede and follow the one you are writing.

If you *start* a story with the Where element, the chances are good that you, an editor, or a producer can place that story almost anywhere in a newscast without later having to rewrite a more specific transition:

```
In Boston, Mayor Richard Roe announced today...
```

—O—

```
On West 23rd Street, a bus jumped a curb this morning...
```

—O—

```
In Seoul, South Korea, student demonstrators clashed...
```

Using "where" as a transition to make a clean break from an as yet unknown preceding story is especially useful in small news departments. In large news departments, producers usually have enough staff to assign a single writer a group of stories destined to run together; the writer will thus have time to link the stories with creative transitions. But in smaller news departments, where the work load tends to be heavier on everyone, writers have little time for such niceties; they will find that using "where" as an opening transition comes in very handy.

But, again, a caution: Do not overdo it. You can't start every story with the Where element without the newscast sounding monotonous.

EXERCISES

1. Slug the following story EXPLOSION and write a 15-second story, being careful to give listeners a mental map of the location.

        MOSCOW (UPI)--Dozens of explosions wrecked a warehouse at
a Soviet rubber factory on Friday, starting fires which
injured a number of workers, Tass news agency reported.
        Tass said the blasts at the Rezinotekhnika works in
Saransk, an industrial town 270 miles southeast of Moscow,
were caused by a glowing cigarette ash in a garbage can.
        It said "several dozen explosions" sent goods stored in
the warehouse flying into the air and shattered the windows of
two adjoining workshops.

2. The following story contains statistics relating to every region of the United States. Slug it TOOTH DECAY and write a 30- to 40-second *localized* version for your area.

Half of US School Children Are Free Of Tooth Decay, Study Says
        WASHINGTON (AP)--Half of America's 43 million school-age
children have never experienced tooth decay, a dental problem
that affected almost all of America's youth just a generation
ago, according to a federal study released Tuesday.
        In a study that included the oral examination of about
40,000 youngsters coast-to-coast, the National Institute of
Dental Research found that dental cavities have declined by 36
percent among children ages 5 to 17, and that 49.9 percent of
these children had no tooth decay at all.
        Officials said the sample population examined was
selected to represent the approximately 43 million school-aged
children in the nation.
        Dr. James P. Carlos, chief of the epidemiology at the
NIDR, said that dental decay, a problem that has plagued
humankind throughout history, has been steadily declining
since the use of fluoride became widespread and that the trend
probably will continue.
        "This disease, which is probably the most chronic disease
of childhood, is being decreased very fast," said Carlos, "It

is declining 35 to 36 percent every seven years and now half
the children in the country have never even experienced dental
decay."

Carlos said the decline in tooth decay follows a pattern
consistent with the increased use of fluoride in the nation's
drinking water, in toothpastes, and in mouth washes.

He said the increased use of dental sealant also has
affected the decline in tooth decay. The sealant is a plastic
material that dentists paint on the chewing surfaces to
protect teeth from decay.

For the survey, specialists counted the amount of decay
or fillings noted on each of the 128 surfaces of a typical set
of 28 teeth in the school children. A missing tooth was
counted as five surfaces. Wisdom teeth were not counted since
few school children have them.

The result showed that the statistical mean of tooth
surfaces with decay was 3.07 per child. The mean in a survey
taken in 1980 was 4.77, reflecting a 36 percent decline in
tooth cavities.

In 1980, the survey found that 36.6 percent of the
children were free of tooth decay. This compares to almost
half, 49.9 percent, found without decay in the recent survey.

Carlos said no similar surveys were taken prior to the
1980 finding, but experts estimate that only 28 percent of the
school children in the 1970s were without tooth decay, and
that a generation earlier virtually every child experienced
some tooth decay between age 5 and 17.

He said in the 1940s, it was estimated that U.S. school
children averaged seven teeth each that were decayed, missing
or filled.

Now, instead of counting teeth, he said, the survey must
count surfaces affected in order to get a meaningful
statistic.

Carlos said school children in the Southwest, which
includes Texas, New Mexico, Arizona and Colorado, showed the
least amount of tooth decay with a mean of 2.4 tooth surfaces
affected per child. That region showed a mean of 3.4 in 1980.

The New England states, Maine, New Hampshire, Vermont,
Massachusetts, Connecticut and Rhode Island, showed the
highest rate, with a mean of 3.6, compared to a mean of 6.1 in
1980.

Other regional findings, with the mean number of tooth
surfaces per child affected and the same mean from the 1980
survey in parenthesis, are:

Northeast (New York, Pennsylvania, New Jersey): 3.4
(5.4).

Midwest (Minnesota, Wisconsin, Michigan, Iowa, Missouri,
Illinois, Indiana, Ohio): 2.9 (4.7).

Southeast (Maryland, Virginia, Delaware, North Carolina,
South Carolina, Georgia, Florida, Alabama, Mississippi,
Tennessee, Kentucky, West Virginia, Arkansas, Louisiana): 3.1
(4.6).

Pacific (Alaska, Hawaii, Washington, Oregon and
California): 3.4 (5.1).

Northwest (North Dakota, South Dakota, Nebraska, Kansas,
Oklahoma, Montana, Idaho, Wyoming, Nevada and Utah): 2.8
(4.4).

Carlos said the reason for the regional difference "has

never been satisfactorily explained and is one of the enduring
mysteries of dental epidemiology."

At one time, he said, experts thought that the varying
amounts of fluoride in the drinking water of the national
regions accounted for the differences, but that has now been
discounted because fluoride is present in about 60 percent of
the water systems in the nation.

Dr. Preston A. Littleton Jr., deputy director of NIDR,
said the decline in childhood dental decay will make it
possible for the agency to concentrate more of its research
efforts toward dental problems experienced among adults and
older Americans.

"The results give us the opportunity to redeploy efforts
and attempt to make similar gains among the older population,"
said Littleton.
AP-NY 1541EDT

10

Language

At times, the job of writing broadcast news is like being a foreign-language interpreter: You translate the language of a newsmaker into a language your audience can easily understand.

English is one of the world's richest languages—and nowadays the most influential. It long ago supplanted French as the language of diplomacy and German as the language of science. U.S. economic, scientific, and cultural hegemony after World War II made English the primary international language; almost everywhere, nonnative speakers and writers study English as a second language.

But despite (or because of) its richness, English lends itself to imprecision. The imprecision ranges from the ungrammatical coarseness of the undereducated, to the color and verbal shorthand of slang, to the dense and sometimes deliberate obfuscation of jargon. Broadcast journalists encounter such language variations on a daily basis, and their task is to translate them, whenever possible, into the kind of informal, yet clear, style we've been stressing in this book. As we've seen (in Chapter 7), people's words must sometimes be quoted directly. Most of the time, paraphrasing does the job more clearly and concisely. And sometimes, paraphrasing is the only way to "translate" the news clearly.

JARGON

A great deal of the joy of writing broadcast news comes in deflating the often stilted, pretentious language of officials, bureaucrats, and "experts" in many fields. If you ask a politician, "Well, Senator, have you decided to run for president?" and get the reply, "I am studying the position with a view toward making a determination on the eventuality of a viable candidacy," you may have a grin on your face as you write, "Senator Smith says he hasn't made up his mind whether to run for president."

The senator's language is a form of jargon, designed in this case to give the impression of activity where there is none, of answering the question without in fact answering it.

Not all jargon is impenetrable. Some is colorful. Most people speak jargon in one context or another, usually job- or peer group-specific. When a broadcast journalist speaks of "sound bites" or "talking heads," the terms are clearly understood by other broadcast journalists. When a police officer announces "the apprehension of a perpetrator," he or she means "the arrest of a suspect". On the other hand, a lot of jargon is so dense as to be mind-numbing. Spend a few hours reading the *Congressional Record,* corporate stockholder reports, or transcripts of speeches at academic conferences or at the U.N. Trusteeship Council, and you expose yourself to an overdose of bloated, jargon-filled prose. And yet that is often the raw material from which news reports are written. To repeat the newsmaker's jargon in a broadcast news story is tantamount to confusing the audience—and that is unacceptable.

Most of the time you will recognize unacceptable jargon when you hear or read it. The words or meaning will not be clear to you. And if they're not clear to *you,* they will probably not be clear to your audience. So you should get in the habit of asking yourself, "If I write something this way, will people I know—friends, family, fellow students, and so forth—understand it?" If the answer is no, rewrite it in words you and they do understand. When in doubt, ask for help.

To treat the matter fully is beyond the scope of this text. But, essentially, objectionable jargon consists of language not readily understandable by a general (that is, broadcast) audience. Journalists, especially in broadcasting, must learn to spot such words (or phrases) and either delete them or replace them with clearer words. Journalists should:

1. Avoid redundancy.
   Politician: "I want the American people to realize their *hopes and aspirations.*" (Strike "aspirations." It means "hopes" and is three syllables longer.)
   Designer: "This skirt is *very unique.*" (Stike "very." Something is either unique or it isn't. There's no middle ground. "Unique" means "one of a kind.")
   Witness: "The truck *narrowly missed hitting* the car." (Strike "hitting," or say "almost hit.")
   Sales Clerk: "This model has many *new innovations.*" (Strike "new." An innovation is something new.)

2. Avoid foreign words and expressions for which there is a clear English equivalent. Translate them colloquially.
   Book Critic: "This novel's sole *raison d'etre* is to make money." ("This novel's only purpose (or aim) is to make money.")
   Professor: "The Soviet Communist *Weltanschauung* results inexorably in

paranoia." ("The Soviet Communist world view results in paranoia.")

[*Note:* Some foreign words entered the broadcast news vocabulary long ago and may be used without losing the audience; examples are *coup* (short for the French *coup d'etat,* meaning the overthrow of a government) and *junta* (from the Spanish for "military regime.") Occasionally, there are newcomers; an example is *glasnost,* Russian for "openness," and meaning the liberalization of the Soviet system.]

3. Avoid bookish, "highbrow" words where simpler words will do.

Restaurant Critic: "The chef's *gustatory* instincts were *awry.*" ("The cook's taste buds were flat.")

Art Critic: "Heaven knows where the gallery acquired its predilection for antediluvian tableaux!" ("I don't know where the gallery got its taste for primitive art.")

4. Avoid cliches, even though they may be all around you.

Guest Speaker: "I'm *pleased as punch* to address this assemblage of *movers and shakers.* ("I'm very happy to address this important group.")

Football Coach: "We're gonna *get up* for this one and really *sock it to 'em* and *come up smellin' like a rose.* ("We're going to win big next Saturday.")

5. Avoid mixed metaphors.

Politician: I'm *throwing* the tax bill for *a long pass* and hoping someone *crosses home plate* with it. (mixing football and baseball)

Historian: Roosevelt was a *colossus,* taking the world of economic troubles *onto his back.* (confusing the Colossus of Rhodes with the Atlas of Greek myth)

6. Avoid trendy, overworked expressions that become clichés.

Reporter 1: The *bottom line* was he had to start all over again. (Make it "result" instead of "bottom line.")

Reporter 2: The administration hopes to get its foreign policy back *on track* by next year. (Make it "straighten out" or "reorganize" or "adjust.")

Remember, the foregoing list of "don'ts" applies to the language *you* use to write the news in broadcast style. Whenever you quote someone directly, you must obviously report the speaker's exact words, jargon and all.

SLANG

Just as jargon and pretentious language must be "translated down," so must substandard or unsuitable language be "translated up." Solecisms such as "ain't got" and "can't hardly" are taboo if they're *your* words. If they're someone else's words, someone you wish to quote, then the matter must be decided on a case-by-case basis. That's because some slangy words or expressions lend color to a story. So let me make this distinction:

Slang is permissible when it is *both* (1) widely understood and (2) spoken by a news*maker*, not a news*caster*. Put another way, you may quote people in the news who use slang, but you yourself may not use it. Examples:

yes: `The senator called the president's remarks "dopey" and "tomfoolish."`

(It's clear that the senator used those words.)

or: `The senator termed the president's remarks stupid.`

(paraphrase)

but
not: `The senator says the president's remarks are dopey and tomfoolish.`

(Sounds like the newscaster is using those words.)

—o—

yes: `In farmer Smith's words, "You can't hardly get them kind of ducks no`

`more."`

(Substandard English quoted for colorful effect.)

or: `Farmer Smith said that breed of duck is a rare bird indeed.`

(Paraphrasing to retain semblance of colorful effect.)

but
not: `Farmer Smith said you can't hardly find them kind of ducks no more.`

(Substandard writer and newscaster.)

Again, space does not permit an exhaustive listing of slangy examples. Your dictionary and language guide will indicate if a word or expression is considered slang. Suffice it here to warn you to keep your ears open to the way you and your friends talk.

Each of us spends most of his or her time in a limited setting among people of the same general group, whether at home, at school, or in the office. We converse so often with these people that we no longer question certain words and expressions, without realizing that people on the next block or on the other side of town may not know what those expressions mean, or may think they mean something entirely different.

For example, a student newscaster wrote,

```
    After his lecture, Professor Carmichael attended a beer and

munchies...
```

On her university campus, the term "beer and munchies" was a well-known way to describe a get-together where food and beverages were served. The food was not necessarily snacks, and the beverage was not necessarily beer. The expression had thus taken on a generic meaning quite apart from its component words. Although virtually everyone on campus understood it, the radio station served several communities well outside the campus. The station was known to have many, many listeners in those areas who were not or had never been students; they simply liked the programming. For them, the term "beer and munchies," especially used as a noun, was either confusing or meaningless. The student newscaster, aware she was addressing an audience not just of students, should have written,

```
    After his lecture, Professor Carmichael joined students for

refreshments.
```

A mistake like this isn't the end of the world, but it's the kind of thing a broadcast newswriter has to watch for.

The same watchful eye should be kept on idiomatic expressions and colloquialisms. Because such language is often colorful, it can and should be used in broadcast newswriting, but *judiciously*. It must truly lend color, be widely understood, and should be grammatically accurate as well.

```
no:        The mayor, looking like Uncle Ned's whiskers, attacked the city

council for what he called "laziness."
```

(Was the mayor angry? Red-faced? Disheveled? This kind of idiomatic expression shouldn't be used; few people understand it.)

```
                                  -0-
```

```
no:        Seriously injured was 34-year-old Yvette Taylor of suburban

Woodfield. The Taylor woman was taken to Saint Francis Hospital.
```

(Colloquial in the South-Central states, but grammatically poor. Make it "Mrs. (or Miss) Taylor.")

Again, one could fill a book (or several) with examples. But you know your specific audience better than I do, and I leave it to you to judge each case on its merits.

IMPACT OF WORDS

Broadcast journalists have a special responsibility to watch their tongues. That's because spoken words drive more deeply into the psyche than do written ones. This becomes apparent even in childhood. Somehow, the words, "Fe, Fi, Fo, Fum, I smell the blood of an Englishman," just don't seem to strike as much terror on the page of a book as they do from the mouth of a parent. And at the very next words, uttered in Dad's best Ugly Giant voice—"Be he live or be he dead, I'll grind his bones to make me bread!"—some youngsters retreat under the covers.

In the broadcast news business, we don't want to send listeners retreating under their figurative covers. We recognize that, even for adults, words invested with the dimension and fullness of the human voice contain a special power to move people emotionally, to grab at their guts, and sometimes to make them act rashly or foolishly.

Above all, broadcasters must remain calm in their words and tone of voice. We've come a long way since a radio program—Orson Welles' *Mercury Theater* production of "War of the Worlds" in 1938—was able to make thousands of Americans believe that Martians had landed. But we can never come so far as to drain spoken words of their emotional impact. Here are a few cases in point.

The word "violence" is tricky and troublesome. It carries more impact spoken than written. If we say,

```
Violent clashes marred an antinuclear demonstration today in West

Germany...
```

we lead listeners to expect some awfully bloody details. But if it turns out that the "violent clashes" amounted to half a dozen people slightly injured in a series of shoving matches, we have grossly overstated the case and robbed the words of their true meaning.

There is a way to avoid this: *Be specific* as to what happened, *without* characterizing it as "violence" or "violent." Let the facts speak for themselves.

A distinction should be made, too, between "wounds" and "injuries." They are *not* synonyms. If we say,

```
The bomb wounded six people...
```

the meaning is that the bomb was *deliberately* detonated. If we say,

```
The bomb injured six people...
```

the meaning is that it went off *accidentally*. In newsroom parlance, injuries happen in accidents, wounds in deliberate violence such as war or terrorism. If you think such distinctions are small or unimportant, you had best stay out of the news business.*

Race and Religion

Even more caution is required for stories involving race or religion. As a first step, you must decide if a story really does involve either of them. If we say,

> A group of Southern congressmen, including two blacks, called today for reform of the income tax laws . . .

we are mentioning race unnecessarily. The race of the congressmen has nothing to do with the issue they are espousing, and should therefore not be mentioned.

And if we say,

> In a rash of anti-Semitism in France, vandals today painted swastikas on two Paris synagogues . . .

we are overstating wildly and irresponsibly. "Paris" does not equal "France," and "two synagogues" defaced do not constitute a "rash of anti-Semitism." The facts of the story are vivid enough and speak for themselves. They do not need "dramatization" through the addition of inaccurate, inappropriate, or irresponsible language.

On the other hand, some stories do require racial specification:

```
     JOHANNESBURG, South Africa (AP)--A special Easter weekend
passenger train jumped the tracks near Pretoria on Friday, and
at least 16 black passengers were killed, authorities said.
     Three locomotives and five passenger cars derailed at
10:45 a.m. about six miles north of Pretoria, the railway
police department said in a statement. The police said the
cause of the accident is unknown.
     Fourteen people were reported dead at the scene. A
spokeswoman for the South African Transport Services said two
more people died later in a hospital. She said 30 people were
injured.
     The train, packed with black travelers from the
Johannesburg and Pretoria areas, was heading to Pietersburg in
the northern Transvaal.
     Both Friday and Monday are holidays in South Africa, and
hundreds of thousands of blacks travel from urban centers to
their traditional homes in rural areas.
```

Because South Africa is a racially segregated society, and because its racial policies are protested by most of the world, the race of the victims is an important part of the story. Thus, a broadcast version might go this way:

---

*There is argument over whether broadcasters should say "people" or "persons." Those who prefer "people" say it is more conversational. Those who prefer "persons" say the word "people" applies only in the cultural or anthropological sense, as in "the American *people*." I strongly favor "people" instead of "persons," and I am using it throughout this book.

An Easter holiday train carrying black workers to their traditional homelands derailed near Pretoria, South Africa, today. Authorities said at least 16 passengers were killed and 30 injured.

Deliberate Cruelty

You have all studied enough modern history to know the depths of cruelty and depravity to which human beings can sink. The Nazi death camps of World War II, in which millions of people were systematically put to death, and the Khmer Rouge atrocities in Cambodia in 1975–1978 mark the twentieth-century (and perhaps all-time) lows in pure evil. If the world is vigilant, you may never have to write news stories about such horrors in the future. But you will quite often have to write stories based on material like the following:

```
     BAKERSFIELD, Cal. (AP)--A man convicted of animal cruelty
for stomping on a kitten, then tossing it to his pit bull
terrier to kill, has been fined nearly $1,000 but will not
have to spend any time in jail.
     Kern County Superior Court Judge Clarence Westra Jr.
rejected a Probation Department recommendation Thursday that
William Robert Graham, 22, of Fellows spend 10 weekends in
jail for the felony conviction. Instead, Graham was fined and
placed on three years' probation.
     His estranged wife, Kathy, gave sheriff's deputies this
account of the incident that began at 2:30 a.m. last Oct. 27,
two days after the couple separated:
     Graham called the home in Taft where she was staying and
said he was coming to beat her up. Kathy Graham and a
girlfriend were waiting on the front porch when he arrived.
     The couple argued, and Graham grabbed the kitten out of
her hand, threw it on the ground and jumped up and down on it.
She tried to rescue the pet, but Graham pushed her down and
pulled her hair. Then he threw the cat to his pit bull terrier
and told the dog to "eat it up."
     Kathy Graham said the kitten was dead by the time she
pried it away from the pit bull, which also bit her.
     But Graham told Deputy Probation Officer Mark L. Jacobus
that the case was "blown out of proportion," and that the dog
killed the cat without him urging it to do so.
     Graham was accused of spouse beating, resisting arrest
and animal cruelty but pleaded guilty in a plea bargain to the
cruelty charge. The other counts were dismissed.
```

Although cruelty to animals does not rank as low as cruelty to humans, it is nevertheless strong stuff, and a broadcast news story of a kitten being stomped and thrown to a pit bull terrier is going to leave many people horrified, or angry, or, at the very least, upset. There may be children in the audience, and they especially are likely to be affected adversely by what they hear.

Such stories pose a real dilemma: Does broadcast journalism's responsibility to report the news outweigh the possible negative effects on the audience? In the real world of competitive news broadcasting, the answer, almost always, is yes. Telling the news is the first consideration.

However, there are ways to mitigate the potential harm. For example, it is not necessary to include all the gory details. And you can prepare the audience for what is to follow—perhaps give parents a chance to momentarily tune out something they don't want their children to see or hear. You might write the story this way:

```
A man convicted of animal cruelty will pay a fine, but won't go to

jail.  That was the ruling today by a judge in Bakersfield, California,

in a case involving a kitten and a pit bull terrier.

    The judge fined 22-year-old William Graham nearly a thousand dollars

and placed him on three years' probation.  Graham's estranged wife had

testified he grabbed her pet kitten, stomped it, and tossed it to his pit

bull terrier, during a domestic fight.
```

That version deliberately suppresses a detailed account of the kitten's death and the alleged command to the pit bull to "eat it up." And by delaying revelation of Graham's alleged actions to the end of the story, parents have at least 15 seconds to lower the volume or divert their children's attention.

To sum up the impact of broadcast language on the audience: Do *not* include details of race, religion, national origin, cruelty, or violence *unless* such details are germane to the point of the story. In fact, it might be a good idea to mutter to yourself, "Fe, Fi, Fo, Fum!" whenever you come across a story involving

race
religion
cruelty
bodily injury (blood and gore)
bodily functions
sexual conduct

Measure the impact of your language on the audience. You are writing and speaking to fellow human beings.

OBSCENITY

Obscenity is in the eye of the beholder. One person's "art" is another person's "pornography." The U.S. Supreme Court has held that obscenity shall be determined by community standards. What may be held to be obscene in Roanoke may not necessarily be held to be obscene in Milwaukee; the people in those two communities may have different standards.

That said, broadcast standards, in actual practice, are far more strict than print standards. Reading is a deliberate act. Listening or viewing can happen by accident. A 3-year-old will not read words that he or she may accidentally hear. All of which is not to say that broadcasters are prudes. It's just that broadcasting, by its very nature, reaches a wider audience than print. And since broadcasters are forever trying to reach an even wider audience, it stands to reason that they do not want to risk offending people.

And make no mistake about it: People *are* easily offended. Although standards in entertainment programming have been relaxed over the years (not long ago it was forbidden to say "hell," "damn," "bastard," or "son-of-a-bitch," even in the context of dramatic dialogue), standards remain strict in news programming. Specifically, it is taboo to use the name of the Lord in a profane way or to use the popular words for excrement, genitalia, or sexual activities.

The vast majority of newsmakers understand this and consequently watch their language in public, especially when cameras and microphones are present. But sometimes they forget themselves and let slip an occasional "Shit!" or "God damn it!" Such language is almost always edited out during preparation for broadcast.

But standards are changing. Some words and expressions once considered obscene are now considered acceptable, depending on context and the hour of the newscast. A newsmaker may talk about being "pissed off" or call someone a "son-of-a-bitch," and such remarks may occasionally be aired—repeat, *occasionally*—because they accurately reflect the speaker's strong feelings, and because such remarks have become publicly acceptable; they have lost their former shock value.

Pornography

Even under today's relatively relaxed standards, it remains a matter of news judgment how far broadcasters should go in reporting *about* alleged obscenity. News agencies almost always warn their subscribers that a story contains potentially offensive material by preceding it with the advisory "note nature." An example:

```
bc-obscene 2ndld-writethru 6-27 0668
MetroWire
editors: note nature
(complete writethru--quotes, details of verdict, background)
     LOS ANGELES (UPI)--A man was convicted Monday of
distributing short stories and a video depicting the sexual
torture and murder of children, becoming the first person to
be found guilty under a new state obscenity law.
     Police said the materials, including "Die Kiddie Die,"
"Kiddie Killer" and "Human Bedpan," plus a recording, are the
most obscene ever uncovered in the city.
     City Attorney James Hahn called Gary Jerome Levinson's
```

obscenity conviction, the first by a Los Angeles jury in 10 years, the "dawn of a new era in obscenity prosecutions."

Hahn said the case also represents the first California prosecution stemming from materials that depict sexual torture and murder and the first conviction in city history involving obscene videos.

Levinson, 38, of Hollywood, is scheduled to be sentenced July 6, when he could be sent to County Jail for up to 3 1/2 years and be fined $7,000. He additionally faces a pending trial in U.S. District Court on federal obscenity charges.

Following the verdict, a bitter-sounding Levinson said his conviction represents "a total encroachment of the freedoms we're supposed to enjoy under the First Amendment."

"But I realize that it's stacked against you in court," he said. "You're there to get buried. If you win, it's a fluke."

Defense lawyer William Grayson said he would appeal the conviction on grounds the law is unconstitutional.

A Municipal Court jury of seven women and five men convicted Levinson of five counts of distributing obscene material and one count each of possession of obscene material with the intent to distribute and advertising obscene materials.

Those charges stem from the distribution of one video, one tape recording, four short stories and a catalog advertising many of the materials, said Deputy City Attorney Michael Guarino.

The jury, which deliberated for three days, acquitted Levinson of one count stemming from the distribution of a video entitled "Little Boy Snuffed."

The jury deadlocked on two other counts stemming from the distribution of two other videos, including one showing adults having sex with animals, Guarino said.

City Attorney James Hahn said the materials, which Levinson distributed through his Hollywood mail-order company, Fischer Publications, was the "most vile type of obscenity that could appeal only to the darkest side of human imagination."

Hahn said Levinson, who produced, performed in and distributed the videos, was the first person in California to be convicted under a new, strengthened state obscenity law.

The law, which became effective Jan. 1, 1987, incorporated the redefinition of obscene material contained in the 1973 U.S. Supreme Court decision, Miller vs. California.

Under the new law, a prosecutor only has to prove that no reasonable person would find the material to have significant value, Hahn said.

"Under the old definition, a prosecutor had to prove that material, regardless of how repugnant it might be, was without any value whatsoever, which was very difficult to do," Hahn said.

Grayson had argued that the materials do not violate the law, that the youngest actor featured in the videos is 21 and that Levinson's right to distribute them to consenting adults is protected by the Constitution.

Levinson said he no longer is involved in pornographic videos and recently helped produce the R-rated, low-budget

```
movie, "Hollywood Chain Saw Hookers," and acted in another
low-budget film, "Surf Nazis Must Die."
------------------
upi 07:25 ped
```

Although that story is obviously of more interest in California than in other states, which have their own laws regarding obscenity, it does have some national interest by virtue of California's reputation as the country's "trend-setting" state: If a child pornographer can be convicted in California, he or she can probably be convicted anywhere in the United States.

The question is, how far can news broadcasters go in telling the story without themselves risking an appeal to prurience? Specifically, should broadcast versions include the titles of the pornographic materials and describe their subject matter?

The handling of the story's details, just like the matter of obscenity itself, will depend on local standards. Stations in some cities and towns will not air the story at all; stations in other cities and towns will report only the conviction and its significance; and some stations, mostly in big cities where obscenity has long been an issue and where pornography is a thriving business, will report the details without fear of offending the vast majority of the audience. Thus, in cities where public life is conditioned by reserve in the discussion of sex and pornography, a broadcast version might be circumspect:

```
A Los Angeles jury today delivered the first guilty verdict under a

new state obscenity law.  The jury convicted a 38-year-old man of

distributing material depicting child pornography.

    Under the new California law, prosecutors must prove only that such

material has no significant value to reasonable people.  Previously, they

had to prove such material has no value whatsoever.

    The convicted man faces a jail term of up to three-and-a-half

years...and a fine of up to seven thousand dollars.
```

That version is sedate. It does not risk offending impressionable or prudish listeners. It is, for lack of a better word, "safe."

However, in big cities, it is not competitive. By that I mean that big-city audiences are used to seeing and hearing about a much wider range of human activities than less urbanized audiences. For better or worse, urban audiences are used to assaults on their sensibilities, and many people will wonder, What could this guy have done that was so bad he'll probably go to jail for it? Big-city stations are likely to tell them:

```
     A Los Angeles jury today convicted a man for distributing "kiddie

porn" -- child pornography.  It was the first conviction under a new

California law making it easier to prosecute pornographers.

     Thirty-eight-year-old Gary Jerome Levinson was found guilty of

distributing printed and videotaped material depicting the sexual torture

and murder of children.  Police called it the most obscene child

pornography ever uncovered in Los Angeles.

     Levinson faces three-and-a-half years in jail and a fine of up to

7,000 dollars.  His lawyer plans an appeal based on the Free Speech

clause of the U-S Constitution.
```

Note that not even that example includes the titles of the pornographic materials. Some stations, however, would name them, knowing full well the disgust they might raise among listeners and viewers. In short, the issue of handling stories about obscenity and pornography is, like so much in the news business, a matter of judgment.

TONGUE-TWISTERS

"Rubber buggy bumpers" is hard to say. So is "Thirteen thieves of Thebes thinned three thickets of thistles." And no newscaster should ever be forced to attempt either one during a broadcast.

We all like "bloopers," those instances of entertainers tripping over their tongues on the air. Such boners are rarely heard these days, since virtually all entertainment programming is recorded on film or tape and the bloopers edited out. Sports is just about the only entertainment still broadcast live.

News, on the other hand, is almost always delivered live. Even in those instances where the East Coast edition of the network news is taped for later replay in the Pacific and Mountain time zones, the content is "protected"; that is, news staffs on the West Coast update and change the newscast as necessary, right up to and during the rebroadcast. Even the 24-hour all-news radio and TV outlets are programmed live.

Live programming inevitably results in occasional mistakes and miscues, both human and electronic. The goal is to keep such miscues to a minimum. There is no need to manufacture them by using the wrong language, the language of tongue-twisters. For example, there is no good reason to write,

Federal narcotics agents have *thwarted* a cocaine smuggling ring.

when it's just as easy to write,

Federal narcotics agents have **broken up** a cocaine smuggling ring.

"Thwart" is hard to say. "Break up" is not. In this context they mean the same thing, but "break up" is better in broadcasting.

The same is true of "furor," which is spoken better as "stir" or "outburst," and "cause a furor" is better put as "cause a scene." Sometimes the problem pops up not in single words but in word combinations:

Governor **S**huster **s**igned the legi**s**lation at **s**even thi**s** morning.

That sentence contains an overabundance of sibilants ("s"-sounds), guaranteed to leave many a newscaster hissing or spitting. We can fix the problem by choosing slightly different wording.

Governor Shuster signed the bill this morning. . .

(By the way, the words "bill" and "law" are far preferable to more formal words such as "legislation," "ordinance," or "statute." In everyday speech, people are more likely to say "drunk driving *law*" than "drunk driving *statute*.")

Another sound to watch out for is the plosive letter "p":

Police a**pp**rehended a dozen **p**icketing gra**p**e-**p**ickers. . .

might be better rendered as

Police arrested a dozen picketing farm workers. . .

("Apprehend" is also a no-no. "Arrest" will do just fine.)

There's no room in this book to list every hard-to-pronounce word or word combination that comes to mind. The point is to sensitize you to the problem. For a career in broadcast news, you must train yourself to recognize potential tongue-twisters and to change your wording when necessary. The best way to do this is to read your copy aloud—always.

EXERCISE

1. The following news agency story is slugged BODY PARTS. It contains material that some in the audience may find disgusting or objectionable. Write a 40-second broadcast version, adapting your language to suit your specific audience.

```
AM-Body Parts, Bjt,0836
Infant Slaughter-Organ Transplant Rumors Frustrate Officials
      WASHINGTON (AP)--U.S. officials are frustrated by
persistent reports, some blamed on Soviet disinformation, that
Latin American children are being butchered for organ
transplants in the United States.
      The reports have been crisscrossing the globe for the
```

past 20 months, confounding U.S. officials who have been trying to locate their genesis, track their progress and provide credible denials.

The latest report surfaced in Paraguay, after police raided a house and found seven infants and several pregnant women who apparently planned to give their babies up for adoption.

A juvenile judge, Angel Campos, said that while he had no proof, he believed some of the babies might be dismembered in the United States for their organs, which could then be sold for hundreds of dollars.

The story, circulated by a respected news agency, has been making the rounds of the world press despite adamant denials from the U.S. Embassy in Asuncion.

The U.S. Information Agency has concluded that all the reports are based on unsubstantiated rumors which began in Honduras. Its yearlong investigation aided by the FBI, the Department of Health and Human Services and other agencies has failed to find any proof of the charges.

"The original misinformation would not have spread so far and wide if it had not been for the way it was cynically used and embellished with deliberate distortions in a disinformation campaign by several communist countries, with the Soviet Union and Cuba taking the lead," according to a report on Soviet disinformation prepared by USIA for Congress.

The United Network for Organ Sharing, which oversees organ transplants in the United States, has also denied the charges.

"It's very frustrating when you don't know who's spreading such rumors," said Kelle Straw, a spokeswoman for the non-profit organization, which receives some of its funds from the government.

Ms. Straw said the United Network had never found any leads to follow in its own investigation of the reports.

"And anyway, it's ridiculous," she said. "Children don't make good donors; their organs aren't fully developed."

In its report to Congress, the U.S. Information Agency cited dozens of other such reports which have surfaced in places as diverse as Bangladesh and Morocco, some in Communist Party newspapers and others in independent publications.

"The rumor is gruesome enough so that it would feed on itself without any help," said Todd Leventhal, an agency official who prepared the report and has been monitoring the "baby parts" case as it is known in the government.

"But because the Soviets are involved, we're seeing more of these reports and with more of an anti-American slant," he added.

Latin America, where thousands of babies are adopted by foreigners every year, is a fertile ground for breeding such rumors.

In its report to Congress, the USIA concluded it is sometimes hard to tell which of the baby parts allegations are "due to misinformation and which is due to disinformation."

But Leventhal said disinformation experts in the United States can tell whether the Soviets are behind a certain report according to the newspapers carrying such a story and the slant that it takes.

In some cases, the Soviet role is quite obvious, he said.

On July 25, 1987, the official Soviet newspaper Izvestia reported that an international Mafia brings up disabled children in Guatemala and sends them to the United States. "There, the butcher medics cut out their hearts, kidneys and eyes," the Izvestia report said.

The newspaper cited officials of the Geneva-based Defense for Children, International, as the source of its information. The organization accused Izvestia of turning out "a veritable masterpiece: an astute mix of quotes taken out of context, journalistic comment, established fact and unfounded allegations."

The course of the baby parts story constitutes a fascinating study in the life of a rumor.

The USIA has traced the original report to Leonardo Villeda Bermudez, formerly Honduras' top social welfare official. Bermudez was quoted as saying in January 1987 that he was told by some social workers several years previously about people seeking to adopt disabled children so they could sell them "for parts" in the United States.

His comments were circulated worldwide by a respected news agency, lending them sufficient credibility and exposure so that they have been cited repeatedly since then despite his retraction the day after his remarks were reported.

In his retraction, Bermudez said "he confused a simple rumor" with facts. Other Honduran officials denied there was any proof of such practices.

But more than a year later, his comments were still circulating, and were quoted among other places in the Venezuelan newspaper El Nacional.

"It just won't die. Just when we think we've managed to get rid of it, it pops up again," said Leventhal.
AP-NY 1141EDT

11

Special Segments

Both on radio and television, a standard local newscast anywhere in the United States covers sports and weather, as well as hard news. Often it contains the latest financial news as well, and, on the lighter side, an amusing item known as a "kicker." Although the weather forecast and the stock market report are usually straightforward in format, sports and kickers give broadcast newswriters broad freedom in both style and content.

SPORTS

Strictly speaking, amateur and professional sports belong to the realm of entertainment rather than news. The fate of the world does not hinge on the outcome of the Super Bowl or the World Series. A sports story must have transcending interest to be included in a network newscast. But at the local level, sports occupies a large chunk of news time, as news departments try to satisfy the audience's apparently unquenchable thirst for information about local teams, be they high school, college, or pro.

Perhaps the most colorful sportswriting in America appears in the major daily newspapers. Print sportswriting almost *has* to be colorful to command readers' interest. After all, readers already know how the games came out. They heard the final scores reported on radio or TV. In the age of television, print sportswriting must concentrate not on who won, but rather on how the game was played.

Because of time limitations, most broadcast sportswriting is composed of reporting interim or final scores. However, in longer newscasts, especially on television, sportswriters and reporters must strive for color and originality in stories about local teams. Unfortunately, few of them succeed, managing instead only to pile cliché upon cliché. One explanation for this shortcoming may be that sportswriting and reporting tend to be "orphans" in college broadcast journalism departments, not deemed worthy of the seriousness accorded to the teaching of hard newswriting. Another may be that sports journalism attracts a different sort of student, the sort oriented toward action rather than the written word.

Whatever the explanation, you can bank on this: If you go into broadcast journalism, sooner or later you *will* find yourself writing sports copy. It matters not that your career goal is to cover the White House for CBS News. Starting out, you'll have to write stories about the president *and* the local volleyball tournament. *You* may not care about sports, but a large chunk of your audience does. So you might as well do your best to tell the sports news as clearly as possible.

Step One is to follow broadcast style and *avoid clichés*. In baseball, for example, there is a very good name for what players use to hit the ball. It's called a "bat." There is no need whatever to find other words for it—words such as "stick," "lumber," "war club," and so on. Such words are all clichés. They do not make sports copy sound better. They do make it sound silly and trite.

Step Two is to keep it short. The news agency copy you receive will contain far more information about the game than you can possibly hope to include in a broadcast version. If a hometown team is involved, you will be able to write longer and include more details. But compared to print, your broadcast version will still be short.

Let's pick a working model:

```
bc-bba-chisox 7-1 0556

     CHICAGO (UPI)--Gary Redus, whose game-winning single in
the ninth inning Friday night lifted the Chicago White Sox to
a 2-1 victory over the New York Yankees, said he was
determined to get a hit because of opportunities he muffed
earlier in the game.
     "My thinking was I've got to do something for the two
mistakes I made earlier," said Redus, who twice flied out
after Ron Karkovice led off with doubles.
     "If I had done my job earlier in the game, it would have
been a different situation. So I kind of feel like I redeemed
myself in that respect."
     Redus's single down the third-base line with one out in
the ninth drove home Fred Manrique and gave the White Sox
their first victory over the Yankees in six attempts this
season.
     Manrique had led off with a single and took second when
Ozzie Guillen's sacrifice was bobbled by reliever Steve
Shields for an error, allowing Guillen to reach first. Dave
Righetti relieved and struck out pinch hitter Darryl Boston.
Cecilio Guante then came on and surrendered Redus's
game-winning hit on the first pitch.
```

```
        Bobby Thigpen pitched one inning to improve to 5-5.
Shields fell to 1-3.
        Chicago starter Jack McDowell allowed one run on three
hits in eight innings. He struck out six and walked two before
being relieved by Thigpen in the ninth.
        "He's still got a lot to learn but I thought he just
pitched the best game I ever saw him pitch," Chicago Manager
Jim Fregosi said of his right-handed rookie.
        The White Sox took a 1-0 lead in the third inning on an
RBI single by Harold Baines after Karkovice led off with a
double and moved to third on Steve Lyons' groundout.
        The Yankees, who had been limited by McDowell to one hit
through six innings, tied the score 1-1 in the seventh. Gary
Ward doubled and scored two outs later on a single by Mike
Pagliarulo.
        New York's Ron Guidry, making his first start of the
season after recuperating from shoulder surgery last December,
gave up six hits over 4 2/3 innings. He was lifted with two
outs in the fifth after the White Sox loaded the bases on
Karkovice's second double, an intentional walk to Baines and a
walk to Greg Walker. Shields fanned pinch hitter Dan Pasqua to
end the inning.
        Guidry, who threw 90 pitches, gave up one run, struck out
one and walked two. "I didn't know what to expect," said
Guidry, who was reactivated from the disabled list when the
Yankees placed Richard Dotson on the 15-day DL with a strained
groin muscle. "I'm not happy with the outcome (of the game),
but personally I was content. I managed to have fairly good
velocity and control, and that's a good sign."
        Yankees Manager Lou Piniella also was pleased with
Guidry's performance.
        "I couldn't be happier," Piniella said. "He threw the
ball well; it was just an excellent outing.
        "We just didn't hit the ball well tonight," he said. "But
you have to give McDowell credit. He held us to three hits.
That's a pretty good performance."
---------------------
upi 12:34 aed
```

Unless you are writing for a station in Chicago or New York, that story will wind up as part of a broadcast roundup of final scores. It will merit a grand total of two seconds' air time!

```
    Chicago, 2, the Yankees, 1
```

(Note the use of figures that in regular news copy would be spelled out. Since sports scores are numbers by definition, there is little chance anchors will be confused by figures.) Maybe it would be phrased as a complete sentence, but it would still merit only two seconds.

```
    Chicago beat the Yankees, 2-1.
```

(Note that the When element is omitted. That's because scores are normally "today's" or "tonight's" results unless specified otherwise.) If the newscast you are writing for contains more time for sports than just the bare-bones scores, but time is still short, the story can contain a few key details:

```
Chicago beat the Yankees 2-1 tonight on a ninth-inning single by

Gary Redus.  It was the first time the White Sox have beaten New York all

season.
```

Except in hometown cities (in this case Chicago and New York), that amount of copy, totalling seven seconds of air time, is just about the maximum for this story on radio.

However, on hometown radio, and on local TV where "highlight" video-tape is available, the story will run longer—anywhere from 15 to 30 seconds. This is where broadcast sportswriting risks sounding trite instead of colorful. To avoid triteness, newcomers are best advised to "play it straight."

```
For the first time this season, the Chicago White Sox beat the New

York Yankees.  Tonight's final score was 2-1.  The game-winning hit came

on a ninth-inning single by Gary Redus off reliever Cecilio Guante.

Veteran lefthander Ron Guidry made his first start of the season for

the Yankees, following shoulder surgery last year.  Guidry was lifted in

the fifth after throwing 90 pitches.  The win went to Chicago reliever

Bobby Thigpen.
```

Admittedly, there is nothing compelling or "sexy" in that version. But it is clear, concise, and tells what was significant (that is, new and different) about the game. Once you have learned to write sports that way, deliberately suppressing the urge to be original, you can move on to try a more colorful style:

```
The Chicago White Sox finally overcame the Yankee hex tonight,

beating New York for the first time in six tries.  Chicago's Gary Redus

singled down the third base line in the bottom of the ninth, for a 2-1

Sox victory.

Yankee southpaw Ron Guidry, his shoulder repaired by surgery, got

his first start of the season.  Guidry went nearly five innings, throwing
```

90 pitches, and allowing only one run before being lifted for Steve

Shields. Shields took the loss, even though Redus's hit came off Cecilio

Guante. The win went to Chicago reliever Bobby Thigpen, his fifth.

Some of you may think the foregoing is not "colorful" enough—and maybe you're right. In fact, I urge you to do better . . . but only after succeeding in "playing it straight." Professional sportswriters and reporters serve a long apprenticeship during which they must develop an idiosyncratic style if they are to succeed in finding jobs in the big cities. Those who fail to learn to write simply and clearly, opting instead for hackneyed prose that they misperceive as colorful, are doomed to remain in the backwaters of sports broadcasting.

Sports Statistics

Apparently, sports fans love statistics. And just as apparently, broadcasters are happy to oblige the fans. Anyone wishing to enter sports broadcasting will have to understand both the shorthand of sports statistics and the rules of the games. A knowledgeable sportswriter will be able to reconstruct a sporting event merely from a statistical analysis of it. For example, the same news agency sports wire that sent the foregoing account of the Chicago–New York baseball game also sent the following "box score":

```
pm-bba-alboxes 2ndadd sked 7-2 0561
NEW YORK          ab   r   h   bi   CHICAGO           ab   r   h   bi
Washington cf      4   0   0   0    Redus lf           5   0   2   1
Ward rf            4   1   1   0    Lyons 3b           4   0   1   0
Mattingly 1b       4   0   1   0    Baines dh          3   0   1   1
Clark dh           3   0   0   0    Walker 1b          3   0   0   0
Pagliarul 3b       3   0   1   1    Williams rf        2   0   1   0
Cruz lf            3   0   0   0    Pasqua rf          2   0   1   0
Buhner rf          1   0   0   0    Gallagher cf       4   0   2   0
Santana ss         3   0   0   0    Manrique 2b        3   1   1   0
Skinner c          2   0   0   0    Guillen ss         3   0   0   0
Meacham 2b         1   0   0   0    Karkovice c        3   1   2   0
Winfield ph        1   0   0   0    Boston ph          1   0   0   0
Randolph 2b        0   0   0   0
Totals......      29#  1#  3#   1   Totals....#       33#  2# 11#   2
One out when winning run scored #..#..
New York#..#..#..#    000 000 100-- 1
Chicago#..#..#..#....#    001 000 001-- 2
    Game-winning RBI -- Redus (3) . E--
Shields. DP--New York 2, Chicago 1.
LOB--New York 5, Chicago 10. 2B--
Karkovice2, Gallagher, Ward. SB--Redus
(19), Williams (4). S--Manrique, Guillen.
#..#..#..#..#..                      IP# H# R  ER  BB  SO
    ..New York
 Guidry                 4 2-3   6     1    1    2    1
 Shields (L 1-3)        3 1-3   4     1    1    0    3
```

```
Righetti                        1-3      0      0      0      0      1
Guante                           0       1      0      0      0      0
   ..Chicago
 McDowell                        8       3      1      1      2      6
Thigpen (W 5-5)                  1       0      0      0      2      0
   Sheilds pitched to 2 batters in 9th:
Guante pitched to 1 batter in 9th, T--
2:49, A--19,798. Umpires--Home, Young:
1b, Evans; 2b, Tischida; 3b, Hendry.----»
```

To people who have little interest in baseball, or in sports generally, the box score is a series of meaningless statistics. But during the 8-month baseball season (spring training through the World Series), it is a staple on the news wires. To a professional sportswriter or reporter, it contains more than enough information to write an unembellished account of the game. Everything about the action of the game itself is listed, enabling a professional to write a detailed story (minus the color).

Sometimes a news agency will supply *only* the box score, without a separate account of the game. Thus, professionals must know how to read it. Space does not permit me to explain the box score line by line. But I urge those of you who want to enter sports broadcasting to seek outside help from someone who does understand it and the statistical shorthand for other sports as well. It's the raw material with which you'll be earning a living.

WEATHER

Like sports, weather reporting and forecasting has become a standard segment of local radio and TV news. And, like sports, it is a segment often filled, unfortunately, with cliché-ridden, substandard prose. On local TV especially, weather writer/anchors tend to be "personalities" rather than journalists, watched chiefly for their entertainment value.

All stations get their weather information from the same source, the U.S. Weather Service's local and regional offices. The forecast and hourly temperatures are carried alike to all newsrooms via the news agencies. So unless the weather is sufficiently harsh as to provide an actual news story, the forecast can be given in about 15 seconds. The weather segment of most local TV newscasts is thus an exercise in making a mountain out of a molehill. Stations employ "entertaining" weather anchors for competitive reasons; they are afraid, perhaps justifiably so, that dropping the weather segment will result in a significant loss of audience for the entire newscast.

So this section is not about how to become a stand-up comic/weather anchor. It is about how to avoid grabbing the nearest cliché such as:

```
Better get out those umbrellas -- the weatherman says it'll rain

tonight...
```

Please resist this temptation. Most of your listeners are wise enough to realize that if rain is forecast, they should probably carry an umbrella. They don't need you to offer childish advice. And *who* is "the weatherman"? Is he related to the Sandman? Leave the silliness to the disk jockey. As for you, just keep it short and to the point:

```
The weather forecast:  Possible rain tonight, with a low around 50.

Clearing by morning, with a high tomorrow around 70.
```

Because the weather is often the closing item in a newscast, it is well to write it in such a way that it can be shortened or lengthened at a glance from the newscaster. That's because, while it's easy to begin a newscast on time, it's tricky to end it on time. A certain amount of flexibility is needed to enable the newscaster to "stretch" or "get off."

Therefore, the weather should be written (on a separate page, of course) something like this:

```
The weather forecast calls for possible rain tonight, with a low

around 50.  Clearing by morning, with a high tomorrow around 70.

(Turning colder by Thursday, and more rain expected by the weekend.)

At _____ o'clock, the airport temperature was _____.

The humidity was _____ per cent.

And the wind was _____ at _____ miles per hour.
```

The blanks are filled in with the latest readings just before air time, and the material in parenthesis, as well as the hourly readings, may be read or deleted as time warrants. Many news departments have standardized format sheets for the weather; the blanks need only be penciled in on the way to the studio.

FINANCIAL NEWS

Afternoon and evening newscasts usually include a brief stockmarket report. Unless the format specifies otherwise, the stock report should be kept very short. It should include only the latest (or closing) Dow Jones industrial average, whether trading has been "light," "moderate," or "heavy," and, time permitting, the closing dollar price of gold in New York and the closing Nikkei (pronounced NEE-kay) average on the Tokyo Stock Exchange.

All this information—and much too much more—arrives in the newsroom via the news agencies. A standard example:

am-stocks 5-20 0828

Editors: Also moving on the financial wires
Stocks end mixed in slow trading
By ALAN KRAUSS
UPI Business Writer
    NEW YORK (UPI)--Stock prices ended mixed Friday in the
slowest session of the year, as one piece of evidence that
inflation remains under control failed to break the doldrums
that held prices down for most of the week.
    The Dow Jones industrial average, which rose 7.63
Thursday, fell 6.13 to close at 1952.59. For the week, the
blue-chip index slipped 37.96 points, or 1.9 percent. It was
the Dow's third straight weekly loss.
    Advances outnumbered declines 837-606 among the 1,954
issues traded, however. Volume was an anemic 120,600,000
shares, compared with 165,160,000 traded Thursday.
    Broad-market indexes posted modest gains. The New York
Stock Exchange composite index gained 0.29 to close at 143.30.
Standard & Poor's 500-stock index rose 0.45 to 253.02. The
price of an average share rose 7 cents.
    Analysts said news that April's increase in U.S. consumer
prices was within the expected range gave the stock market an
early boost, but failed to overcome inflation worries.
    Before the market opened, the Labor Department reported
that the Consumer Price Index rose a seasonally adjusted 0.4
percent in April, a 5.3 percent annual rate.
    Chester Pado, director of technical research at Jefferies
& Co. in Los Angeles, said the CPI figure was offset by rising
commodities future prices, interpreted as an inflationary
portent.
    Pado said a key commodities index broke through an
important resistance point at midweek, leading investors to
discount the CPI figure released Friday.
    Jim Andrews, head of the institutional trading desk at
Janney Montgomery Scott Inc. in Philadelphia, said bargain
hunting among blue chips that pushed prices higher late in
Thursday's session carried over into early trading Friday.
    "The market seems to want to firm up and get better,"
Andrews said, but has seemed unable to shake off the doldrums.
    "That's the kind of market we're in," he continued. "If
the news is bad, they sell. If the news is good, the reaction
is blase."
    Analysts believe a generalized lack of confidence
triggered a slide of nearly 57 points on the Dow on Tuesday
and Wednesday following news of a substantial contraction in
the nation's trade deficit in March.
    The government reported Tuesday the trade deficit for
March narrowed to $9.7 billion from $13.8 billion in February.
The seemingly good news had sparked fears of inflation and
higher interest rates because it indicates the economy may be
expanding too quickly.
    The nervousness was also apparent in Tokyo, where prices
ended mixed in directionless trading. The key Nikkei average
of 225 industrial issues, which fell 394.34 points Thursday in
its steepest single-day loss of the year, recovered a modest
20.62 points to close at 27,393.85. Declines outpaced
advances, however, 455-429.

```
     London stock prices gained. The Financial Times 100-stock
index advanced 9.6 points to 1770.2 in light trading.
     On the NYSE trading floor, Ohio Edison was the most
active listed issue, up 1/8 to 18.
     It was followed by Browning Ferris Industries, up 1/2 to
21 3/4.
     Union Carbide was third on the actives list, up 1/2 to
18 5/8.
     AT&T rose 1/8 to 26 3/4. IBM fell 11/8 to 109 3/8.

     Among other blue chips, General Motors fell 3/8 to 74 5/8,
General Electric slipped 1/8 to 40 1/4, USX sagged 1/4 to 31 1/4
and Ford dropped 1/4.
     Texaco fell 1 3/4 to 47 5/8 amid continued rumors the
giant oil company is engaged in talks that could lead to an
amicable resolution of its disagreements with its largest
shareholder, TWA Chairman Carl Icahn.
     Payless Cashways slipped 1/8 to 21 1/2. Investor Asher
Edelman revealed he had accumulated nearly 10 percent of the
Kansas City, Mo.-based company, which indicated it would
resist an Edelman acquisition bid.
     Lucky Stores closed unchanged at 64 3/8. Lucky Stores
accepted a $65-a-share bid by American Stores: which was off 1
to 53 1/4.
     Volume of NYSE-listed issues, including trades in stocks
on regional exchanges and in the over-the-counter market,
totaled 142,486,810 shares, compared with 190,258,310
Thursday.
     Prices rose in light trading on the American Stock
Exchange.
     The Amex market value index added 0.05 to close at
291.84. The price of an average Amex share was unchanged,
Advances led declines 290-267 among the 842 issues traded.
Composite volume totaled 9,108,260 shares, compared with
13,262,100 Thursday.
     Dome Petroleum led the Amex actives, up 1-32 to 1 3-32.
     The National Association of Securities Dealers composite
index fell 0.22 to close at 366.03.
------------------
upi 11:39 ped
```

Whew! Most people interested in such detailed financial information (chiefly brokers and stockholders with specific holdings) will consult a newspaper for it. For broadcast, the entire welter of statistics should be reduced to the following:

```
On Wall Street today, the slowest session of the year.  The Dow

Jones industrials lost six points in extremely light trading.  In Tokyo,

the Nikkei average gained 20-and-a-half points.
```

Short and sweet.

(There are radio and cable TV services broadcasting financial news exclusively. Their stories are much, much longer. The scripted statistics are keyed to identical figures on the TV screen. These broadcasters serve audiences who want to learn the specific numbers and who therefore have a high level of tolerance for statistics.)

KICKERS

By its very nature, any newscast is overwhelmingly devoted to stories involving serious issues. Seldom is there any time for lighter human interest stories, except at the very end of a newscast or just before the local sports and weather. Such a lighter item is known in broadcasting as a "kicker."

Kickers are important psychologically—a way of saying to listeners that the world is not coming to an immediate end despite the bleak picture painted by the news stories they have heard so far. And for the newswriter/newscaster, writing kickers is a sort of release from the tension of writing sober, issue-oriented copy all day.

There are no firm rules on which stories make good kickers. However, there are a few rules on what *not* to use:

1. Kickers should never treat serious issues lightly.
2. Kickers should never make fun of people or beliefs.
3. Kickers should never be cruel to people, animals, or religious institutions.

Here, for example, is the type of story to *avoid* as a potential kicker:

```
     DENVER (AP)--A man angry about the haircut he received
returned to the barbershop with a gun and killed the barber,
police said.
     Robert Willis, owner of Barber Bob's Barber Shop in east
Denver, was shot at least five times Saturday by a man whose
hair he had cut earlier in the day, witnesses said.
```

Let's face it: That is the kind of story that lends itself to "sick humor." There's probably not a newsroom in the country where staffers wouldn't kid around by shouting outrageous comments to one another—or pinning the story on a bulletin board and adding a remark or two. But sick humor is not—repeat *not*—a fit subject for a kicker. Yes, the event was bizarre and the story is attention-getting. But a person *was killed!* That makes it a straight news story, not a kicker.

Kickers must be in good taste. While most can be funny, they need provide only a pleasant contrast to the serious news stories that precede them. They are the news department's way of saying, "Things may be pretty bad today—but here's something that isn't."

The following kickers from ABC Radio News illustrate the style and tone to aim for:

A new weapon in the age—old battle between man and mosquito: Two scientists in New Delhi say garlic does the trick. They've discovered garlic not only helps stimulate the human system and fight bacteria —— a little spray of garlic also kills the mosquito. However, at the dosage they're recommending, it could kill your social life as well.

—O—

Eight million dollars is a lot of overtime —— but that's how much doctors at three university clinics in West Germany collected last year. Officials decided they'd look into the matter, and they found an easy explanation: The doctors were cheating. They put in for extra pay for working on special days —— February Thirtieth...June Thirty—first —— days that don't exist on any calendar.

As you scan the news agency copy coming over the teletype machine or computer screen, some stories virtually leap out as possible kickers. They are offbeat, tasteful and usually uplifting. Here's one that's *literally* uplifting:

MOUNTAIN VIEW, Cal. (AP)——Little DeAndra Anrig was flying her kite when it suddenly started to fly her, her parents say. It was just a short hop, but one the 8—year—old isn't likely to forget.

A twin—engine plane caught the 200—pound nylon test line of DeAndra's kite, lifted her several feet off the ground——over her father's head and almost into a tree——and carried her about 100 feet, she said Tuesday.

She let go and landed safely, but said she was still sore after two days' rest. The plane, meanwhile, is grounded because of damage apparently caused by getting tangled in the kite string.

DeAndra and her parents, who live in the East Bay community of Dublin, were picnicking with friends at the Shoreline Park about 30 miles south of San Francisco and about two miles from the Palo Alto Airport on Sunday and taking turns flying a glider—type kite with a 12—foot wingspan.

While it was DeAndra's turn, a plane descending for the airport snagged the line, her parents said.

"She said it was just a big jerk that lifted her into the air," said DeAndra's mother, Debby. "It carried her right over my husband's head. All he saw was a shadow going over his head. I'm just thankful she let go.

"We always said, "Hold on tight. Don't let go, honey'," the mother said, recalling their advice on proper kite—flying techniques.

DeAndra said she was doing just that, until she saw what
was looming in front of her: "I thought that I was going to
hit a tree."

Lenore Deaville, a pilot, was at the airport watching a
friend make her first solo flight. She said the pilot of the
twin-engine Rockwell Turbo Commander, Jake Uranga of Reno,
told her that "he was at 800 feet doing about 140 knots (160
m.p.h.) when this thing came at him."

Uranga, who was flying a patient destined for Stanford
University Hospital, said he tried to avoid it, but couldn't.
He landed safely.

An FAA official said one of the two propellers on
Uranga's plane suffered a 2-inch gash.

If your mental wheels have been spinning, you're probably ready to start rewriting this one. But a word of caution: One thing you do *not* want to do is use the same wording as the news agency writer, especially in the lead. There's no law against "stealing" a lead—but doing so is a violation of professional etiquette. It is much better to be original, to come up with your own version. A couple of possibilities:

An eight-year-old California girl knows what it's like to be Peter

Pan, if only for a scary moment. The other day she found herself sailing

through the air when a small plane snagged the line of a kite she was

flying. Her parents say she held on and was airborne for about 100 feet,

dropping safely to the ground just before she would have smacked into a

tree.

She's spent the past two days in bed...sore but otherwise unhurt.

As for the plane, a twin-engine Rockwell Turbo Commander: It's been

grounded with a damaged propeller, a gash caused by the nylon kite line.

-0-

Kite-flying may be a safe and sane thing to do -- but don't tell

that to 8-year-old DeAndra Anrig of Dublin, California. DeAndra was

flying a large kite the other day when a small plane coming in for a

landing at a nearby airport snagged the kite line. DeAndra held on for

dear life...and was airborne for about 100 feet. Her parents say she let

go and dropped safely to the ground just in time to avoid hitting a tree.

```
She's still a little sore, but otherwise okay -- which is more than can

be said for the plane: It's been grounded with a damaged propeller.
```

If you are the type of person who just can't wait to sink your teeth into this story and devise your own version, the chances are good that you will become a successful broadcast journalist. If you can't have fun doing this kind of story, you may never have fun in a newsroom. And if you can't have fun doing something, if you can't enjoy it, why do it at all?

HEADLINES AND TEASERS

"Headline" is a term borrowed from print journalism that changed its meaning in the process. In broadcast news, a headline (or just "head" for short) is a one-sentence, capsule version of a news story. Some stations use headlines, usually about 30 seconds' worth, instead of full newscasts at certain times of day. On radio, they may be used at half past the hour on stations with regular newscasts on the hour, or, in the case of all-news radio, every 20 minutes or so. On television, heads may be used during breaks in entertainment programming or as an introduction to a full newscast.

Headlines are not to be confused with "teasers" (which we'll consider in a moment). Headlines simply boil down the essence of the hour's (or day's) major news stories into a series of rapidly delivered sentences, one per story. They may be put in the present tense, past tense, or present perfect tense, depending on the style set by management. A headline package for some of the stories used in this book might go as follows:

```
     Good evening  In tonight's news...

     Supreme Court nominee Douglas Ginsburg admits to having smoked

marijuana...

     An Israeli court issues a death sentence for ex-concentration camp

guard John Demjanjuk (Dem-YAHN-yook)...

     The Senate votes to indemnify Japanese-Americans who were interned

in World War Two...

     And...authorities uncover an alleged plot to murder the mayor of San

Antonio.
```

Another use of a headline in both radio and TV news is as a "preview" of an upcoming story, just before a commercial break:

```
The president says "no" to a tax increase.  That story in a
```

```
moment...
```

It is important to note that a properly phrased headline tells the essence of the news story to which it refers. It does *not* attempt to withhold the essence. A so-called headline that does conceal the essence of story is called a "teaser," aptly named because it attempts to "tease" the audience into staying tuned if it wants to hear the story.

Many news departments frown on the use of teasers because they say, in effect, "Hey, *we* know the news, but if *you* want to learn it, you'll have to sit through a couple of commercials." That is not the sort of image many news departments want to project.

Nevertheless, teasers are a fact of life in many newsrooms, and, using the foregoing stories, they might be phrased this way:

```
Good evening.  In the news tonight...
```

```
A surprising revelation from Supreme Court nominee Douglas
```

```
Ginsburg...
```

```
A death sentence in Israel...
```

```
Good news for Japanese-Americans interned in World War Two...
```

```
And...an alleged plot to murder a big-city mayor.
```

And, as a segment break:

```
The president's decision on a tax increase.  Details when we come
```

```
back...
```

By now you should be training a critical eye on your local news programs and be able to recognize many of the techniques described in this book. It is likely you have formed your own opinion on which techniques you prefer, which you think journalistically proper, and which you think designed to package the news as entertainment. But remember, it is top management that has the last word; in the workplace, you may have to keep your opinion to yourself.

TRANSITIONS

In broadcasting, a transition—sometimes called a "tie-in" or "link"—refers to the word or words connecting two different stories, whether they are related or unrelated. Print's way of linking related stories is to write them as a "roundup" in one overall story, a structure that, as we've seen, does not work well in broadcasting. And print doesn't link different stories at all; it merely publishes them in a different column or page. That, too, doesn't work in broadcasting, since there are no "columns" or "pages"; a newscast goes from beginning to end, leaving the listener with no option but to stay tuned or to tune out altogether. Thus, *occasional* transitions are necessary to help the newscast flow smoothly.

I stress the word "occasional" because, as with so much of broadcast style, effective use of a technique depends on using it sparingly. On average, there should be no more than one or two transitions per newscast. Otherwise, they call attention to themselves and detract from the stories themselves.

A few transitions are so standard that they long ago reached the status of cliché: *meanwhile, meantime, in the meantime,* and *elsewhere.* Sometimes, because of the pressure of the clock, newswriter/newscasters will grab one of those cliché transitions, however reluctantly, because there's no time to come up with something more inventive.

However, as noted in Chapter 9, the location of a story—the where element—often makes a simple, handy transition, one which the writer can use to open a story even though he or she doesn't yet know its ultimate position in a newscast:

```
In New York, Mayor Ed Koch said today...


               -0-


In Washington today, the Labor Department reported...
```

Stories begun that way will fit almost anywhere in a newscast. If the first of these two examples winds up following another story set in New York, then the copy would be changed at the last minute to read *"Also in New York,"* or *"New York's Mayor Ed Koch,"* or something similar.

In the second example, the writer knows that a Labor Department story always comes out of Washington and therefore normally would not even mention the city; but here the writer does so to make a smooth transition from the preceding story, which he or she knows will be on a different subject.

Often the best transitions are those that specifically tie one story to another:

```
Federal spending wasn't the only thing on the president's mind

today...


               -0-


While the Israelis remained adamant, the P-L-O was showing some

flexibility...


               -0-
```

```
Arizona's loss was Nevada's gain...
```

Such specific tie-ins work only if they are strictly accurate. If the writer has to stretch too far for them, they fall flat and call undue attention to themselves. So unless a good transition springs to mind quickly, suggesting itself, as it were, it is best to keep it simple:

```
At the same time...
```

—0—

```
In other economic (medical, political, etc.) news...
```

—0—

```
Also downstate (upstate, etc.)...
```

Remember that transitions should be used sparingly. A well-written newscast may require no transitions at all, as long as the writer has varied his or her approach to stories that are *inherently* related. For example, here are three grouped stories that took a total of 40 seconds of air time:

```
(HONDURAS)
Terrorists in Honduras holding 105 hostages say they will start killing

their captives one at a time, starting two hours from now, if their

demands are not met.  The terrorists are demanding freedom for some 80

political prisoners in Honduras, and softening of the country's three—

month old anti—terroism law.

    (BRUSSELS)
Four people were wounded today in Brussels when a man with a machine gun

opened fire on a synagogue during Rosh Hashanah services.  The gunman

escaped.

    (PARIS)
French police have arrested 14 people and uncovered a cache of weapons

and explosives in Paris.  Officials say they believe the 14 are part of

the terrorist group "Direct Action."  That group has claimed
```

responsibility for recent anti—Jewish violence in France.

(Rob Armstrong, CBS Radio)

Note that those three stories, whose common thread is terrorism, could have been read *in any order*. If the writer had used a transition, the flexibility of story order would have been destroyed. Instead, each was written on a separate page to stand on its own and eventually linked with the others by placement (story order) rather than transitional words.

EXERCISES

1. Slug your story WIMBLEDON SEMIS and write two versions of the following sports story: First, a one-sentence item for inclusion in an eventual sports roundup, and second, a 30-second stand-alone story.

```
PM-TEN--Wimbledon General, 2nd Ld-DATARECAP,0949
```

WIMBLEDON, England (AP)--Boris Becker advanced to his third Wimbledon men's final in four years Saturday by beating Ivan Lendl in a match spread over two days.

Becker, champion in 1985-86, completed a 6-4, 6-3, 6-7, 6-4 victory on his ninth match point to gain a spot in Sunday's title match against Stefan Edberg.

On a day dotted by rain showers, the women's singles championship was decided as top-seeded Steffi Graf met defending champion Martina Navratilova.

Becker held a two-set-to-one lead when play was suspended by darkness Friday night. He blew three match points in the third-set tiebreaker and five more in the 10th game of the fourth set Saturday before driving a forehand right at Lendl at the net.

The top-seeded Lendl had to duck out of the way. The ball struck just inside the baseline and Becker thrust his fists overhead, letting his head flop back in exhaustion, the match finally won.

When play resumed today, Lendl appeared with a heavy bandage protecting torn muscle fibres in the upper part of his left thigh. He showed his usual power, producing service winners one after the other as he saved four break points in the sixth game.

After two rain delays totalling 71 minutes, the sun stayed out and the players stayed on serve. Becker took a 5-4 lead at love, then used two forehand volley errors by Lendl to gain double-match point at 15-40 on the Czechoslovak's serve.

Becker hit a backhand off the netcord wide, then a forehand down the line that was just long to send the game to deuce. He got match point No. 6 on a backhand passing shot, but Lendl saved that with a service winner.

Lendl had his chances to hold service, taking the advantage when Becker hit a forehand long. But a service return by Becker took the game to deuce, and match point No. 7

came on a netted backhand volley. Becker promptly hit a backhand volley into the net himself.

He got match point No. 8 on a backhand passing shot, and walked over to a line judge to ask advice on how to hold on. Umpire Richard Kaufman called, "Let's play," and Lendl promptly fired a cannonball serve that just nipped Becker's racket.

Eight chances, and eight chances missed. But No. 9 did not get away.

A running backing passing shot down the line gave Becker the ninth match point, and he put it away with his drive.

Edberg advanced to his first Wimbledon final with a comeback that would have made Bjorn Borg proud.

Seven years after Borg rallied from two sets down to make the final of his last Wimbledon, another blond Swede, Edberg, turned the clock back Friday with a recovery that was equally remarkable.

"It was hard to believe I could come back today," Edberg said after his 4-6, 2-6, 6-4, 6-3, 6-4 victory over Miloslav Mecir. "It felt such a long way off."

AP-NY 1056EDT —

2. Write a maximum 35-second kicker slugged CASH DASH based on the following news agency story:

SAN FRANCISCO (AP)--Three people apparently made off with at least $460,000 after a crate of money bags fell off an armored car Tuesday, police said.

The unidentified individuals scooped up the cash-stuffed bags and drove away after the crate, containing more than $1.5 million, fell out of a moving Loomis Armored Inc. truck when the rear door flew open in the Mission District.

The truck driver was unaware of the loss until he stopped two blocks away after a motorist honked his horn and said the truck's door was ajar, according to Police Officer Harry Soulette, who was flagged down by the driver.

By the time Soulette and the Loomis driver went back to the crate, a crowd had gathered around the fallen bags. About $1 million was recovered.

Some people were putting the sacks back in the crate, but a few had other ideas.

"There was a gentleman from the post office grabbing bags of money out of people's hands and putting them back in the crate," Soulette said. "At least three people looked at him and told him what he could do with his suggestion.... Several people decided they were going to take advantage of what happened, threw the bags into their cars and left."

Witnesses were able to give detailed descriptions of three of the people and their cars. If found, they could face felony grand theft charges, police said.

"My advice to them is to turn it in," Soulette said.

12

Tape I: Actualities and Sound Bites

Modern broadcast news owes much of its style and content to the development of portable sound and picture recording equipment. Such gear made its first practical appearance in the early 1960s, and since then hardly a month has gone by without some new technological refinement. Most dramatic has been the development of lightweight video cameras and editing gear, coupled with mobile satellite transmission equipment, enabling broadcast journalists to send live and instant-replay TV coverage of news events from almost anywhere in the world—as well as occasionally from outer space. Television has thus caught up to radio in the built-in immediacy of its news presentation.

Learning to use the technical tools of broadcast news is, quite obviously, a hands-on enterprise. You've got to see and hear what the machines can do to appreciate their use. Except at big-city stations where labor unions restrict editorial personnel from operating the equipment, broadcast journalists are expected to know how to record and edit audiotape, shoot and edit videotape, and run the playback equipment during newscasts.

All this poses a major problem for journalism instructors. The problem is that schools and universities, just like professional news departments, use different equipment; there is no such thing as "standard equipment." And, to compound the problem, the rapid pace of technological change requires that broadcast journalists be retrained on the job to operate new generations of machines. Thus, no journalism textbook can teach which buttons to push, because the buttons are everywhere different.

What a textbook *can* do, however, is attempt to teach the style of writing required to integrate taped segments into news stories and newscasts. Fortunately, the writing techniques are the same, regardless of the specific technology employed in producing the final product.

The ability effectively to integrate writing and tape is a skill *demanded* of today's broadcast journalists. Roughly one-third to one-half of any given radio or television newscast is on tape, either in the form of brief excerpts (called "actualities" in radio, "sound bites" in television), or longer pieces from reporters in the field (called "spots" in radio and "packages" in television). Job competition is so intense in broadcast news that writing-to-tape (like broadcast style itself) is not taught on the job; a newcomer must demonstrate the requisite skill, in a pre-hiring exam called an "audition," before he or she is offered an editorial position (that is, as a writer, reporter, or producer) in a professional newsroom.

If I'm making it sound tough, that's because it *is* tough. Employers won't accept your word that you can do something. They will want to see proof of it. But take heart. If you can assimilate the material in this and ensuing chapters, and if you are well on your way toward writing clearly in broadcast style, you will probably do well enough on your first audition to land that all-important first job. So pay attention. The integration of sound and pictures into the news is what makes broadcast journalism radically different from print journalism. Nothing of what follows has its equivalent anywhere in newspapers or magazines.

(For the sake of simplicity, we will use the term "actuality" to refer to taped excerpts in both radio and television. Wherever there are differences in their selection or handling, these will be specifically noted.)

TYPES OF ACTUALITIES

Voices and Moving Pictures of Newsmakers

These are by far the most frequently seen and heard kinds of actualities. Nothing conveys the "feel" of a news event as well as the voice and/or moving picture of someone who took part in it or witnessed it. Yes, there is a writer's skill to paraphrase. But what writer can convey the emotional power of Rev. Martin Luther King, Jr.'s "I have a dream!" speech? The forlorness of Richard Nixon's announcement that "I shall resign the presidency effective at noon tomorrow"? The faraway yet breathtaking essence of Neil Armstrong's "A small step for a man, a giant leap for mankind" as he set foot on the moon?

Those words and pictures are lodged deep within our individual and collective memories not only for their substance, but also for the way in which we saw and heard them. In particles of magnetic tape, they are preserved for generations to come.

At first glance, voice actualities appear to be the equivalent of print's direct quotes. But they are not, and it is misleading to consider them as such. Quotes in print have no "voice" or "image." They are disembodied, appearing only as ink on paper. As such, a direct quote in print, preceded or followed by an identification of who said it, seems to flow in context. But on the air, the quote and the identification of the speaker are heard and seen as *two voices and/or pictures,* two different sounds and/or pictures emanating from two different electronic sources. Unless handled in a special way, they might not seem to flow; instead, they might seem jarring or incongruous.

Before detailing how to make writing and actualities flow, let's examine the actualities themselves. How do you choose them? What standards guide their selection and use? Answering these questions is tricky, because, in the last analysis, each case must be decided on its own merits. But by and large, there are six standards by which to judge actualities:

1. *Informational Content.* This is by far the most frequent basis for selection. Almost every speech, news conference, or interview contains one or more portions, brief excerpts, which reflect the crux of the remarks as a whole. Journalistically speaking, the crux is overwhelmingly the "what" or the "why," perhaps both. In short, the *main point* (or points) of a spoken context is what most often makes the best actuality (or series of actualities).

2. *Colorful Details.* Sometimes, the main point of a spoken context can be stated more quickly and clearly by the newswriter than by the speaker. In such cases, the colorful or quirky remark might make the better actuality. Suppose that the president of the United States, in a speech somewhere, proposes a long series of controls on the food industry to guarantee the purity and safety of food products on supermarket shelves. And suppose his recitation is so long-winded and boring that a newswriter could summarize the proposal in two sentences. Good-bye, actuality. But suppose that the president had ad libbed, "You know, the only reason I'm making these proposals is because I found a staple in my Corn Flakes this morning," followed by audience laughter. Suddenly, you've got your actuality: that remark, *including* the audience reaction.

3. *Emotional Impact.* Very often the flavor or weight of a set of remarks is carried not so much by the words as by the speaker's tone of voice or facial expression. Someone's reaction to a piece of good or bad news is a frequent example. If you ask the winner of a multi-million-dollar state lottery for his or her reaction, you are obviously going to hear words to the effect, "I'm very, very happy." But the tone of voice or facial expression will tell you just *how* happy; the words themselves mean little without their emotional coloring.

4. *Sound Quality.* Except in rare cases (as when a piece of tape is of historic value or, in television, where the picture itself is important), actualities must sound clear technically. Every word must be understandable. The voice or accent can't sound mushy or "off-mike."

    Obviously, you can't control the quality of the receiving equipment used by the audience. But at the point of transmission (that is, the newsroom or studio), there must be no straining of ears or shaking of heads over the text of an actuality. In radio, a common standard for judging sound quality is to ask the question, "Will this be understood over a commuter's car radio while driving at 55 miles an hour in moderate traffic?" If the answer is no, the tape should not be used.

    In television, the text of a hard-to-understand actuality may be presented simultaneously on the screen in an electronic graphic or title.

5. *Picture Quality.* On television, an actuality may consist of silence—or at least a lack of spoken words. A facial expression or emotional reaction (such as laughter or tears) can speak volumes. A handshake between two former enemies is an actuality (even though some news departments, instead of labeling it a "sound bite," refer to it as NATSOT; more on this in a moment). So is a punch thrown in anger. Or a public official stonily refusing to reply to a question.

6. *Length.* There is no "best" length for an actuality. By that I mean that each actuality depends on context (cf. the five preceding standards) and therefore has its own inherent "best" length. Further, you can't control the way people express themselves (beyond editing the tape afterwards); therefore, some actualities will be short, others long.

   As we've noted repeatedly, however, broadcast news prizes brevity. Thus, the shorter an actuality, the better. As a rule of thumb, no actuality should run less than 5 seconds in radio; it takes a second or two for listeners to "digest" the second voice. But on television, where the picture of the speaker immediately establishes a new presence, the modern trend is to use actualities as short as 3 seconds, the time required for a single pithy remark.

Natural Sound (NATSOT)

Sometimes the best actualities are not words in the form of prepared or ad-lib remarks. Sometimes they are the natural sounds of events, such as chanting, singing, sirens, police bullhorns, railroad cars clacking on rails, machinery in operation, computers beeping, and so on. In television, "natural sound" also means "natural picture." We can watch people doing something, performing some action; they need not be saying anything. Or we can watch a building collapse, a rocket blast off, or a child eating an ice cream cone. When President Ronald Reagan signed a bill making the third Monday in January a national holiday in honor of Rev. Martin Luther King, Jr., the crowd of onlookers in the White House Rose Garden spontaneously began singing "We Shall Overcome"; the natural sound and picture of the crowd in song was a memorable actuality on both radio and television, more telling than anyone's prepared remarks.

Broadcast reporters and producers are always on the lookout for such natural sounds and pictures, which are recorded "in the clear" (that is, without spoken commentary) and then incorporated into stories and newscasts.

In television news, natural sound is designated NATSOT—short for "natural sound on tape." In radio, natural sound is often called "wild-track audio."

Q-and-A

Sometimes written as "Q/A," Q-and-A is short for "question and answer." It is an actuality that includes the reporter's voice (or voice and picture) as well as the newsmaker's. A typical Q/A actuality opens with a newsmaker's remark, continues with a reporter's follow-up question, and ends with the newsmaker's reply. Q/A's inherently run longer than simple actualities, and, as a general rule, they are used only if both parties' remarks are succinct or if the interview from which they are excerpted is a newsmaking exclusive.

There is a second type of Q/A that does not even include the voice of a newsmaker. It is composed either entirely of a reporter's voice (or voice and picture) or of a combination of the reporter and an in-studio staffer. For example, a reporter at the scene of an event may be interviewed (by phone in radio, by satellite in TV) by a colleague (a writer, producer, or even the anchor) about what he or she has witnessed. The interview (a form of debriefing) may be broadcast live, but more often it is taped; excerpts are then edited for broadcast. In radio, the edited Q/A may in fact be just the reporter's "answer," typically a first-hand description or assessment. In television, Q/A typically runs longer and does include a portion of both ends of the conversation. It has become a common practice in TV news to follow a reporter's recorded package with a live Q/A portion in which the reporter delivers later information or responds to the anchor's questions on story angles not covered in the package itself.

INTERNAL EDITING

Content

The content of taped actualities is an editorial decision in the same way that print journalists decide which of their notes to include in a story and which to reject. Journalists, *not* the newsmakers, control the structure and content of their stories in all media.

This means freedom to edit out extraneous remarks, as long as such editing *does not distort the speaker's meaning or intent.* Clearly, internal editing demands a high degree of journalistic integrity. Former President Richard Nixon once declared, "I am not a crook." Any journalist who edited out the word "not" would deservedly have been fired on the spot.

More than likely, the case will be something like this: Mayor Smith says,

> The tax bill is a sham from stem to stern. *Now wait a minute, folks, let me answer this question.* It takes money from the poor and puts it into the pockets of the rich.

Clearly, the second sentence (in italics) is an interruption of some kind and not a part of the mayor's train of thought. You as a journalist would edit that sentence out, butting together the first and third sentences into a single actuality.

Of course, internal editing can get much trickier. Suppose that the mayor had said.

> The tax bill is a sham from stem to stern. *Its proposal at this time is a blight on the citizens of our fair city, a stain on our civic pride, a caving in to greedy instincts.* It takes money from the poor and puts it into the pockets of the rich.

This time the radio journalist has a choice: to use the remark unedited *or,* for the sake of brevity, to edit out the second sentence. Again, the meaning is not distorted.

However, suppose Mayor Smith had said,

The tax bill is a sham from stem to stern. *And the property assessment indicator is no bargain, either.* It takes money from the poor and puts it into the pockets of the rich.

Much as you might like to edit out the second sentence, you can't do it honestly. That's because the "it" at the start of the third sentence could refer to the tax bill, the assessment indicator, or both. You just don't know for sure. So your choices are to use the actuality in its entirety, or not to use it at all.

Internal edits need not be confined to single sentences. A remark from one part of the text may be butted to a remark that came minutes later (but not hours or days), as long as the resulting actuality is faithful to the sense of the remarks as a whole. I can't stress this too strongly. Responsibility in editing is at the heart of broadcast journalism.

Inflections

Sometimes you won't be able to edit an actuality for the most desirable content. That's because human speech patterns won't always let you.

All human languages rely, to varying degrees, on rhythms and inflections to help convey meaning. Some Oriental languages rely on inflections so heavily that, in Chinese, for example, one word can have four or five different meanings, depending on its tonal inflection.

English, on the other hand, uses inflections sparingly, usually at the end of a phrase or sentence. The sentence, "You are going," ends in a *down* inflection. But if we add a question mark, "You are going?" the inflection is now *up*, indicating doubt or that something is to follow.

Many speakers tend to ramble, unsure of where the thought or sentence will end. Such speakers end their sentences with unnatural *up* inflections. The result, in tape editing, is that it's hard to find a place to end the actuality without letting it go on to an undesirable length. For the sake of flow and normal speech patterns, actualities should end with *down* inflections. In other words, natural speech rhythms should be retained in editing and ending actualities. Otherwise, they sound unnatural, in fact, sound "edited."

Most beginners discover the inflection problem through trial and error. But they soon develop an ear for inflections and can predict in advance whether a certain edit will work.

SOURCES OF TAPE

Radio and TV news departments get their taped material from a wide variety of sources. For local news, the main source is their own staffers armed with equipment to record interviews, news conferences, demonstrations, and so forth.

(Many college journalism departments have audio- and videotape recording and editing equipment for student use. These electronic devices are everyday tools of the trade in broadcast news, and you should learn how to handle them.)

At local stations, the main source of taped material for world and national stories is the network with which they are affiliated or an independent supplier such as AP or UPI Broadcast News.

A third main source is the telephone, which is used to record people's remarks on breaking news or for reporters to call in their stories. (Although laws differ across the country, it is generally a firm rule to request permission to record a person's remarks before proceeding with an interview; except in rare cases, people may not be recorded surreptitiously or their voices broadcast against their will.) For obvious reasons, "foners" (as they are called) are a staple of radio news. But they are also used in television when it is not possible to establish a video link on a breaking story either before or during a broadcast.

Audiotape

The Audio material is fed to contracting stations at regular intervals throughout the day. At the same time, a description of the material being fed is sent by telex or over the broadcast wire. Here's a sample audio advisory from UPI:

```
NU--R
Z2271NU--R
        R R NETWORK-HOURLY NEWSFEED 0377
10-29 810P(
FOLLOWING CUTS FED AT 8:10 and 10:10PM EDT=
(
(
83 :45 V-A WA -(ARMS)- (VICKI BARKER W-PRES(
REAGAN) PRES RESTATES COMMITMENT TO NUCLEAR(
ARMS REDUCTION IN WKLY RADIO ADDRESS(
(
84 :41 V-A WA -(DEMS)- (VICKI BARKER W-REP(
LEE HAMILTON, D-IND) DEMOCRATIC RESPONDENT(
URGES GOVT TO KEEP MARINES IN LEBANON(
(
85 :46 V NEW YORK -(SPRINT)-(
(MICHAEL LYSAK W-MARK HOCHMAN,(
OF SUMERVILLE, N J) PHONE SERVICE(
CUSTOMER ALLEGES RIPOFF(
86 :46 V NEW YORK -(REAGAN)-(
(JACK VAIL) SURVEY SHOWS PRES(
REAGAN GETTING FAVORABLE REACTIONS(
TO BEIRUT AND GRENADA POLICIES(
(
87 :25 A TULSA, OKL -(GRENADA)-(
(U-S AMBASSADOR TO UNITED NATIONS(
JEANE KIRKPATRICK) VOTING MEMBERS(
IN THE GENERAL ASSEMBLY SHOULD KEEP(
THEIR STORIES STRAIGHT (TIRED OF THAT)(
88 :16 A TULSA, OKL -(GRENADA)-(
(U-S AMBASSADOR TO UNITED NATIONS(
JEANE KIRKPATRICK) THEIR DEAL OF(
SUPPORT FOR U-S MILITARY ACTION IN(
GRENADA (WORLD TODAY)(
(EDS: CUTS 87-88 REFER TO A RECENT VOTE(
TAKEN IN THE U N GENERAL ASSEMBLY CONDEMNING(
U-S INVASION OF GRENADA, WHICH THE U-S VETOED)(
```

Each item to be fed at the times specified (in this case 8:10 and 10:10 P.M. Eastern Daylight Time) is called a "cut." Each is numbered consecutively throughout the day. This particular UPI Newsfeed contains cuts 83 through 88.

Following each cut number is its *exact* running time (to the second, *not* rounded off. This is on *tape,* and in both radio and TV, everything on tape is timed *exactly.*). That's followed by a letter or two. "V" stands for "voicer," a voice report *without* an actuality. "V-A" stands for "voice-actuality," meaning that the report contains the voice of a newsmaker as well as that of the reporter. In the business, this is known as a "wraparound," or just "wrap," because of the reporter's voice "wrapping around" someone else's.

Next comes an abbreviation for the location of the report. In cuts 83 and 84, "WA" stands for Washington, D.C.

Then, in parentheses, comes the name of the reporter and, where applicable, the name of the voice in the actuality, followed by a brief description of the report's content. The information in parentheses also serves as the slug.

Cuts 87 and 88 are denoted "A," which stands for "actuality," in other words the voice of a newsmaker. In this case, it's U.N. Ambassador Jeane Kirkpatrick, speaking in Tulsa. The words in parentheses at the ends of cuts 87 and 88—"tired of that" and "world today," respectively—are called "outcues" or "endcues." An outcue is the final few words of an actuality or report.

Videotape

Even in the space age, TV networks and local stations continue to use black-and-white still photographs of news events from around the world—the same photos you are likely to see in your local newspaper. But they use them only as a last resort—that is, when no video camera was nearby to provide moving pictures in full color. And these days, that's a rare case indeed.

The still photos usually come from AP or UPI, transmitted to networks and subscribing local stations. They're usually called "wirephotos," despite the fact that transmission by wire has now given way to transmission by laser (the equivalent of replacing a spear with a bullet).

Television's overwhelming effort is aimed at getting videotape from wherever events are taking place around the world. Not long ago, this was so complicated and expensive that only a major news event warranted the effort. It's still expensive, but now, in what has been described as television's "global village," it is a routine matter to cover the news by satellite—and to watch the "CBS Evening News" in Paris and French TV's *Journal Télévisé* in Los Angeles.

Until the mid-1980s, only networks, in cooperation with foreign broadcast organizations, had the resources to obtain and transmit such visuals. Now, however, satellites and mobile transmitter/receivers have enabled local TV stations to cover world and national stories with their own personnel. In addition, there is a host of TV news syndication services available for purchase. Technology and the rise of cable television have broken the traditional network monopoly on world and national video coverage. Local stations willing to spend the money on travel and satellite transmissions can and do compete with networks for coverage of world and national stories of interest to their own audiences.

On an everyday basis, however, local TV stations continue to rely on networks for most of their world and national videotape.* The tape is fed to local stations at preset times of day, with extra coverage available at any time for major breaking stories. Networks used to reserve their "best pictures" for their own nightly newscasts; nowadays they feed them as quickly as possible to their local affiliates to keep the affiliates competitive in the "global village."

Private, Corporate, and Governmental Sources

To an ever-growing extent, TV news departments are getting videotape from sources outside the news industry. The widespread use and increased quality of consumer video gear (VHS, Beta, and 8mm) enable private citizens to act as adjuncts to the TV news business. It is now commonplace for TV news to broadcast tape shot by amateurs at the scenes of events. (The stations pay the amateurs who had the luck or foresight to bring their video cameras and switch them on at just the right moment.)

A growing number of private companies maintain a public affairs (that is, public relations) department fully equipped with video gear. Although the primary purpose of such departments is to present the companies' "good side," the tape they shoot is often the only visual record of goings-on that eventually make news. The companies frequently make the tape available to TV news departments.

Government, too, has entered the wide world of video in a big way. Many government agencies keep up-to-date video records of their activities and frequently make the tapes available to the media. The Defense Department in particular is the source of virtually all visuals showing military aircraft, ships, and weapons systems. The State Department maintains full video facilities in order to produce programs aimed at foreign outlets. And NASA is the source of almost all visuals of the space program.

All proprietary videotape—whether private, corporate, or governmental—is supposed to be clearly labeled when shown on TV news. By means of an electronic title (be patient, we'll come to this in Chapters 15 and 16), such as "NASA tape" or "General Motors tape," stations inform viewers of the source of the visuals. In other words, the rules of attribution apply to pictures as well as to words.

WRITING TO ACTUALITIES

To understand the way broadcast journalists prepare stories containing taped actualities, let's begin at the beginning—with a text spoken by a newsmaker.

During most of his term in the White House, President Ronald Reagan delivered a five-minute radio speech every Saturday. Originally billed as a "fireside chat" in emulation of President Franklin Roosevelt's method of addressing the nation, Mr. Reagan's Saturday talk was devoted to an issue of the day or to a

---

*According to the FCC (Federal Communications Commission), more than 600 of the 850 commercial VHF and UHF television stations in the United States are affiliated with ABC, NBC, or CBS. The remaining stations, known as "independents," buy their nonlocal videotape from other suppliers. Noncommercial stations also have limited access to network and nonnetwork material.

partisan attack on his Democratic opponents in Congress, sometimes both. In broadcast newsrooms across the United States, the "Reagan Talk" became a standard story every Saturday.

As you read the following verbatim transcript of his talk of August 27, 1988 (when Mr. Reagan had only five months left in his term of office), remember that as a broadcaster you will be looking and listening in a different way from print journalists. First and foremost, you will be assessing its news value in the realization that, barring a major presidential announcement, your eventual air time will be very short. At the same time, you will be on the alert for those portions of the remarks that will make good actualities.

The text, as broadcast that Saturday:

My fellow Americans, I want to talk to you today about some good things that are happening around the world—a move toward peace that shows how successful this nation's commitment to peace through strength has been.

In the Persian Gulf, a ceasefire has been declared in one of this era's most horrendous conflicts, the Iran-Iraq war. In Asia, half the Soviet Union's invasion force has left Afghanistan, and the rest are due out early next year. In Southeast Asia, Vietnam has promised to withdraw its occupation force from Cambodia. In Southern Africa, we're brokering an agreement that may lead to the departure of all Cuban and South African forces from Angola. And we seem to have a more constructive relationship with the Soviet Union, because of the Afghanistan withdrawal, human rights improvements, and the INF treaty that eliminates an entire class of U.S. and Soviet nuclear missiles.

Peace is gaining ground. But the gains haven't just come in the last few months. It's taken seven and a half years of effort. We came into office convinced that the word "peace" is just an empty slogan unless the word "strength" follows hard upon it. Peace is a godly thing, but men are seldom godly. What we've learned is that peace is hard to achieve unless the forces of good have the strength to stand firmly for it.

Before we took office in 1981, the globe was reeling from an explosion of international turbulence. Our nation had neglected its defenses for years, while some assured us that a passive America would enjoy a peace that was more, not less, secure. But that's not how things turned out. Soon we saw Vietnam invade Cambodia, and the Soviet Union invade Afghanistan. Iraq and Iran began their war during this period as well. Over and over, we Americans saw that when our nation does not maintain her strength, peace has no anchor in the world.

Our resolve was tested early on. The Soviet Union had deployed highly destabilizing intermediate-range missiles in Europe and Asia—a threat to peace. With our NATO allies, we went to the Soviets with a proposal: Get rid of those missiles, we said, before we match them with missiles of our own. The Soviets turned us down. They were daring us to deliver. And we did. Our determination and that of our allies to see our missiles installed in Europe convinced the Soviet Union that the days of unilateral disarmament were over. And once the Soviets learned they could not intimidate us or cajole us into giving them the advantage, they came to the bargaining table. They did business because we proved we meant business.

We also meant business when we said we would not sit idly by as noble and brave Afghan freedom fighters resisted an invasion of their country. Our aid to the

Afghan resistance has been of critical importance in the Soviet decision to go home. Once again, they did business because we proved we meant business.

In Angola, Jonas Savimbi's UNITA has been fighting for 13 years against the Marxist regime and its Cuban protectors. In 1975, President Gerald Ford wanted to help—but some in Congress felt our standing with the freedom fighters would only prolong hostilities. A law was passed that made aid illegal. The war dragged on. The Cubans multiplied. In 1985, Congress repealed the law and began supporting UNITA. Now the Cubans are talking of a pullout. They're doing business because we showed them we meant business.

We've proved that we can stand united as a country that means business—business for peace.

Our bipartisan policy in the Persian Gulf has been to stand firm against Iranian aggression and for the principle of free navigation. Now the Iran-Iraq war's coming to a close. Why? One reason, as retired admirals Elmo Zumwalt and Worth Bagley put it, was that the allied naval operation, designed to be a deterrent, worked.

Contrast these successes with the tragic situation in Nicaragua. It's been almost two years since Congress has approved any military aid to the brave freedom fighters there. Here's the results: The Sandinistas come to the bargaining table making promises to bring democracy and end the war. And then they violate those promises with impunity. They kick out our ambassadors, oppress their people, arrest their opposition, muzzle the media, and engage in vicious assaults on civilians to get them to stop aiding the freedom fighters. They feel free to do all this because they do not believe that we mean business.

Our policy of peace through strength has been vindicated wherever it's been tried. There is still time to turn the tide in Nicaragua. We shouldn't be overly optimistic, for freedom still faces serious challenges, whether in South Asia or Eastern Europe. But the future for world peace is bright if we Americans continue to stand firm, stand tall, and stand for freedom.

Until next week, thank you for listening, and God bless you.

First, what was the news, if any, in Mr. Reagan's talk? If you put that question to any ten professional journalists picked at random, it's a safe bet that all ten would agree that the President's call for renewed military aid to the Contra rebels (whom he chose to call "freedom fighters") in Nicaragua was the most newsworthy part of his remarks. The story, no matter its length, would be built around that issue.

If your assignment were to write that story without tape, you could do so quite easily in 15 or 20 seconds.

But since your assignment is to write a story containing tape, you cannot begin to structure your story until after choosing your actualities. So let's look again at those portions of Mr. Reagan's remarks that concerned Contra aid, and consider which ones best serve to help us tell the story:

> Contrast these successes with the tragic situation in Nicaragua. It's been almost two years since Congress has approved any military aid to the brave freedom fighters there. Here's the results: The Sandinistas come to the bargaining table making promises to bring democracy and end the war. And then they violate those promises with impunity. They kick out our am-

bassadors, oppress their people, arrest their opposition, muzzle the media, and engage in vicious assaults on civilians to get them to stop aiding the freedom fighters. They feel free to do all this because they do not believe that we mean business.

Our policy of peace through strength has been vindicated wherever it's been tried. There is still time to turn the tide in Nicaragua. We shouldn't be overly optimistic, for freedom still faces serious challenges, whether in South Asia or Eastern Europe. But the future for world peace is bright if we Americans continue to stand firm, stand tall, and stand for freedom.

Taken together, those words run 59 seconds—too long, obviously, for the time constraints of broadcast news. So we must edit short excerpts that run between 10 and 35 seconds. Here are a few choices and their running times:

REAGAN/CONTRAS #1

It's been almost two years since Congress has approved any military aid to the brave freedom fighters there. Here's the results: The Sandinistas come to the bargaining table making promises to bring democracy and end the war. And then they violate those promises with impunity. They kick out our ambassadors, oppress their people, arrest their opposition, muzzle the media, and engage in vicious assaults on civilians to get them to stop aiding the freedom fighters. They feel free to do all this because they do not believe that we mean business.

(runs :33)

REAGAN/CONTRAS #2

The Sandinistas come to the bargaining table making promises to bring democracy and end the war. And then they violate those promises with impunity. They kick out our ambassadors, oppress their people, arrest their opposition, muzzle the media, and engage in vicious assaults on civilians to get them to stop aiding the freedom fighters. They feel free to do all this because they do not believe that we mean business.

(runs :24)

REAGAN/CONTRAS #3

Our policy of peace through strength has been vindicated wherever it's been tried. There is still time to turn the tide in Nicaragua. We shouldn't be overly optimistic, for freedom still faces serious challenges, whether in South Asia or Eastern Europe. But the future for world peace is bright if we Americans continue to stand firm, stand tall, and stand for freedom.

(runs :21)

REAGAN/CONTRAS #4

Our policy of peace through strength has been vindicated wherever it's been tried. There is still time to turn the tide in Nicaragua. (. . .) The future for world peace is bright if we Americans continue to stand firm, stand tall, and stand for freedom.

(runs :14)

(Notice that cut #2 is merely a shorter version of cut #1 and that cut #4 is a shorter version of cut #3, made possible by an internal edit.)

Okay, we've decided what the news is, and we've picked our actualities. Now we must decide which cut we will use in our first version of the story.

Please note that we have adopted a very different approach from print journalism. Print journalists may compose a lead sentence and then flesh it out with direct quotes selected afterwards. We, on the other hand, must know first which "quote" we will use *even before* we write our lead. Why? In order *not* to say the same thing in the lead as the newsmaker will say in the tape. Our time on the air is too short to waste in redundancy and repetition. And once we choose our actuality, we can't suddenly change our minds without switching tapes and thus losing time while our competition is busy putting its own version on the air.

Let's say we decide to use cut #4. We know its text. Thus, we know we must not use the phrases "peace through strength" or "turn the tide in Nicaragua" in our written copy. Okay, let's try it:

```
President Reagan called on Congress today to pass a new military aid

package for the Contra rebels in Nicaragua.

In his weekly radio talk, Mr. Reagan accused the Sandinista

government of bad faith in recent peace negotiations, and of brutally

suppressing its opponents.  Only through military strength backed by the

United States, the president said, will there be true democracy in

Nicaragua:
```

> Our policy of peace through strength has been vindicated wherever it's been tried. There is still time to turn the tide in Nicaragua. (. . .) The future for world peace is bright if we Americans continue to stand firm, stand tall, and stand for freedom.

```
Congress voted to end Contra military aid nearly two years ago.
```

That story runs a total of 40 seconds (14 seconds of tape time plus about 26 seconds of written copy), just about right for a story containing an actuality. We could make it even shorter:

```
President Reagan called on Congress today to pass a new military aid

package for the Contra rebels in Nicaragua.

In his weekly radio talk, Mr. Reagan said that only through military

strength backed by the United States will there be true democracy in

Nicaragua:
```

> Our policy of peace through strength has been vindicated wherever it's been tried. There is still time to turn the tide in Nicaragua. (. . .) The future for world peace is bright if we Americans continue to stand firm, stand tall, and stand for freedom.

```
Congress voted to end Contra military aid nearly two years ago.
```

That reduces the story to 30 seconds (14 seconds of tape + 16 seconds of written copy). Yes, that's very short. It doesn't contain much detail or nuance. But it does cover the main point—and that is the everyday nature of broadcast news.

Now let's try a longer version and see how much detail we can pack in. We'll use cut #2:

```
President Reagan is calling once again for military aid to the

Contras.  Congress cut off such aid nearly two years ago -- which the

president says has allowed the Nicaraguan Sandinista government to

bargain in bad faith:
```

> The Sandinistas come to the bargaining table making promises to bring democracy and end the war. And then they violate those promises with impunity. They kick out our ambassadors, oppress their people, arrest their opposition, muzzle the media, and engage in vicious assaults on civilians to get them to stop aiding the freedom fighters. They feel free to do all this because they do not believe that we mean business.

```
In his weekly radio address, Mr. Reagan said only U-S military

backing of the Contras will force the Sandinistas to seek real peace.
```

That version runs 45 seconds (24 seconds of tape + 19 seconds of written copy = 43 seconds; rounded off = 45 seconds). It's got a little more flavor, but not much more substance. And that, in sum, is the nature of broadcast news. Compare the foregoing broadcast versions with the following print version:

```
PM-Reagan     APTVvar    Sat Aug 27 11:37

Reagan Again Asks for New Contra Aid
     LOS ANGELES (AP)--President Reagan, renewing his plea for
aid to the Nicaraguan Contra rebels, cautioned today that
world peace cannot be achieved unless Americans "stand firm,
stand tall and stand for freedom."
     Reagan used his weekly radio address to celebrate
advances toward international peace in several of the world's
hotspots, which he credited to the efforts of his
administration and his policy of "peace through strength."
```

    He also put in a plug for renewed aid to the Contras,
which is stalled in Congress.
    Reagan cited the cease-fire in the Persian Gulf, the
Soviet withdrawal from Afghanistan, work toward an agreement
for Cuban and South African withdrawals from Angola, as well
as the improvement in relations with the Soviet Union.
    "Peace is gaining ground. But the gains haven't just come
in the last few months. It's taken seven and a half years of
effort," Reagan said. "We came into office convinced that the
word peace is just an empty slogan, unless the word strength
follows hard upon it."
    The president said the United States has supported "noble
and brave" freedom fighters, such as the Afghan rebels, and
stood firm to the military threat of the Soviet Union.
    "Once the Soviets learned they could not intimidate us or
cajole us into giving them the advantages, they came to the
bargaining table," Reagan said. "They did business because we
proved we meant business."
    Reagan complained that it has been almost two years since
Congress has approved any military aid to the rebels battling
the leftist Sandinista government.
    "Here's the results: The Sandinistas come to the
bargaining table making promises to bring democracy and end
the war. And then they violate those promises with impunity.
They feel free to do all this because they do not believe that
we mean business," Reagan said.
    The President warned that "there is still time to turn
the tide in Nicaragua.... The future for world peace is bright
if we Americans continue to stand firm, stand tall, and stand
for freedom."
    Reagan's radio address was taped prior to his departure
today for a round of fund raising for the California
Republican Party.

Because the news agency was not under the same time constraints as broadcast writers, its writer was able to respect the president's overall structure, making clear that he was claiming victories in many world hotspots while blaming Congress for the Contra failure in Nicaragua. Only in broadcast newsrooms willing to give at least one minute's air time to this story is it possible to add a fuller context. There are such newsrooms, but they are a minority.

Before continuing with other examples of broadcast style in stories containing actualities, we need to define a few terms that are used in broadcast newsrooms throughout the United States. These terms are part of the everyday vocabulary of broadcast journalism.

Lead-ins

The written copy *preceding* a taped actuality or report is called the "lead-in" (LEED-in). Although a few news departments call it an "intro," the term lead-in is more apt, because the copy is supposed to "lead the listener in" to the taped voice or natural sound. In other words, listeners must not be surprised by the tape; they must be expecting it—because the written copy has prepared them for it. Thus, lead-ins must

1. open the story, and
2. set the stage for the tape.

Tags

The written copy *following* the tape is called the "tag." It, too, serves a double function:

1. to reidentify the voice or sound we've just heard, and
2. to finish the story or carry it one step further.

The modern practice in many cases is to dispense with the tag altogether, especially if (1) the voice is familiar to the audience, and/or (2) the final words of the actuality make a natural end to the story.

Bridges

A "bridge" refers to the written copy that comes *between* two actualities within the same story. It's called a bridge because it links one actuality to another. (We'll show an example shortly.)

Cue Lines

The *first three words* of an actuality are called the "incue." Thus, the incue of the preceding REAGAN/CONTRAS #2 is "The Sandinistas come. . . ."

The *last three words* of an actuality are called the "outcue." The outcue of that same cut is ". . . we mean business."

As we shall see, the outcue is a critical script component and must indicate precisely the final *sound* of the tape.

Slugs and Time Cues

It is essential that written stories and tapes bear the same identifying slug. Otherwise, they might be mixed up during playback in a newscast.

A playback (edited, ready for broadcast) tape is labeled with the date, the slug, the cut number, the exact running time, the name of the speaker (or natural sound), and the outcue.

Note that tape is timed exactly to the second, instead of rounded off to the nearest 5 seconds like written copy.

SCRIPTING

A radio news script does not contain a verbatim transcript of the taped portion. That would be cumbersome and unnecessarily time-consuming. But it does contain the cue lines and timings. Otherwise, the form is identical to the sample scripts in Chapter 4.

Here are model scripts for two of the foregoing REAGAN/CONTRA stories:

Bard, 11/27/ 1p

REAGAN/CONTRAS

:30

President Reagan called on Congress today to pass a new military aid package for the Contra rebels in Nicaragua.

In his weekly radio talk, Mr. Reagan said that only through military strength backed by the United States will there be true democracy in Nicaragua:

> REAGAN/CONTRAS #4
> RUNS: :14
> OUT: "...stand for freedom."

Congress voted to end Contra military air nearly two years ago.

Bard, 11/27, 2p

REAGAN/CONTRAS

:45

President Reagan is calling once again for military aid to the Contras. Congress cut off such aid nearly two years ago -- which the president says has allowed the Nicaraguan Sandinista government to bargain in bad faith:

> REAGAN/CONTRAS #2
> RUNS: :24
> OUT: "...we mean business."

In his weekly radio address, Mr. Reagan said only U-S military backing of the Contras will force the Sandinistas to seek real peace.

Okay, now for some more examples of integrating tape:

(lead-
in)   President Reagan is in New Jersey today, campaigning for the G-O-P

candidate for the U-S Senate, Congresswoman Millicent Fenwick. The

president used the occasion to call for a crackdown on crime:

(actuality)   (Reagan) Many of you have written to me how afraid you are to walk the
                                               streets at night. Many older citizens are frightened to go out even during the
                                               daytime. It's time to get the hardened criminal off the street and into jail.
                                               (applause)

(tag)   The president also denied charges by Democrats that his

administration has been hard-hearted when it comes to America's poor.

 The president said his battle against inflation has delivered more

purchasing power to poverty-level families.

(Stephanie Shelton, CBS Radio)

That manner of handling the story is special to broadcast journalism. In print journalism, the writer would have to have led with something on the order of, "President Ronald Reagan, declaring 'it's time to get the hardened criminal off the street and into jail,' called Monday for stricter anticrime legislation."

But if this broadcast newswriter had begun that way, she would have obviated the need to use that particular actuality. It would have been redundant and would have wasted precious air time. Since she was given an actuality with that text, she had to find a way to tell the story without upstaging the news contained in it

Note that the actuality was edited to include the applause in reaction to the president's remarks. If he had been booed, that, too, would have been included. A crowd's reaction is part of the scene, part of the "feel." Including the applause also enabled the newscaster to begin the tag *over* (hence the term "voice/over") the last second or two of the actuality. This resulted in a continuous flow of sound.

All right, here's another:

(lead-
in)   A special honor today for Steven Spielberg, who directed the summer

box-office smash "E-T." Spielberg was in New York, where he received the

United Nations Peace Medal. In accepting the medal, Spielberg compared

the U-N with E-T:

(actuality)   (Spielberg) They both have the desire and the need to communicate, often to "phone home," (laughter) to understand the care and the love, regardless of nationality. This film is dedicated to all such children, of all ages, in all the world. Thank you very much. (applause)

(tag)   Movie Director Steven Spielberg.

(Bill Diehl, ABC Radio)

Note that the actuality cannot stand on its own. It begins with the pronoun "they." Thus, the lead-in had not only to identify the speaker and establish the context, it had also to spell out who "they" are. Otherwise, the actuality would make no sense.

Note also that the tag is a simple reidentification of the speaker. The writer could have gone on to report more of Spielberg's remarks, but this would have been anticlimactic.

Now let's move on to something more difficult—a story with *two* actualities, requiring a "bridge" of copy tying the two together:

(lead-in)   The government's new off-shore oil and gas leasing plan came under

fire today at a hearing on Capitol Hill. Leading the attack was

Democratic Senator Walter Metzenbaum of Ohio:

(actuality 1)   (Metzenbaum) It would seem to me that the program to lease 200 million acres a year for five years is absurd. And its only conceivable result will be the most monumental giveaway in the nation's history: vast and immensely valuable public resources leased out at bargain basement prices, and in all probability leased out to the largest corporations in America.

(bridge)   But Interior Secretary James Watt said Metzenbaum and others were

off-base in their criticism of the leasing plan:

(actuality 2)   (Watt) There's a basic lack of understanding that what we're talking about is the far-out lands under the oceans—not the coastal beach areas. And too many people have, without understanding or intentionally without understanding, have made comments and conclusions that are not accurate or fair.

(tag)   Watt, who was testifying before the Senate Energy Subcommittee, said

the plan would create jobs, strengthen national security, protect the

environment, and reduce the nation's dependence on foreign oil.

(George Engle, ABC Radio)

In a one-sentence bridge, the writer has reidentified Metzenbaum while at the same time setting up the context of Watt. This kind of writing is not easy for most newcomers; it requires a lot of practice, a lot of experience working with tape. But the key to it, I think, is the acceptance of the non-inverted-pyramid structure of broadcast news. The first thing out of the newscaster's mouth does not have to be the essence of the story (although it may very well be), just as long as the essence is contained somewhere by the end of the story.

How about a story incorporating natural sound?

(actuality
1)
                        (CHANTING) "Win, Jesse, win, . . . win, Jesse, win . . .

(bridge)   (VOICE/OVER) To the chant of "Win, Jesse, win," civil rights leader

Jesse Jackson announced today he's a candidate for the Democratic

presidential nomination. (TAPE OUT) Jackson says that he is running for

office to affirm his belief that leadership has no color or gender.

(actuality
2)
                        (Jackson) I seek the presidency because there is a need to inspire the young
                        to hold fast to the American dream, and assume their rightful place in the
                        political process.

(tag)   With Jackson in the race, there are now 8 announced candidates for

the Democratic presidential nomination.

                                        (Ann Taylor, NBC Radio)

It was a bit risky to have begun that story with natural sound because the writer couldn't be sure what kind of story would precede it. In any case, it worked here. The bridge (which, you'll recall, is a kind of tag/lead-in between two pieces of tape) repeated the words "Win, Jesse, win" because it was possible some listeners wouldn't understand the tape. This way, the writer left no doubt.

Please note how absolutely impossible it would be for print journalism to attempt this sort of structure. It just wouldn't work.

Here's an example of Q-and-A, where the reporter himself is treated as an actuality:

(lead-
in)
        A few moments of high drama today...amid the hours of tedium at the

occupied Polish embassy in Bern, Switzerland. A diplomat the terrorists

did not know was hiding in the building all this time...got away...with

some help from Swiss police. ABC's Bob Dyke, who's been covering the

story in Bern, says it began to unfold when police units showed up at the

embassy building in force:

(actuality,
Q/A)

(Dyke) A van with blankets over the window drove away. Later, we learned that police had rescued from inside the embassy someone, uh, who was not a hostage, but had managed to hide away in the building when the compound was seized last Monday.

(tag)

Correspondent Dyke says photographers had spotted the man several hours earlier when the man held a piece of paper up to the top floor window. But police asked reporters not to mention it so the terrorists wouldn't find him. They didn't. He's now been identified as Polish diplomat YO—seff SO—zee—ak...his post at the embassy unknown.

(ABC Radio)

Because some of the foregoing stories required specific script cues with which you are not yet familiar, we will reproduce them now to show you the proper way to set up your own scripts in the future.

In the REAGAN/CRIME script, note that the outcue specifically shows that the tape ends with "applause." This is important. The anchor and technicians must know precisely the last *sound* on the tape.

Shelton, 10/28, 2p
$\quad\quad\quad\quad\quad\quad\quad\quad\quad\quad\quad\quad\quad\quad\quad\quad\quad\quad\quad\quad$ (:35)

REAGAN/CRIME

$\quad\quad$President Reagan is in New Jersey today, campaigning for the G-O-P candidate for the U-S Senate, Congresswoman Millicent Fenwick. The president used the occasion to call for a crackdown on crime:

> REAGAN/CRIME #2
>
> RUNS: :16
>
> OUT: "...into jail (applause)."

$\quad\quad$The president also denied charges by Democrats that his administration has been hard-hearted when it comes to America's poor. The president said his battle against inflation has delivered more purchasing power to poverty-level families.

Engle, 11/4, 1130a

LEASE HEARINGS

The government's new offshore oil and gas leasing plan came under
fire today at a hearing on Capitol Hill. Leading the attack was
Democratic Senator Walter Metzenbaum of Ohio:

METZENBAUM #1

RUNS: :23

OUT: "...corporations in America."

But Interior Secretary James Watt said Metzenbaum and others were
off base in their criticism of the leasing plan:

WATT #3

RUNS: :20

OUT: "...accurate or fair."

Watt, who was testifying before the Senate energy Subcommittee,
said the plan would create jobs, strengthen national security, protect
the environment, and reduce the nation's dependence on foreign oil.

Taylor, 11/3, 5p

JACKSON

(OPENS W/TAPE)

> CHANTING #1 -- (ESTABLISH AND FADE)
>
> RUNS: :15
>
> OUT: "...(chanting) win, Jesse, win!"

    (VOICE OVER) To the chant of "Win, Jesse, win," civil rights leader Jesse Jackson announced today he's a candidate for the Democratic presidential nomination.

    (TAPE OUT) Jackson says that he is running for office to affirm his belief that leadership has no color or gender:

> JACKSON #2
>
> RUNS: :14
>
> OUT: "...the political process."

    With Jackson in the race, there are now eight announced candidates for the Democratic presidential nomination.

In the LEASE HEARINGS script (see p. 170), note the importance of indenting the tape cues and setting them off by brackets. This keeps the page visually tidy and leaves no doubt where and when to play the tapes.

And in the JACKSON script (see p. 171), the most complicated we've shown so far, there are specific instructions where, when, and how to play the tapes. These instructions are in parentheses *and* in all caps, setting them apart from the standard upper/lower style, and thus warning the anchor not to read them aloud by mistake.

TRICKY LEAD-INS AND OUTCUES

Suppose that we have an actuality of the president of the United States with the following text:

> The world cannot tolerate this kind of behavior. It amounts to international piracy. We will ask the United Nations for a resolution demanding a Soviet withdrawal—an IMMEDIATE Soviet withdrawal.

As previously noted, the lead-in should *not* use the same words or tell the same information as the actuality. If it did, there would be no point in using the actuality at all. For example, the lead-in should *not* say,

```
President Jones reacted angrily today to the Soviet seizure of a

disputed island in the Sea of Japan. The president said the world cannot

tolerate such behavior:
```

Those are the wrong words because they are redundant. For the same reason, the lead-in should not use the words "international piracy," again because they're already in the actuality. The trick is to find the kind of language that tells part of the news, without telling the *same* news. For example,

```
An angry reaction from President Jones today to the Soviet seizure

of that disputed island in the Sea of Japan.  The president called for

international action:
```

Now the actuality fits right into the flow of the narrative.

As for the matter of inflections, lead-ins, too, must pay heed to normal speech patterns. Suppose that I lead in this way to the preceding actuality:

```
President Jones reacted angrily today to the Soviet seizure of a

disputed island in the Sea of Japan. The president said:
```

Try reading that out loud. Notice where your voice is on the word "said"? The inflection is "up." It would end "up" even higher if it had been phrased, "Said the president:"

What's wrong with that? Well, nothing, provided that the tape plays *immediately.* If there's a long pause between your voice and the start of the tape, the result is dead air. And dead air is disorienting. So in all things *live,* do *not* end lead-ins with "up" inflections. Save such razzle-dazzle for *recorded* reports, where there is no chance for a miscue. Besides, "down" inflections sound more natural. And in the event of dead air, the effect is not as disorienting.

As for the outcue to that actuality, read it carefully. The president *repeats* the final words—"Soviet withdrawal." If we typed the outcue this way,

```
OUT: "...Soviet withdrawal."
```

the newscaster might come in *too soon* with the tag copy. This must be prevented. Here's how:

```
OUT: "...Soviet withdrawal." (DOUBLE OUTCUE)
```

The additional words "DOUBLE OUTCUE" in parentheses and capital letters ensure that the newscaster and the engineer both know that the words of the outcue will be heard twice.

EXERCISES

1. With the following news agency story and selection of actualities as your pool of resources, write a 45-second radio story slugged WILDFIRES.

```
am-wildfires sub7thgraf-writethru
By United Press International
     Despite raging wildfires that have closed roads and
created smog-like layers of choking smoke, tourists remained
true Saturday to Yellowstone National Park's most famous
attraction, Old Faithful.
     Seven major fires continued to burn on more than 400,000
acres, and officials who have already spent $30 million
fighting the fires are now conceding to nature, figuring the
blazes will remain unchecked until autumn rains and winter
snows fall on the 2.2 million-acre park.
     Much of the park's road system was closed, forcing some
visitors to take circuitous journeys to get to the big geyser.
     The road from the park's West Entrance to Old Faithful
remained open but could be closed "at any time," park
officials said.
     Jodi Mauck, of Fort Collins, Colo., visiting with her
family, said road conditions forced them on a five-hour detour
through Wyoming and Montana to get to Old Faithful, but they
made the trip anyway.
```

"It's interesting," she said of the fires, a tourist attraction in themselves. "But I'm not sure I like it. You can still see a lot of the park, if you're determined," she added.

Park officials estimated about 10,000 visitors were in the park over the weekend but none were in immediate danger.

New activity was reported on the adjoining North Fork and Wolf Lake fires, which burned a total of 116,000 acres and were spreading toward Canyon, a developed area. A total of 1,300 firefighters were trying to hold the fire back.

Also, the Red-Shoshone Fire in the southern half of the park grew overnight by an estimated 20,000 acres to about 112,000 acres, spokeswoman Linda Miller said.

But cooler temperatures and lighter winds were helping firefighters hold their own against the other blazes. Miller said the weather was "making it easier to build containment lines."

Rangers have taken to explaining the U.S. Forest Service's policy of allowing most fires to burn as part of the park's natural ecological cycle. Most visitors have taken the policy in stride.

Letting the fires burn is expected to have long-term benefits, including a major regeneration of old, insect-ridden woodlands.

"People question whether (the policy) is a good idea, but we found out that it was what they needed," said Larry Gaddin, Redwood City, Calif.

An army of 3,500 firefighters, aided by 1,200 Army and National Guard troops, continued to battle the fires that have laid waste to 1,000 square miles, or one-fifth of the park's land area.

Visibility in the worst areas remained near zero. Tourists with respiratory problems were advised to consult their physicians before entering the park, spokeswoman Joan Anzelmo said.

Other fires continued to burn in Wyoming, Utah, Idaho, California, Montana, Oregon and Washington. Most were started by lightning strikes.

In southwestern Oregon, the lightning-sparked Walker Mountain fire crept within a half mile of a subdivision of about 1,000 people north of Grants Pass. In the northeastern corner of the state, the Ward Canyon fire spread to within a mile of the tiny community of Troy, authorities said.

Both communities were placed on evacuation alert. The Ward Canyon blaze had burned 15 unoccupied structures, mostly hunting cabins.

About 120 second-grade children from the Fir Point Bible Camp were taken to a school about 25 miles north of Grants Pass "as a precautionary move" after the Woods Creek fire grew to 500 acres, said Jim Fisher, a state Forestry Department spokesman. He said the children headed home Friday and the fire was 75 percent contained.

Also in the state's northeast corner, the Tepee Butte fire exploded to 26,300 acres of grass and timber by Friday night from 150 acres Thursday afternoon, and firefighters said it could spread to as many as 80,000 acres,

"It appears as though we may have lost the left flank of

that fire," said Wallowa-Whitman National Forest spokeswoman
Gail Aschenbrenner.

WILDFIRES #1 (Gregg Kroll, Yellowstone Park spokesman)

The fires are still definitely burning, but they are not at the present time endangering any structures within the park.

(runs :08)

WILDFIRES #2 (Amy Vanderbilt, Yellowstone Park spokeswoman)

We do advise possible visitors that if they might have a respiratory problem, that they might want to consult with a personal physician before traveling to the Park. We are seeing a forecast calling for high temperatures and low humidity again, with westerly winds, and those will be conditions that will keep firefighters ever diligent to protect the structures and try to keep those fires contained.

(runs :25)

WILDFIRES #3 (Ken Paylin, Oregon Forestry Dept. spokesman)

We have just about all of our resources out on the fires, so that we're, uh, doing everything we can at this point to get things under control.

(runs :09)

WILDFIRES #4 (Dave Morman, Oregon Fire Information Officer)

We're hangin' on by our fingernails, day by day. It seems like we're losing some ground every day, but now that, uh, loss to the fire is decreasing each day.

(runs :11)

2. Write a second version of your **WILDFIRES** story, using a different actuality from the one (or two) you used in your first version.

13

Tape II: Reports

Reports, either written in the newsroom or at the scenes of events, constitute the second major type of broadcast newswriting involving taped segments.

As we've noted, modern technology permits field reporters to exploit broadcasting's immediacy by "going live" from the scene. In many cases, especially where the news is still breaking, reporters ad-lib their stories, speaking extemporaneously with the aid of a few hastily scribbled notes. Most reports, however, are tape-recorded for playback during specific newscasts. And despite the hectic pace of broadcast news, this means that reporters and writers have time (but not much) to organize their thoughts and choose their words with care.

We should note before proceeding that reports differ in radio and television. Radio reports are much shorter, running around 45 seconds on average. A TV news field report is typically twice as long—around 1:30 (a minute and a half) Occasionally, this means that a TV writer/reporter has twice as much time to devote to a single subject. But that is not normally the case. Instead, a TV report normally encompasses many facets of a story (the facets are called "story elements"), whereas a radio report concentrates on a single facet. A TV report also shows several different locations. A radio report focuses on events at a single location; story elements at other locations are told in separate reports from those locations.

Because of these structural differences, we will deal with TV reports separately (in Chapter 16). We'll confine ourselves for now to the structuring and writing of radio reports and the lead-ins to them.

TYPES OF REPORTS

First our customary vocabulary lesson:

A radio report (or "spot") that contains only the reporter's voice telling a story is called a *voicer*. No actuality or sound of any other kind is included.

A report containing one or more actualities is called a *wraparound,* or just "wrap" for short. The name derives from the structure: The reporter's voice "wraps around" the actuality. A wrap's basic structure is thus lead-in/actuality/tag/signoff.

Still another basic type of radio spot is called a *ROSR*—pronounced "ROzer"—short for "Radio On-Scene Report." A ROSR is simply this: A reporter in the field talks into his or her tape recorder, either extemporaneously or from prepared notes, describing a scene or event as it occurs before his or her very eyes. In other words, the reporter acts as if he or she is going live, trying to capture the color and feel of an event. This running eyewitness narrative is then fed (transmitted) back to the newsroom, where 30- or 40-second chunks of it are excerpted and aired in the same manner as a voicer or wrap.

Signoffs

Every spot, whether voicer, wrap, or ROSR, concludes with a signoff. Signoffs in broadcasting are roughly the equivalent of a combination of a newspaper byline and dateline—roughly but not exactly. For one thing, signoffs do not contain the date. They do contain at least two elements:

1. The reporter's name
2. The reporter's location

```
...Pye Chamberlayne, Washington.
```

(UPI Audio)

```
...Jack Vail, New York
```

(UPI Audio)

And most signoffs contain a third element:

3. The reporter's news organization

```
...David Rush, NBC News, Washington.
```

```
...Richard C. Hottelet, CBS News, at the United Nations.
```

Whenever possible, signoffs emphasize the *closeness* of the reporter to the story:

```
...Bill Plante, CBS News, with the president in New Orleans.

...Larry Pintak, CBS News, with Israeli forces in Lebanon.
```

There are strict rules for expressing proximity to the story in a signoff. Obviously, the president of the United States was not looking over Bill Plante's shoulder as Plante filed his report. They weren't in the same room. Maybe not in the same building. But Plante (and the rest of the White House press corps) had followed the presidential party around all day. Their assignment was to cover the president, to be with him whenever possible (or allowed by the White House). So the signoff "with the president" is correct. If Plante had merely rewritten his copy from wire services—in fact had not been "with the president"—he could *not* use those words in his signoff.

Rule:
No reporter may ever sign off from where he or she has not been
in connection with a story.

The reporter need not be at that location at the moment of filing the story. But the reporter must have been there to cover it, at least in part.

And in fact many spots in radio are merely rewrites from wire service copy or are based on telephone interviews. In those cases the signoff contains the reporter's name, news organization, and *city*. No further specification is legitimate. No reporter must ever give the impression of having been somewhere he or she has not in fact been.

There are a few other twists to signoffs. The general public is largely unaware of them, but they are understood inside the industry.

One is a matter of professional standing. Only a full-time staff member of a news organization may use the name of that organization unqualifiedly in a signoff. Nonstaff reporters, such as part-time "stringers" or local staffers of independent or network-affiliated stations, must include the word "for" in the signoff:

```
...Jeff Grant, for CBS News, Newark, New Jersey.

...JoAnne Nader, for NBC News, Boston Heights, Ohio.
```

These two signoffs are examples of local reporters who, either by volunteering or by request, got their voices onto network newscasts. For this they were paid a fee by the network.

Still another signoff variation is one that *omits* the reporter's location altogether:

```
...Garrick Utley, NBC News.

...Lynn Scherr, ABC News.
```

Such signoffs might indicate that the reporter voicing the spot did not actually cover the story in person. Typically, the story that is the subject matter of the spot might have taken place in a location different from the reporter's. Or such a signoff might indicate that the reporter is merely narrating material written by someone else.

Some news organizations—CBS, for one—strictly forbid such ambiguous signoffs. And if the correspondent did not personally write the report, then the lead-in uses tip-off wording such as, "Our report is narrated by . . ."

Note that signoffs to *newscasts* are not subject to the rule of stating location. In local radio, it's assumed that the newscaster is in town and in the studio, not announcing from a vacation cottage in Acapulco. And in network radio, although most newscasts originate from New York or Washington, the practice is to omit the location in the signoff as a kind of gimmick to make the news organization seem omnipresent—sort of like saying, "If we don't tell 'em where we are, maybe they'll think we're everywhere." (On such matters are careers sometimes made or broken.)

To sum up: signoffs to reports must be accurate. It is unethical to "invent" a signoff.

STRUCTURE OF SPOTS

To attempt to tell you exactly how to write a radio news spot would be just as impossible as telling you how to construct a snowflake. Each is different. Writing (hence, journalism) is an art, not a science.

However, we can offer guidelines regarding the content and structure of spots in general. And this much we can state unequivocally: It is impossible to tell the history of the world in 45 seconds. So don't even try.

Beginners have a tendency to think that their spots must be comprehensive, must trace the history of an event from its early beginnings, through its current developments, and on to an analysis of its possible ramifications. That is far, far too much territory for a radio spot. Instead, the focus must be kept narrow, on the current developments. History (background) should be kept to a minimum—only enough, in fact, to make the current developments clear. And the analysis should be kept out altogether or confined to the telling of what will (or might) happen next. (And I do mean *next*—not down the road a decade or two.)

Specifically,

1. Spots should be limited in subject matter. A spot should deal only with the story immediately at hand: its facts, limited background, and significance. Spots should *not* deal with related stories; related developments will be treated in separate stories scripted by the newswriter/newscaster and/or by other reporters in their own spots. Limit the content to what *you* have seen or learned.

2. Spots should be limited geographically. A spot should treat events that occur at the location stated in the signoff or close to it—*not* events occurring elsewhere. Again, events elsewhere, however related, will be treated in spots from those locations, not yours.

Okay, we're ready to examine the structure and style of the various kinds of spots. To do so, we'll use an actual story, but, for the purposes of demonstration, to put you in the role of a reporter/writer in a lifelike situation, we'll have to give you a new identity and move you to another location.

We'll call you "Jim Deadline" (or, in the name of equal opportunity, "Jill Deadline"). You are a staffer at KQKQ Radio (a fictional station) on the island of Maui, Hawaii. Shortly after 2 P.M., the newsroom police and fire radios alert you that an airliner has made an emergency landing at Kahului (Ka-HOO-loo-ee) airport. You grab your tape recorder, jump into a station vehicle (equipped with a 2-way transmitter), and rush to the airport. It is immediately clear that you have come upon a major news story, of importance to a national and international audience as well as to your local one. Your first task is to go on the air live (via your vehicle's transmitter) to describe what you see. Your station, recognizing that this is a major story, will send other staffers to help cover it while you rush to interview anyone and everyone you can find to help you piece the story together.

And here, as represented by the following news agency copy, is what you learn:

```
PM-Jet Blast, 2nd Ld--Writethru: 1021
One Person Missing, 60 Injured In Jetliner Explosion
     KAHULUI, Hawaii (AP)--A mysterious explosion ripped open
an Aloha Airlines jet "like a convertible" at 24,000 feet,
injuring 60 people and tossing a flight attendant to her death
before the pilot landed safely.
     The Boeing 737, with one of its two engines aflame and
about 15 to 20 feet of its cabin exposed, flew for 25 miles
after the blast and made an emergency landing at Kahului
Airport at 2 p.m. Thursday (8 p.m. EDT), airline officials
said.
     "There was big bang when it happened and everybody looked
up and we were looking at blue sky," said passenger Bill Fink
of Honolulu.
     The cause of the blast was unknown, said Kevin Morimatsu,
a spokesman for the state Department of Transportation.
     The National Transportation Safety Board was sending
investigators to the scene and FBI agents were sent from
Honolulu to determine whether the blast was caused by a bomb,
said FBI spokesman Robert Heafner.
     Another passenger, Alice Godwin of Boulder City, Nev.,
said she put on a life jacket and put her head between her
knees. "I sang all the hymns I knew," she said. "That kept me
busy."
     "Everybody screamed," said Dan Dennin, also of Honolulu.
"However, it was very brief, the panic.... The rest of the
plane was intact, and we did not go into any unusual attitudes
or anything like that. I think that people realized the plane
was still flying and they quickly went about the business of
doing whatever they could do to save their lives."
     Mark Eberly, a ramp supervisor at the airport, said he
dropped to his knees in shock as he watched the plane land
with one of its engines smoking and a section of the top
missing. "I saw hair flying in the wind and arms dangling," he
said.
```

Craig Nichols of Pocatello, Idaho, said after the plane came to a stop on the ground, he saw "some really mangled people (passengers)," including one with an arm almost severed.

"It looked like a normal landing with the whole top of the plane gone," he said, adding that the damage began behind the cockpit, "clear down to the windows," and extended to the rear.

"It looked like a convertible," said Joe Ronderos of Los Angeles.

"It was like somebody had peeled off a layer of skin. You could just see all the passengers sitting there," said George Harvey, area coordinator for the Federal Aviation Administration in Honolulu.

"I give credit to the pilot. He brought that plane down so smoothly. It was just like riding in a Cadillac," said passenger John Lopez, 40, of Hilo.

"I've had worse landings in normal aircraft," Dennin said.

Sixty people were taken to Maui Memorial Hospital and 12 were admitted, two in critical condition and four serious, said Dr. Charles Mitchell, emergency room director. Injuries included burns, bruises and cuts, he said.

The missing flight attendant, identified as Clarabelle B. Lansing of Honolulu, was probably ejected by the blast or blown out of the plane by the wind, said Clifford Hue, another FAA area manager.

"I think the stewardess (Mrs. Lansing) had just picked up the microphone to start talking" when the explosion occurred, Fink said.

Fink and Dennin said some of the passengers hung on to another standing flight attendant so she would not be sucked out of the plane, and they praised the cabin crew for helping calm the passengers.

The U.S. Coast Guard mounted a search that included a cutter, a C-130 search and rescue aircraft and two helicopters, said Coast Guard spokesman Petty Officer Jeffrey Crawley.

However, searchers found no trace of Mrs. Lansing, or the missing section of the plane, he said.

The explosion occurred southeast of Maui while the plane was at an altitude of 24,000 feet, the airline said. It said the 110-mile flight from Hilo on Hawaii Island to Kahului carried 89 passengers, five crew members and an air traffic controller from Hilo Airport.

Passengers reported hearing an explosion in the forward part of the plane, apparently around the first-class section, said assistant hospital administrator Alan Lee.

"They told me there was a loud, sudden explosion and the roof of the plane literally flew off," said Mitchell.

VOICERS

Hard Leads

Your first spots (the first of what may be dozens before very long) will be *voicers*. Because almost anything you report at this time will be listeners' first hearing of the story, you will concentrate on the hard information—the Who, What, When, and Where. Thus, you will structure your first voicer much like a traditional news story, giving the latest information at the top. An example:

```
JET BLAST #1

     An Aloha Airlines jet made an emergency landing here this afternoon

after a midair explosion blew away part of the passenger cabin.

Officials say a flight attendant was killed, and 60 of the 95 people

aboard were injured.

     The Boeing 7-37 was on an inter-island flight from Hilo to Honolulu,

flying at 24-thousand feet.  Passengers say an explosion blew the roof

off the forward passenger cabin, causing a momentary panic.  Somehow, the

pilot managed to fly the stricken aircraft 25 miles to a safe landing.

     Officials identified the single fatality as flight attendant

Clarabelle Lansing of Honolulu.  They say she was apparently blown out of

the plane by the explosion.

     For the moment, officials are unable to say what caused the

explosion.  But an investigation is under way.

     The injured were taken to Maui Memorial Hospital, where two are

listed in critical condition.

     Jim Deadline, KQKQ News, at Kahului airport.


                         (runs :48)
```

There's nothing fancy about that spot. The writing is bare-bones. As the character Joe Friday used to say on the old "Dragnet" program, "Just the facts, Ma'am."

This is what's known as a "hard" spot with a "hard lead." That means the spot stands by itself as a story. It needs no preceding information to put it in context. It stresses immediacy wherever possible, making frequent use of the present tense to report what is happening "now."

It thus contains information that may become dated very quickly—such as the total number of deaths (the two people in critical condition might succumb at any time) and the cause of the explosion (which may also be learned very shortly). A spot containing material that can quickly be rendered inaccurate by later information is said to be "unprotected"; it is "unprotected" against fresh details.

Thus, a hard, unprotected spot is meant to go on the air as quickly as possible, before events overtake it. As long as a reporter/writer is in a position to update and transmit fresh details, the "hard lead" approach is the right one.

However, because you cannot gather information and go on the air simultaneously, you can tailor at least some of your spots to cover the time you spend gathering and preparing fresh material. The tailoring process is called "soft leading."

Soft Leads

The structure of this second type of spot is very different from the foregoing hard lead. It is called a "soft lead" because it *begins* by assuming that the audience has *already heard* the hard news from the anchor. In other words, the reporter/writer assumes the anchor will tell the audience that there has been an apparent explosion on the airliner and that X number of people have been killed or injured.

In addition, you would write the spot in a "protected" manner. That is, you would make *no reference* to story elements that might change very quickly. Therefore, you would *not* give the total number of casualties, the condition of survivors, or speculation about the cause of the explosion. Instead, you would confine yourself to those story elements that cannot change because they are in the past. This "protects" your spot, permitting your station to air it in a later newscast while you are busy rounding up fresh information.

(*Note:* If you wanted to protect your spot for a longer time, from a period of several hours to as long as overnight, you would also leave out any reference to the day or time of day—no "today," "this afternoon," "tonight," "yesterday," etc.)

A typical soft-lead, protected voicer would go this way:

```
JET BLAST #2


    The explosion took place at an altitude of 24-thousand feet, while

the jetliner was en route from Hilo to Honolulu.  Passengers said there

was a "big bang" and then, suddenly, the top of the forward passenger

cabin simply wasn't there.  They said there was momentary panic, but when

they realized the plane was still flying, they calmed down enough to

buckle themselves in.

    With two of the plane's engines aflame and part of the

superstructure missing, the pilot managed to guide the stricken plane 25

miles here to the airport.  An airport employee said he gazed in stunned

amazement as the jetliner came in for an emergency landing.  Clearly
```

```
visible, he said, were passengers with arms dangling, their hair flying

in the wind.

     The explosion's one immediate fatality was flight attendant

Clarabelle Lansing of Honolulu.  Officials say she was literally blown

out of the plane.

     Jill Deadline, KQKQ News, at Kahului airport.


                         (runs :48)
```

A soft-lead, protected spot such as this offers some clear advantages in addition to providing breathing space. It enables the writer/reporter to concentrate on the details that make a story vivid for listeners. Precious time not spent on the basic facts, which can be left to the anchor, becomes available for color and quotes. And that's especially important when actualities are included—because they eat up time.

WRAPAROUNDS

During the breathing space afforded by having sent the foregoing protected voicer, you (as "Jim/Jill Deadline") have been busy preparing some wraparounds. You have chosen the following actualities from interviews recorded at the airport:

PASSENGER #1 (Dan Dennin, of Honolulu, passenger)

Everybody screamed. However, it was very brief, the panic. The explosion happened, the rest of the plane was intact, and we did not go into any unusual attitudes or anything like that.

(runs :11)

PASSENGER #2 (Dan Dennin again)

I think that people realized the plane was still flying and they quickly went about their business of doing whatever they could do to save their lives. I think we flew for almost 15 minutes with half an airplane, so we were all well aware of what was going on.

(runs :14)

PASSENGER #3 (Alice Godwin, of Boulder City, Nevada, passenger)

We all prayed. As long as those engines were running, the more secure I felt. I sang all the hymns I knew. That kept me busy.

(runs :09)

In a story of this nature, which goes under the heading of "near-catastrophe," the entire news industry—news agencies, newspapers, news-weeklies, network radio and television, local radio and television, etc.—throw vast effort and resources into the competition for news, sounds, and pictures. Within moments of a story like this breaking on the wires, editors, reporters, and producers will be calling anyone they can think of who might shed light on how it could have happened. In this case, calls flooded the Boeing company in Seattle, the main office of Aloha Airlines in Honolulu, as well as the Federal Aviation Administration (FAA) and the National Transportation Safety Board (NTSB) local and regional offices.

In short, a lot of people will have a lot to say, and the news media will be busy reporting it.

Jim/Jill's role in all this is to concentrate on those story angles that he/she is in the best position to report. In this case, which is perfectly typical in such situations, Jim/Jill had access to surviving passengers at the airport.

And so Jim/Jill's wraps might go this way:

```
JET BLAST #3


    They were scared, very scared.  Passenger Dan Dennin of Honolulu

says the explosion caused momentary panic:

          PASSENGER #1

          RUNS: :11

          OUT: "...anything like that."

    Another passenger, Alice Godwin of Boulder City, Nevada, says she

tucked her head between her knees:

          PASSENGER #3

          RUNS: :09

          OUT: "...kept me busy."

    Maybe it was the prayers.  Maybe just a skilled pilot.  Maybe both.

Whatever it was, the plane -- what was left of it -- landed safely.

    Jim Deadline, KQKQ News, at Kahului airport.


                         (runs :43)


                            -0-


JET BLAST #4
```

If it had been a movie, it might have been called "Terror at 24–thousand Feet." But it wasn't a movie.

Torn off was a 20–foot section of the jetliner's front passenger cabin. One passenger said when he looked up, all he could see was blue sky.

Another passenger, Dan Dennin of Honolulu, said there was a moment of panic, but then everyone recovered:

PASSENGER #2

RUNS: :14

OUT: "...was going on."

People on the ground who watched the plane come in could scarcely believe their eyes. And the passengers could scarcely believe their luck.

Jill Deadline, KQKQ News, at Kahului aiport.

(runs :44)

Both versions are protected soft leads. They can be used and reused as desired, with other reporters and writers updating the hard, breaking information as it becomes available.

ROSRs

At some point, Jim/Jill might have started talking into his/her tape recorder, to voice some of the things that might occur to almost anyone witnessing such an unusual event. And the resulting ROSR might have gone like this:

I'm standing near the Aloha Airlines jetliner, and it's hard to believe a plane with this much damage could fly at all, much less 25 miles from a height of 24–thousand feet. A 20–foot chunk of the fuselage is missing, blown out in the explosion. Two engines are charred by fire. The front passenger seats are exposed to the open air. It must have felt like riding in a Ferris wheel gone out of control. But of course, this

was no amusement park ride. It's amazing so many survived.

    The purpose of a ROSR is not so much to impart hard facts—although it can do that—as to provide listeners with the feel of an event. In this case, the truly unusual thing is that there was only one death in this bizarre event. But a death is a death, and you can't very well report "only one death" as good news. In all likelihood, someone among the passengers or spectators on the ground would say in the course of an interview, "It was a miracle more people weren't killed . . . ," and that could have been broadcast as an actuality. Without that, there remains only the reporter to act as a surrogate on behalf of the audience. A ROSR or Q/A thus becomes an effective way to give voice to eyewitness reportage.

    Take a look at a couple of ROSRs that were broadcast on network radio. The first is by a CBS reporter accompanying Israeli armored units on an assault against Palestine Liberation Army forces in Beirut, Lebanon:

I'm with a forward Israeli tank unit...rolling forward in the center

of West Beirut...(gunshots)...tanks are coming up...(tanks

firing)...heavy machine guns on the tanks (machine gun firing) trying to

pick out sniper positions in the buildings above us. Israeli troops back

against the walls of this street, amid the rubble...thick black smoke

rising just in front of the tanks (tank shell explosions). The tank's

now charging forward, turret swinging...machine guns and sniper

fire)...firing toward sniper positions, the machine guns opening up.

It's twin firing its heavy cannons into the buildings...thick smoke

clouding everything in front of us. Israeli troops here with us against

the walls of the buildings...(more tank fire). Larry Pintak, CBS News,

with the Israelis in West Beirut.

(runs 1:03)

    Not long afterwards, an NBC reporter sent a ROSR while accompanying Israeli forces out of Beirut. No gunshots or exploding shells this time, but the steady rumble of army vehicles is heard in the background:

    I'm standing beside a column of Israeli soldiers who're beginning

their individual pullout of West Beirut. This has been going on now for

several days...but tomorrow, all of the Israelis are supposed to be out

of this section of the city, which was once a stronghold of the Palestine

Liberation Army...(sirens). Their pullout has been controversial. The

multinational force...has refused...to come in until the Israelis get out

of West Beirut. But another French unit arrived today, after another 350

French paratroopers came in yesterday. Ike Seamans, NBC News, West

Beirut.

                              (runs :39)

Hard versus Soft Leads

The concepts of hard leading and soft leading are sometimes difficult for newcomers to understand. But understand them you must, because reporters are
expected to write both kinds of spots for every story they cover (in TV as well as
radio). And, back in the newsroom, writers and anchors must know how to
integrate them into newscasts.

    The single hard-lead voicer we've looked at so far was unprotected. It had
to be aired quickly, or it would have become out of date. But I don't want to leave
the impression that all hard-lead spots should be left unprotected or that, conversely, all soft-lead spots should be protected. In fact, the styles may be mixed at
the discretion of the reporter/writer and the editor/producer.

    As further illustration, here is a pair of network radio voicers on the same
story, the first hard-led, the second soft. The writer was Richard C. Hottelet,
formerly of CBS News:

#1: (HARD LEAD)

    The Arab states, which have been talking about expelling Israel from

the current session of the General Assembly, have now decided to pull

back. Instead of challenging Israel's credentials in a routine vote next

Monday, the Arabs and others will express reservations about Israel's

presence in drastic terms. They will denounce Israel as a member which

violates international law and specifically refuses to obey numerous

Assembly resolutions on Palestinian rights and withdrawal from occupied

territory. Many Arab and Islamic states, as well as African and Western
countries, were appalled by the idea of trying to expel Israel. They saw
it derailing a Middle East process which may just be starting to move
again. And some of the Arabs argued privately that it could only heal
the breach between the Reagan administration and the Begin government.
Most did not have the confidence to make these points publicly, but they
seemed to have sunk in. Unless the radical Arabs go back to the original
idea, or Iran picks it up next Monday, the issue appears to have been
shelved for this year. Richard C. Hottelet, CBS News, United Nations.

(runs 1:03)

#2: (SOFT LEAD)

Two weeks ago, radical Arab states proposed that Israel be thrown
out of the current session of the U—N General Assembly. The idea was to
call for rejection of Israel's credentials when the report of the
Credentials Committee comes up for approval next Monday. The proposal
stirred up a storm. Most Western countries saw it as unwarranted and
illegal distortion of the spirit and letter of the United Nations
charter. Washington served official notice that if Israel were excluded
in this fashion, the United States would walk out with it and, more than
that, would withhold American payments to the United Nations' regular
budget. Since the United States pays 25 per cent or more of the U—N's
expenses, this would have been a disastrous political as well as
financial blow to the organization. Many of the Arab states, and of the
larger Conference of Islamic Countries, opposed the action of expelling
Israel, especially at a time when Arab leaders are consulting with the
United States about plans for peace in the Middle East. **This afternoon,**
the Arab group of nations at the U—N decided NOT to try to reject

```
Israel's credentials, but simply to express their reservations about

Israel's presence.   Richard C. Hottelet, CBS News, United Nations.
```

(runs 1:09)

Spot #1, the hard lead, tells the latest information in the very first sentence. Spot No. 2, the soft lead, defers telling the lastest information until the very last sentence.

But that sentence in spot No. 2 contains the words "this afternoon." This dates the spot, leaving it unprotected after a few hours. Thus, CBS Radio aired it quickly, at 3 o'clock in the afternoon.

Spot #1 is protected. It contains no reference to the day or time of day. It could thus be held for later use. And in fact it was: CBS Radio aired it at 8 o'clock the next morning.

Now we're ready to examine why the hard/soft distinction is important to the technique of integrating spots into newscasts.

LEAD-INS TO SPOTS

Spots do not exist in a void. Because they represent a second sound source (the first source being the voice of the anchor of the newscast), usually on tape, they must be integrated into newscasts in the same way as actualities. In other words, they require carefully written lead-ins to make them flow.

The exact wording of a lead-in to a spot depends both on the overall content of the spot and on its opening words. Listeners must be prepared both for the new voice *and* for the context in which it is speaking. Neither must come as a surprise. Writers must tailor the language of their lead-ins to suit the opening language of the reporter.

Here is the news department's working method:

1. A reporter covers a story.
2. The reporter writes one to three spots on the story and feeds (transmits) them to the newsroom.
3. The editor (or producer) gives the hardest spot, the one with the freshest information, to a writer or writer/anchor for inclusion in the next newscast, reserving the other spot(s) for later newscasts.
4. The writer or writer/anchor tailors the lead-ins to fit the content and opening wording of the spots.

Now we come to the importance of the hard/soft distinction:

1. If a spot begins with a hard lead, the lead-in should be soft. In other words, if the reporter tells the important news in his or her first sentence, the writer's lead-in should *not* do the same. Instead, it should tell just enough to key the listener's attention and understanding. If the lead-in and reporter's

first sentence are both hard, the result is needless repetition; to the listener, it sounds as if the people in the newsroom aren't paying attention.

2. Conversely, if the reporter begins his or her spot with a soft lead, deferring the hardest news till the end or omitting it altogether, then the lead-in must be hard; it must state the latest, most important news. If the lead-in and reporter's opening are both soft, it will take too long for the listener to learn what the real news is—or never learn it at all.

You could almost reduce this to a formula:

Soft-led spot requires hard lead-in.
Hard-led spot requires soft lead-in.

But enough lecturing. Let's see how this works in practice—beginning with the lead-ins to the foregoing two Richard C. Hottelet spots:

```
At the United Nations, Arab nations have backed away from their

campaign to oust Israel from the General Assembly.  The story from

Richard C. Hottelet:

          HOTTELET #2

          RUNS: 1:09

          OUT: ". . . CBS News, United Nations."
```
                                        (lead-in by Stephanie Shelton, CBS Radio)

The spot began soft, so the lead-in was hard.

```
Here in New York, the United Nations has apparently been spared a

crisis that Richard C. Hottelet says could have put it out of business:

          HOTTELET #1

          RUNS: 1:03

          OUT: ". . . CBS News, United Nations."
```
                                        (lead-in by Dallas Townsend, CBS Radio)

The spot began hard, so the lead-in was soft.

Note that the lead-in tells the name of the reporter. That prepares listeners for the new voice. Most lead-ins also tell the reporter's location.

(A few news departments follow a format of *not* identifying the reporter or his or her location in the lead-in. Writers in such newsrooms are instructed to make the lead-in and reporter's opening words flow without this information.

This approach risks leaving listeners disoriented—which is why most news departments don't do it that way.)

Now let's tailor lead-ins to suit the spots filed by our alter egos, "Jim and Jill Deadline." We are at the station, putting together the next newscast, and we get JET BLAST #1. We listen to it and realize that it has a hard lead—Jim tells the hard news up front. All we need to do is set the stage:

```
A jetliner made an emergency landing at Kahului Airport a short time

ago.  Jim Deadline is there with details:

        JET BLAST #1

        RUNS:  :48

        OUT:  "...at Kahului airport."
```

Half an hour later, we air spot #2. The text of Jill's spot leaves it up to us to give the basic information in the lead-in:

```
At least one person was killed and 60 injured this afternoon aboard

an Aloha Airlines 7-37.  As we hear from our Jill Deadline, the plane

made an emergency landing at Kahului airport after being damaged in

midair:

        JET BLAST #2

        RUNS:  :40

        OUT:  "...at Kahului airport."
```

Please go back and read the lead-ins and spots together. Do you see how we've made them flow? We have figuratively taken listeners by the hand and led them through the story, making sure they don't get lost along the way.

Before doing the lead-ins for spots #3 and #4, let's say it is now around 11 P.M., many hours since the mishap. We can safely assume that all but a handful of the audience have heard (or seen, or read) the story by now. We are eagerly awaiting new developments. And we get them: Over our news agency printer (or CRT) comes the following update:

```
AM-Jet Blast, 5th Ld
Investigators Seek Cause of Mid-Air Explosion of Jetliner
Eds: LEADS with 7 grafs to UPDATE with comments from press
conference targeting structural failure as likely cause. Picks
up 5th graf, "The Federal ...
    KAHULUI, Hawaii (AP)--A structural failure, not a bomb,
likely caused the "big bang" that ripped open an Aloha
```

Airlines jet, injuring 61 people and apparently sucking a
flight attendant from the cabin to her death, a federal
official said Friday.
    The Boeing 737, which was cruising at 24,000 feet on an
island hop from Hilo to Honolulu, made a safe emergency
landing at Kahului airport Thursday, after flying about 15
minutes with 20 feet of its upper fuselage just behind the
front passenger door torn away to the floor. Witnesses said
one engine was on fire.
    "There was a big bang when it happened and everybody
looked up and we were looking at blue sky," said passenger
Bill Fink of Honolulu.
    At a news conference late Friday night, a member of the
National Transportation Safety Board said investigators
believed the cause of the accident was a structural problem
with the aging jet.
    "I think it's fair to say the focus of the investigation
is on the structure itself, the hole itself, and what if any
causes might have been to create hull fractures or hull
fatigue," said NTSB member Joseph T. Nall.

Obviously, this updates our story in a major way. The injury toll has risen by
one, but, more important, authorities report a likely cause of the incident. Even
so, we can still use the protected spots from "Jim/Jill." Here's how:

A federal investigator says it was probably structural failure that

tore open that Aloha Airlines jet. The official says the investigation

is now focusing on what he called "hull fracture" or "hull fatigue."

One person was killed and 61 injured in what passengers described as

a mid-flight explosion. Our Jim Deadline was at Kahului airport shortly

after the jet came in for an emergency landing:

        JET BLAST #3

        RUNS: :43

        OUT: "...at Kahului airport."

Even after midnight, we can still use our final spot. We use the lead-in copy to
retain our immediacy; the spot itself is undated, and therefore protected. Thus:

"Structural failure." That, investigators are now saying, is

probably what caused yesterday's near-catastrophe on an Aloha Airlines

jetliner. One person died, and 61 were injured, in what passengers

```
described as a mid-flight explosion.  Our Jill Deadline talked with many

of them after they landed safely at Kahului Airport:

        JET BLAST #4

        RUNS:  :44

        OUT:  "...at Kahului airport."
```

TAGS TO SPOTS

Normally, there is not (repeat *not*) a tag after a spot. That is because the sound source (the reporter) includes his or her own reidentification in the form of a signoff, which makes a natural break from one story to the next. Structurally, the spot amounts (or should amount, if it's been written correctly) to the last word in the newscast on the specific story it concerns.

Occasionally, however, there may be a late-breaking development that updates a spot in a significant way. A news agency, for example, may report new information between the time a spot was filed and the time it is to go on the air. In such a case, the newsroom must choose between two editorial options:

1. Junk the spot and substitute a fresh spot or writer-written version containing the new information.
2. Play the spot and update it with a tag.

The choice depends on the individual case. If, logistically, it is a relatively easy matter to get an updated spot by air time from the reporter, so much the better; the new spot will simply be substituted for the old. If, however, the reporter is unavailable (for example, he or she may be covering another story by then), or if time is very short (which is often the case), and the original spot is well written and otherwise rich in content, then a tag is in order.

Suppose, for example, that a reporter covering a union meeting on whether to strike says, in concluding his spot, "Results of the strike vote are expected shortly." And just before air time, AP sends a bulletin announcing the result of the vote in favor of a strike. This is quite clearly a major update. To include the information in the lead-in to the spot would negate any reason for using it, because it ends with dated information. So instead a tag would be written to this effect:

```
And, we've just received late word that the union HAS voted to

strike.
```

To repeat, the use of such tags is rare. Newsrooms would rather not use them at all, preferring to have the latest word from the reporter. Unfortunately, for logistical and technical reasons, it isn't always possible.

OVERNIGHTS

Let's say you are working the PM shift in radio—3 P.M. to 11 P.M. or 4 P.M. to midnight. Unless you're at a network or exceptionally well-staffed local station, you will turn out the lights as you leave the newsroom, because the AM shift won't be in for four or five hours yet. The wire machines will be left running, but for all intents and purposes, the news department will be closed overnight.

All right, in walks the AM shift. They check the wires. But what do they do for fresh tape? There's been no one to prepare it, right?

Wrong. *You* prepared it before you left last night. How? By writing and recording a spot or two on events that occurred late in your shift. You tailored them specifically for use during AM Drive by rewriting the "when" element to suit the circumstances.

Suppose, for example, that you covered a fire that was brought under control at around 10 P.M. In your spots that evening, you spoke of "tonight's fire" and concluded by saying that "Officials suspect arson and have begun an investigation." Fine. But in your overnight versions, which are simply called "overnights" or "o'nites," you must change the wording to correspond to the projected time of broadcast. You might say

```
Arson investigators this morning are looking into last night's fire

on the West Side...
```

or

```
Arson is one possible explanation fire officials are giving for the

fire that destroyed a warehouse on the West Side...
```

Yes, the AM shift could simply have rewritten fresh copy from the overnight wire service material. But that's not what your news director wants. What he or she wants is fresh *tape* to enliven and enrich newscasts, tape that only *you* as the reporter of the story can provide.

EXERCISES

1. Using the following news agency copy and actualities as your pool of resources, write two wraparounds slugged KING MARCH #1 and KING MARCH #2, signing off your name and "Washington" (you should *not* pretend to have covered the event in person). Select only one actuality per spot.

   Make KING MARCH #1 a hard lead, and date it, leaving it unprotected after an hour or two.

   Make KING MARCH #2 a soft lead, and leave it undated, thereby protecting it for possible use after midnight.

Each spot should run between 40 and 50 seconds.

```
AM-March on Washington, 2nd Ld
Thousands March on 25th Anniversary of King's "I Have a Dream'
Speech
     WASHINGTON (AP)--Tens of thousands of civil rights
marchers tried to recapture the spirit of Martin Luther King
on the 25th anniversary of his "I Have a Dream" speech
Saturday with warnings that the struggle to fulfill King's
dream of equality is far from over.
     Singing "We Shall Overcome," demonstrators led by Jesse
Jackson, Democratic presidential candidate Michael Dukakis and
Coretta Scott King, widow of the slain civil rights leader,
marched from the Washington Monument to the Lincoln Memorial
waving signs and banners in the hot midday sun.
     U.S. Park Police estimated the crowd at 55,000 people,
far fewer than the 250,000 who thronged the National Mall for
King's famous oration climaxing the March on Washington on
Aug. 28, 1963, a crowd that was equalled five years ago at a
20th anniversary march.
     Dukakis' appeal to banish all forms of racism and
discrimination was greeted warmly, but it was Jackson, his
former rival for the Democratic nomination, who got the
biggest cheers of the day with a scathing attack on Republican
nominee George Bush.
     "George Bush is not in Washington today," Jackson said to
a roar of approval. "He must not be here for the Inauguration
next January."
     The civil rights activist said that a quarter-century
ago, "we looked forward to new frontiers" under President
Kennedy.
     "Today, Reagan and Bush attempt to return us to an old
fortress," he said. "They are trying to rebuild old walls.
They have fought to crush the dream."
     Jackson made no mention of the Dukakis or the Democratic
ticket, but he appealed for his predominantly black audience
to vote in the Nov. 8 elections.
     "Hands that once picked cotton can now pick mayors,
legislators, governors, and presidents," he declared.
     Others at the rally echoed Jackson's message.
     "Twenty-five years later, we are here stronger and more
determined than ever," said Rep. John Conyers, D-Mich.
     Conyers told the demonstrators they were not marching so
Jackson could be the next president, "but so that your son or
daughter can be a future president of the United States."
     Dukakis and Jackson met on the front ranks of the march
for the first time since the Massachusetts governor defeated
the civil rights activist for the Democratic nomination at
last month's party convention in Atlanta.
     Jackson led the monument rally in chants of "Keep Hope
Alive!" and Dukakis claimed that only a Democratic president
could help meet the demonstrators' demands for full social and
economic equality.
     From the Washington Monument the demonstrators retraced
King's steps to the Lincoln Memorial, where Dukakis invoked
King's "I Have a Dream" speech a quarter-century ago.
```

"Let us, in the words of Dr. King, 'transform the
jangling discords of our nation into a beautiful symphony of
brotherhood,'" Dukakis said to polite and friendly applause.

"We have to march not just so that some of us can reach
the top of the hill," Dukakis said. "We must march until every
American has reached the bright sunshine of opportunity, until
we can stand, and stand together, in the golden glow of our
shared dream."

"We must march until racism and anti-Semitism and
discrimination of all kinds are banished from this land, until
we have a Justice Department that understands the meaning of
the word "justice,' until we have a civil rights commission
that believes in civil rights, and until we have a president
who understands and respects the Constitution of the United
States."

Bush and his running mate, Dan Quayle, did not respond to
invitations to attend the rally, march organizers said. Bush
was campaigning Saturday in Texas.

Jackson, in a speech on the eve of the rally, pledged to
help get out the vote this fall for the Democratic ticket of
Dukakis and Lloyd Bentsen. "We do have a choice and a chance
in November," Jackson said. "Dukakis and Bentsen represent an
alternative, a chance to change."

At the time, the 1963 demonstration was the biggest ever
held in Washington. The peaceful, orderly march and King's
galvanizing speech are credited with spurring Congress to pass
the landmark Civil Rights Act of 1964 under pressure from
President Johnson.

Mrs. King said the 1963 march "helped break the spine of
racial segregation" in the United States, and that today "we
still have a dream of a nation free of the cancer of racism."

The Rev. Joseph E. Lowery, president of the Southern
Christian Leadership Conference, recalled that King had said,
"America has given the Negro people a bad check, a check which
has come back marked 'insufficient funds'."

Lowery said the marchers had returned to cash that check.

"It's not that there are no funds," he said. "It's that
your ways of accounting are faulty. We know the money is
there. If you don't cash it now, we will be back again and
again and again."

Actualities (excerpted from remarks to the marchers):

CORETTA #1 (Coretta Scott King, widow of Rev. M.L. King, Jr.)

If we, the heirs of the dream of Martin Luther King, Junior, can find the
courage and commitment to rise to the challenge of his dream, we will lead a
mighty chorus of humanity in singing "Free at last, free at last, thank God
almighty, we're free at last!"

(runs :22)

JACKSON #1 (Rev. Jesse Jackson, former King aide and former presidential candidate, attacking the Reagan/Bush record)

They deregulated justice. They deregulated trucking. They deregulated foreign policy. They exchanged drugs for arms. They brought shame to our government. George Bush is not in Washington today. He must not be here for inauguration on January the 20th! (applause)

(runs :23)

JACKSON #2 (on the King legacy)

The torch has passed to a new generation. The challenge to keep the dream alive, a dream generated by the power of love and boundless hope, that is our charge to keep.

(runs :15)

DUKAKIS #1 (Democratic presidential nominee)

Let us march on, and little by little—poco a poco—step by step—paso a paso—hand in hand—mano en mano—together—juntos—we will overcome!

(runs :22)

2. Write lead-ins for each of your spots. Be careful to tailor your lead-ins to suit the time of day and the nature of your spots.

KING MARCH #1 (your hard spot) airs at 3 P.M., less than an hour after the completion of the march and rally.

KING MARCH #2 (your soft-led, protected spot) airs at 3 A.M. the following morning.

14

Newscasting

JOB SKILLS

Most newcomers to broadcast news find their first job in radio rather than television.

The first and most obvious reason is that there are more jobs in radio news. Even though producing TV news requires larger staffs, radio stations in the United States outnumber TV stations by roughly ten to one. Thus, in the aggregate, radio news employs more people.

Second, job competition is much greater in TV than in radio. TV's impact on our society is far greater than radio's; most budding broadcasters want to be "where the action is," thus creating fierce competition for the few available entry-level positions. There's also the fact that, by and large, the pay is higher in TV news, and employers are very selective about whom they hire.*

---

*The broadcasting industry categorizes local audiences according to the number of "TV households" within receiving distance of local radio and TV signals. By far the largest category is designated "small markets"—population areas with fewer than 500,000 TV households. Next come the "medium markets"—areas with from 500,000 to 1,500,000 TV households. And last are "major markets"—areas with more than 1,500,000 TV households.

Market designations correspond roughly to population density: New York is the #1 major market, Los Angeles is #2, Chicago is #3, and so on. However, U.S. geography and population patterns are such that neighboring cities, while each a medium market if considered separately, can be raised into the major market category if they are served by the same local stations. Thus, Dallas

199

Third, newcomers in TV journalism are expected to possess an array of technical skills not required of radio journalists. TV news is inherently preoccupied with gathering and transmitting pictures. Thus, despite the specialization of job skills characteristic of large staffs in big cities, networks, and all-news cable, most newcomers start at small stations where they are expected to shoot and edit videotape, operate studio and control room gear, and face the camera—as well as to write, report, and "package" the news. Many college journalism departments do offer advanced courses in TV newsgathering, but because of the enormous cost of equipment, the gear used at the undergraduate level is rarely of the same standard or complexity as that used professionally. On the other hand, college journalism departments and radio stations frequently use the same kind of hand-held audiotape recorders and studio editing equipment as professional radio stations.

In short, the majority of newcomers arrive on the job market with the skills (writing, reporting, audiotape recording and editing) suitable for radio but insufficient for television.

That said, beginners in radio must usually possess one talent not required of most beginners in TV: They must go on the air, either as reporters or newscasters, more likely as both. Radio staffers generally write *and* announce the news.

In radio's heyday, the requirement was for a deep, resonant, authoritative voice and delivery. Women anchors were virtually excluded; broadcast journalism used to be a predominantly male profession, and employers felt the audience would consider women's voices insufficiently authoritative. As women enter the field in ever larger numbers, such attitudes are considered prehistoric. Voices in radio news now run the range from basso profundo to lyric soprano. What does remain, however, is a requirement to enunciate clearly and fluently—an ability acquired through constant practice. Broadcast journalism students are thus encouraged to take an announcing course, if offered, and/or to work part-time writing and anchoring newscasts at the campus radio station.

THE FUNCTION OF A RADIO NEWSCAST

It is well to bear in mind the *nature* of most radio news in the United States (and overseas, too), which is overwhelmingly the reporting of late-breaking developments, told briefly. Although most newscasts are short, they come hard and fast—every hour or half-hour, depending on the station—a fresh "edition" as many as 24 or 48 times a day. Each newscast is different, consisting of a different

---

and Fort Worth make one major market in the eyes of broadcasters; the same is true of San Francisco-Oakland. By the same token, the city of Denver has a larger population than Tampa, Saint Petersburg, or Sarasota; however, because these last three cities are geographically close and are served by the same TV stations, the Tampa/St. Petersburg/Sarasota market has a higher designation than Denver.

In broadcast journalism, the standards of news judgment and performance grow higher, by and large, as you climb the market ranking scale. (The pay scale, too, grows correspondingly higher.) At the top of the competence and pay scales are the major networks, whose news staffers are recruited from among the very best broadcast journalists at local stations.

mix of stories of different lengths, rewritten, updated, and handled differently from hour to hour.

Thus, it is necessary to approach the writing and assembling of radio newscasts with an attitude different from newspapers and television, whose "editions" are longer but fewer and farther between. One cannot expect from a single short radio newscast the same sort of "definitive" treatment of the day's news as from a single edition of a newspaper or a single telecast. Instead, a day's radio newscasts must be regarded as a whole for any true assessment of quality of coverage.

This is important psychologically as well as journalistically. A newswriter/newscaster need not feel that he or she has failed if an important story gets only 10 seconds on one newscast, as long as it receives adequate time on a different newscast. Radio newscasts are trade-offs whose value can only be assessed in the aggregate.

All of which is not to say that a single newscast, however ephemeral its nature, cannot be a creative, skillful, tasteful, sensitive, and perceptive account of the day's news. Quite the contrary. Those are precisely the qualities to strive for.

NEWSCAST LENGTH AND STRUCTURE (FORMATS)

In this book we've examined the various elements of newscasts: scripted stories without tape, actualities, and reports, as well as attendant matters such as transitions, headlines, and so forth. Putting them all together to form a modern radio newscast is by and large a job assigned to a single staffer: a newswriter/newscaster. (A notable exception to the one-person norm is all-news radio, which requires a sizable staff to perpetually crank the news machine.) In local radio, this lone staffer selects which stories, actualities, and reports to include, writes the entire newscast, then reads it on the air. With the exception of a few stations in the biggest cities, there is no "editor" or "producer" to proofread the newscast to guard against errors of fact or style. The newswriter/newscaster is on his or her own, writing and voicing as many as 8 or 16 newscasts within a single work shift. Although those newscasts may be short (say, 4 minutes on the hour and 90 seconds on the half-hour), and although the use of radio wire copy is often permitted, the writing demands are great, the pace unrelenting.

The length and the structure of each newscast follow a tightly controlled formula called a "format." A station's news format dictates virtually everything about the newscast except its specific content: the time it goes on the air, how long it runs, the average number of stories to include, whether and where to include local sports and weather, the wording of the sign-on and signoff, and so forth.

With so many variables, it's obvious that formats differ markedly from station to station. Nevertheless, your listening habits have probably shown that one format in particular appears to typify modern radio newscasts: 5 minutes, beginning on the hour. In local radio, the emphasis is, of course, on local news. But there is also a mix of world and national news, as well as the local weather forecast and latest scores involving local sports teams. Typically, the 5 minutes of news are reduced to four because of one minute set aside for commercials. A typical five-minute local newscast is thus formatted like the following:

SECTION 1

Sign-on at 00:00:00
Lead local or non-local story
Related stories (if any)
Secondary stories (local or non-local)
(COMMERCIAL)

SECTION 2

More secondary stories (local or non-local)
Local sports (if any that day)
Local weather
Sign-off at 00:05:00

The only hard-bound rules in this format are

1. The newscast must start precisely on the hour.
2. The commercial must be included *somewhere* in the newscast.
3. The newscast must conclude with the local weather forecast.
4. The newscast must be off the air *no later than* 5 minutes past the hour. (Ending a few seconds early is okay, but *not* a few seconds late.)

Everything else—the number of stories, their lengths, their placement, the mix of local and non-local, which ones will include tape, exactly where to break for the commercial—is up to the newswriter/newscaster. He or she thus has *complete editorial control.* Whatever the editorial choices, they are guided by three basic considerations:

1. To tell the *latest* news.
2. To tell the *most important* news.
3. To maintain listener interest and attention.

Consideration 1 is a matter of keeping up with the news wires and the reporters in the field. Consideration 2 is a matter of news judgment and experience. And consideration 3 is a matter of ability to write and communicate.

STORY COUNT AND READING IN

Only in rare cases—maybe a few times a year—will an entire newscast be devoted to just one or two stories of transcendent importance. At all other times, the "typical" 4 minutes available for news must be parceled out, stingily, to a host of stories, all crying in various degrees for attention.

Thus, our model newscast, at any given hour, would contain anywhere from 6 to 10 different or related stories, each of different length.

Since newswriter/newscasters cannot know precisely what will be the latest or most important news by air time, their first task is to prepare for all eventualities. They do this by

1. Reading and "tearing down" (separating and reassembling) all available wire service copy from the preceding several hours and arraying it story by story in a convenient place (usually a desktop)
2. Familiarizing themselves with all available tape, both actualities and reports
3. Reading the station's newscasts from the preceding 4 to 8 hours
4. Ascertaining the whereabouts of all reporters, with an eye toward the tape they are likely to be feeding within the next few hours

This preparatory process—known as "reading in"—is essential as a first step. The material being read and sifted will almost always be fresh news—that is, news that has not yet appeared in the newspapers or on television. Only radio, with its built-in speed and immediacy, can for technical reasons afford to concern itself chiefly with "the top of the news."

Each newswriter/newscaster evolves his or her own system of reassembling wire service copy. Since wire copy continues to pour in without stop, it can quickly clutter one's work space. Most newswriter/newscasters thus form a habit of throwing away immediately all wire copy that they know they will not need—stale news, long features, esoteric sidebars, and so on. Some divide the copy into neat piles of "local," "foreign," and "domestic." Others divide into piles of "set" (stories not likely to change by air time) and "breaking" (stories that are likely to change by air time).

Whatever the system, the essential thing is to read *everything* before deciding which stories to include in a newscast. Once writing begins, it is best to leave the breaking stories for last, since they are the most likely to change and, tackled too early, could entail unnecessary or time-consuming rewrites.

(In a computerized newsroom, reading in is a different process. There is no news agency hard copy to tear down. The wire copy is stored electronically and read on the screen. The newswriter/newscaster can either print hard copies of the stories he or she wishes to rewrite, or transfer them electronically to his or her own "file" in the computer. During writing and rewriting, the screen can be split, one half showing the news agency original, the other the blank page of the eventual script; the broadcast version can thus be written with constant reference to the original.

(Separate computer files detail the day's reporting assignments, the tape that is already prepared for broadcast as well as that which will come in shortly, the latest weather forecast and the hourly temperatures, the latest sports scores, the texts of preceding newscasts, and—let's not forget—the date, time, and location of the office Christmas party. In short, the computer workstation centralizes every clerical and editorial function of the news department.

(Some newsroom computer systems enable staffers to access the mainframe from terminals in outlying bureaus or at home. But do not expect to find such systems at the small stations with entry-level positions.)

STORY LENGTH

Deciding how much air time each story is "worth" is a matter on which reasonable men and women will differ. There is no such thing as an "optimum" length, all length being relative to the structure as a whole. One person's "short" is another person's "long."

In radio, where the range is from 10 seconds to about 1:15 maximum (for an important story involving tape), one need not become preoccupied with the "worth" of most stories within a single newscast, for a story that gets only 15 seconds in one newscast may get 1:15 in the next. (Or it may be left out altogether in favor of a different story.)

What can be said definitively about story lengths is that they should vary widely within each newscast. For better or worse, a newscast is a kind of "show" or "performance." Sameness of length results in a dull show. And a dull show fails to fulfill consideration 3, maintaining listener interest.

So a newswriter/newscaster must make a deliberate effort to vary the running times of the stories chosen for the newscast. This goes along with a writing approach that has been stressed throughout this book: Decide the time of a story *before* writing it. It may come out a few seconds long or a few seconds short, but you will have a target to shoot for as well as an almost certain knowledge of what details you can include.

LEAD STORIES

Deciding the lead story of a newscast—a decision often made only moments before air time—usually provokes the most heated discussion in the newsroom. Again, reasonable men and women will differ, and differ strongly.

Much of the time, of course, the lead story will jump out and grab you by the throat. Stories with great immediacy, importance, or impact virtually "tell themselves."

But at other times, on slow news days, you could literally begin digging into the waste basket to find a lead story, hoping against hope that it was buried in a piece of wire copy you overlooked or rejected.

There is an unfortunate tendency in some news organizations, on slow news days, to "hype" stories out of proportion to their true importance, to use overly dramatic language such as "war of words" or "dropped a bombshell" when there was neither hostility nor air raid. This technique, almost always employed for strictly commercial reasons to attract an audience, debases the English language and, in the long run, debases listeners' trust in the offending station's news team.

So what to do if there's no clear or obvious lead story? Well, some newswriter/newscasters flip a coin. However, certain other solutions are much better. One is to lead with a human-interest story instead of with a hard news story, especially if the former involves health, medicine, or everyday science (a new household invention, for example). Another is to lead, in a general way, with the weather, returning to the specific forecast at the end of the newscast.

Whatever the merits of one possible lead versus another, it is well not to waste too much time in deciding. Remember, if you lead with story "A" at 10 A.M., you can lead with story "B" at 11 A.M. One newscast is just one *installment* of the news, not the day's definitive record.

Still another way to resolve the problem of stale or slow news is to rewrite stories to stress what is *about* to happen or what is *expected* to happen. This technique works best during early-morning newscasts, especially when there have been no major news developments since the previous evening. Sometimes, what is *going* to happen is more immediate and newsworthy than what has already happened.

STORY PLACEMENT

Following selection of the lead story, the rest of the stories are not just thrown together helter-skelter. Instead, they are grouped in some sensible or logical way so that, as much as possible, they flow one to another until they come to a natural break. Modest transitions may be required either between groups of stories or between stories in a group. But if stories are clearly written at the outset, only a slight pause between them by the newscaster will be sufficient.

The intention to group related stories should be in the newswriter/newscaster's mind even as he or she writes the newscast. This makes it possible to write smooth transitions and to order the newscast by grouped rather than individual stories, without getting caught short for time just before air.

There are several bases on which to group stories:

1. *By subject matter,* such as labor relations, politics, economic news, medicine, science, and weather, among others
2. *By geography,* such as U.S. region, Western Europe, Eastern Europe, the Far East, the Middle East, and so on
3. *By newsmaker,* such as Congress, the Supreme Court, the president, governor, or mayor taking different actions on different matters

Remember that grouped stories, however related, should still be typed one story per page. This is to permit the sudden deletion, if necessary, of just one story and the subtraction of that story's running time from the total.

TAPE PLACEMENT

There is a sort of Eleventh Commandment in radio newscasting: "Thou shalt use tape." Based on studies of listening habits and patterns, commercial station managements are convinced that audiences quickly become bored with "static" newscasts, that is, where the only thing heard is the voice of the newscaster. So they instruct newswriter/newscasters to include tape in every newscast, the object being to enliven the "sound" of the news as well as its content. The risk in such a policy is that, depending on circumstances, the tape available may not be newsworthy—in which case its use amounts to cosmetics only. Management's answer to such criticism is, "If you don't like the tape you've got, do foners until you *are* satisfied." So one way or another, there *will* be tape in just about every commercial newscast.

In structuring a newscast, the rule is not to use all the tape in the same place. Rather, it should be divided among newscast sections. Our model newscast, with its two sections, would ideally have one piece of tape in each section, not two in one and none in the other. It doesn't matter if the total tape is two actualities, two reports, or one actuality and one report. The point is to vary the newscast's pacing, both in story length and in tape placement.

As with all things in this book, I don't want you to accept my word alone on this. Listen to the stations in your area. Take notes if you have to—or a rundown of several newscasts, noting story count, length, placement, and tape. Or better yet, arrange to visit one or two of your local stations. Talk to the staff newsmen and women. Ask them about their news departments' formats and policies about the use of tape and so on. Unless it's a very heavy news day, professional broadcast journalists are, as a rule, pleased to welcome students and "show them the ropes."

UPDATING

As noted, newswriter/newscasters write many more versions of the same story than do writers in print or in television. A staffer in local radio may air up to 16 newscasts per shift. In all-news radio, the work load is heavier still. In the case of a major story, the demand is for a fresh version every 20 minutes. By and large, staffers are *not* permitted to air the same version twice, no matter how much time has elapsed between the two.

This can and does become challenging. Once you have written two long versions, two medium versions and two short versions, all of the same story, where do you go from there?

Fortunately, the solution comes in most cases through the natural development of the story itself, the twists and turns it takes as new information becomes known. Each twist and turn can be used to revise the story and perhaps give it a new lead. This process is called "updating." Here's how one network, CBS Radio, updated one major story throughout much of the broadcast day:

```
TIME  ORDER  Text

12p   lead   The battle over the Equal Rights Amendment is back in

             Congress.  One year after the first unsuccessful effort to

             pass it, backers are hoping they will have better luck this

             time around.  Neil Strawser reports:

             (wrap) Backers of the E-R-A are pleased with the strategy

             they have chosen.  It takes a two-thirds vote to bring the
```

Amendment up under suspension of the rules, but it also takes
a two-thirds vote to pass it.   They believe they have the
votes.   The procedure prohibits amendments and limits debate.
The backers say E-R-A has already been debated for years.
But Republicans are outraged...including their leader, Bob
Michel (MY-kel):

> (act.) I think that just does violence to the whole legislative process. I'm sure they're going to be many many members on our side who would support E-R-A and would hope to do so next year, when we have an opportunity to consider it under an open rule, offer amendments, and all the rest.

Senate Leader Howard Baker said he won't tie up the Senate
with E-R-A in the closing days of this session, but some
knowledgeable sources say E-R-A may not reach the Senate
floor until after the 1984 elections.   Neil Strawser, CBS
News, Capitol Hill.

-0-

lp   #2   The House has begun debate on a revived Equal Rights
Amendment.   Under rules set by Speaker Thomas O'Neill, total
discussion is limited to 40 minutes, and amendments are
prohibited.   This has caused an uproar among Republicans.

> (act.) I don't really believe that anybody expects that E-R-A is gonna pass this way, on a suspension of the rules. And I tell ya, it's not gonna pass in the last three days of the Senate. I'm for E-R-A. I supported it in the past. But I'm not gonna support it in the Senate in the last three or four days. So I think it does injury to the cause of the E-R-A to bring it up in this way.

Senate Majority Leader Howard Baker.   Womens' rights groups
and Right-to-Life advocates were reminding members of the
House today that they'll be held accountable for the way they
vote on the E-R-A bill.

-0-

2p lead Debate is under way in the House on a new Equal Rights

     Amendment. Tempers flared over a Democratic maneuver

     limiting the debate and prohibiting opponents from tacking on

     amendments to the bill.

—0—

3p lead The House is now taking a roll—call vote on a revised version

     of the Equal Rights Amendment. The surprise development has

     angered Republicans, who charge "steam—roller" tactics by the

     Democrats in an effort to embarrass the Republicans. They

     say the Democrats were not allowing debate or amendments, a

     breach of normal House procedure. Republican Hamilton Fish

     of New York said the effort does not do justice to the E—R—A:

> (act.) I suggest it is less a commitment to equal rights, that it is more of what we have witnessed repeatedly this fall: partisan politics in search of a campaign issue. We should refuse to cooperate with this approach. A no vote, my colleagues, is not a vote against E-R-A, but a vote for respect for the United States Constitution.

     Several Democrats said they wanted members of Congress to be

     on the record on this issue...as Election Year approaches.

—0—

4p lead An attempt to revive the Equal Rights Amendment failed today

     in the House of Representatives. Neil Strawser reports:

     (wrap) A switch of six votes would have meant victory for

     E—R—A. It took two—thirds. E—R—A lost by a vote of 278 yeas

     to 147 nays. Republicans and some Democrats had argued that

     the Democratic leadership was trying to ramrod the bill

     through without allowing amendments, to make sure E—R—A did

     not mandate abortion or require women to go into combat. And

     Republican Hamilton Fish, an E—R—A supporter, charged

     Democrats with trying to put Republicans on the spot:

(act.) A no vote, my colleagues, is not a vote against E-R-A, but a vote for respect for the United States Constitution (applause).

Speaker O'Neill, winding up debate, scoffed at opponents for trying to hide behind such arguments:

(act.) If you think this is the escape, then vote no. If you truly believe in a constitutional amendment for women's rights, now is the time, and vote yes (applause).

But O'Neill lost, and Fish announced he will attempt to bring E—R—A back to the floor under a rule allowing amendments. But apparently it can't happen yet this session.   Neil Strawser, CBS News, Capitol Hill.

(anchor tag) Senate Republican Leader Howard Baker said he didn't think the Senate would take up E—R—A until next year...and perhaps not until after the 1984 elections. Baker also said...

(tag used as transition to another Senate story)

5p   lead   (opens w/actuality)

(act.) By this vote, the ayes are 278, the nays 147, one member voting "present." Therefore, the two-thirds not having voted yes, the rules are not suspended.

That's the Clerk of the House, with parliamentary talk meaning the Equal Rights Amendment was defeated today, six votes short.   This despite the wagging finger of House Speaker Thomas O'Neill.   House Republicans were infuriated because O'Neill and the rest of the Democratic leadership barred them from modifying the E—R—A proposal in any way. O'Neill issued a warning to those members who declared their opposition because of insufficient debate and no amendments. Said the Speaker, wagging the finger, "You're not fooling anybody.   In your hearts you were never with us."   To which,

Republican Representative Larry Craig of Idaho replied, challenging the leadership's tactics and saying, "Shame on you, Mr. Speaker, shame on you."

-0-

6p   #2   Another attempt to put an Equal Rights Amendment into the U-S Constitution died today in the House of Representatives. The final vote, 278 to 147, was six votes shy of the two-thirds necessary for passage. Republicans were angered by a parliamentary move that prohibited amendments and limited debate to 40 minutes. Some Republicans said they wanted to discuss such issues as abortion and women in combat. Democratic Representative Mary Rose Oakar of Ohio says those issues just provided a handy excuse for voting no:

> (act.) There can be no other more pro-life issue than to be for the Equal Rights Amendment. And I suspect, without impugning the reputations of any of my colleagues, that a lot of people use that as an excuse to oppose us. And they can dream up all kinds of reasons, emotional issues, that are divisive among those of us who believe strongly, simply to see the defeat of this amendment.

-0-

7p   #3   The battered Equal Rights Amendment came to a vote in the House of Representatives again today...and went down to defeat. The vote, 278 to 147. Jacquilyne Adams covered the story:

(wrap) With only six more votes, supporters of the Equal Rights Amendment could have won passage in the House. But a number of members, like Republican Hamilton Fish, argued and voted against the E-R-A, because the amendment was brought to the floor under a procedure normally used for non-controversial amendments, and because it prohibited

debate on abortion and women in combat:

> (act.) I suggest it is less a commitment to equal rights, that it is more of what
> we have witnessed repeatedly this fall: partisan politics in search of a
> campaign issue.

But Speaker Thomas O'Neill discounted the opponents'

arguments:

> (act.) You want to hide behind something that we have done, the strategy
> which we have brought out? You're not fooling anybody. In your heart you
> were never with us. You were looking for the escape.

After the vote, E-R-A supporters said they were sorely

disappointed, but glad that now they have the names of their

opponents. Women's groups say they'll target each one for

defeat--15 percent of House Democrats, two-thirds of House

Republicans. The E-R-A is expected to return to the House

floor next year...before the 1984 election. Jacquilyne

Adams, CBS News, on Capitol Hill.

-0-

8p   lead   It's called the Equal Rights Amendment. It says equality of

rights under the law shall not be denied or abridged by the

United States, or by any state, on account of sex. Today a

revived effort to make the E-R-A a part of the Constitution

went down to defeat in the House of Representatives. The

proposal fell six votes short of the two-thirds majority

needed. Republicans were angered by the restrictions set by

the Democratic leadership to limit debate and bar amendments

to the measure. As might be expected, women's groups such as

the National Organization for Women denounced the House

action. Judy Goldsmith, the president of NOW:

(act.) Votes such as today's virtually assure that the gender gap will continue to grow, as women become more determined to remove from office those who do not support our rights.

−0−

9p   #3   The House of Representatives today killed a new version of the Equal Rights Amendment. The House vote was six votes short of the two-thirds majority needed to send the measure along to the next step in the ratification process. Republicans in the House said they were angry over a parliamentary move that limited debate to 40 minutes. But Cathy Wilson of the National Political Women's Caucus says that's a weak excuse:

        (act.) I think that they are influenced by the right-wing tone that has been set by the president of our country, Ronald Reagan.

−0−

10p   #3   An effort to revive the Equal Rights Amendment failed today in the House of Representatives, coming up six votes shy of the two-thirds majority required for approval. The Democratic leadership ruffled the feathers of many Republicans, and some within Democratic ranks, by limiting debate and barring any amendments to the proposal. House Speaker O'Neill accused E−R−A opponents of using the restrictions as an out for voting no.

By now, you should understand enough of broadcast style and structure to be aware on many levels of the way CBS Radio handled that story. You noticed how the content kept pace with the breaking elements of the story, stressing their immediacy, and yet always retaining the main point, the essence.

You noticed how the story length varied, from as short as around 15 seconds to as long as around 1:30.

You noticed how the story placement varied, sometimes as the lead, but moving up and down in order until, finally, when there were no further developments, dropping well back in the newscast. (By midnight, the story was not even included in the hourly newscast.)

You noticed how the approach and treatment varied, from a straightforward reader, to a lead-in and a spot, to a lead-in with an actuality, sometimes with a tag, sometimes without.

Of course, CBS News is a large organization of many experienced, talented people. This may not be the case in the places you first find work. But your job in updating the news will be the same no matter where you are, even if you have to do it all by yourself.

"FILL" (PAD AND PROTECTION)

As you've no doubt noticed, radio and TV news does not always air as smoothly as planned. Technical foul-ups—"glitches"—occur often. Mislabeling, inattention, or plain carelessness can lead to a tape mix-up. Or the tape mechanism itself can fail. Be it human or mechanical, the failure can force the newscaster to "bail out" of the wrong tape or to fill an uncomfortable silence.

To minimize the damage, experienced newscasters go into the studio prepared for disaster. They always bring more news copy than normally necessary. This excess copy is called "fill"—because it fills the empty time, the silence, caused by human or mechanical error.

There are two types of fill copy. Extra copy of a nonspecific nature, stories of varying lengths that can stand on their own, is called "pad"; it "pads out" (lengthens) a newscast that would otherwise be too short because of the lost tape time.

The other type of fill is designed to replace a specific story lost because of tape failure. Called "protection," this copy is a scripted version of the story that was to have played on tape. If the tape fails to play as scheduled, the newscaster reads the protection copy as smoothly as possible, ad-libbing a transition from the preceding lead-in.

In modern radio news, the writing of protection copy is characteristic only of networks and the largest local stations, places with staffs given enough time to prepare for most eventualities. Elsewhere, staffs are too small and the work loads too heavy to allow for such niceties. At the same time, no newswriter/newscaster can risk going on the air completely unarmed. Thus, fill copy in the form of a pad is a must.

The best time to write fill copy is at the start of a work shift, immediately after reading in. Select at least three stories of marginal interest—stories you consider newsworthy but not as important as the day's other news—and write them for a total of 60 seconds. Vary their running time (say 15, 15, and 30 seconds) because you can't know in advance how much air time you may have to fill. Set the fill copy aside, but remember to bring it with you to the studio for your first newscast. Once it's there, leave it there. (But at the end of your shift, you might have the courtesy to offer it to a hard-pressed colleague.)

SPECIAL TECHNICAL MATTERS

Scripts

Broadcast scripts are never stapled or clipped together until *after* they've been aired. The pages must be kept loose. That's to permit the newscaster to slide the pages noiselessly as they are read on the air. It also permits him or her to drop or rearrange pages at will either before or during a newscast.

Slug and Time Placement

There is a practical reason for insisting that slugs and times be written in the *extreme* upper edge of a page. A newscast script is customarily held in one hand, slightly fanned vertically. This permits the newscaster to see at a glance, without fumbling pages, which stories remain and how long each runs, in order to get off the air on time.

Backtiming

Okay, you've written a terrific kicker. It runs 20 seconds. You want to end the newscast with it, just before signoff. How do you *ensure* you will begin reading it on time, in order to get off the air on time?

By "backtiming" it. You *subtract* the time of your kicker from the time you must be off the air (00:05:00):

$$
\begin{array}{r}
:05:00 \\
-\quad :20 \\
\hline
=\;\; :04:40
\end{array}
$$

You write and circle the notation

$$\left(\text{BY } :04:40\right)$$

in the upper right corner of the copy page. This reminds you at a glance of the latest time you may begin reading the story and still get off the air on time.

The technique of backtiming may be used for the weather or any other item with which you want to end a newscast. It may seem a bit complicated to you now, but after a few months on the job, you'll be doing double and triple backtiming, just to give yourself a challenge.

EXERCISES

1. Using the model format described in this chapter, write a 5-minute newscast as it might be broadcast on your campus or other local radio station. For raw material, use either same-day news agency copy or the latest edition of your local newspaper. Assume you

will have two pieces of tape: a 45-second report on your biggest local story and a 15-second actuality of a newsmaker quoted in one of your world or national stories. Remember that the amount of news copy you must write is reduced by one 60-second commercial and by another 60 seconds of newstape. Thus, you will need to write only 3 minutes of news copy—plus, of course, a few "fill" stories.

(*Note:* Even though you are new at this, you should be able by now to write and assemble the entire newscast in less than two hours. Bear in mind that in a professional radio newsroom, you would typically have less than one hour to do it—in addition to other duties such as doing foners and editing tape.)

15

TV Writing: Graphics and Titles

First the good news: TV newswriting follows essentially the same style as radio newswriting. With only minor variations, the same rules apply in both media—the rules we have been systematically examining in this book. Thus, you will not have to "unlearn" what you have learned to this point.

Now the bad news: From the technical standpoint, TV news is far more complicated than radio news. In addition to the news copy itself, TV scripts include an array of technical instructions to assure the smooth integration of sounds and pictures from many electronic sources. One result is that TV journalists can become so preoccupied with the technology that they have relatively little time to spend on the *words*. This is not meant as a criticism but rather as a statement of fact.

Recent technological advances in computerization and miniaturization have enabled TV news departments to use a vast array of visual special effects in their newscasts. These include computer animation, split- and multiple-screen imagery, forward and reverse "squeezes" (reducing or enlarging moving pictures to various portions of the screen), multicolor titling, variable fonts, etc. The goal of such special effects is to give viewers a clearer "visual understanding" of news stories and/or to provide some "visual spice" to an otherwise static presentation. Sometimes that goal is reached. But sometimes the result is confusion and clutter—known derisively as "flash," form without substance.

Complicating matters further is the fact that different news organizations use different equipment and different techniques. They also use differing terminology, which makes it difficult for a textbook such as this one to specify terms that newcomers will encounter in the workplace. Under the circumstances, the

216

best we can do is to use generic terms to describe the various elements of TV news scripts, on the understanding that interested students will learn about specific technologies at some later point.

Whatever the technology and terminology you eventually encounter, I must stress that effective TV newswriting requires both an understanding of what the electronic gadgetry can do and an ability to dominate the machines, to make them serve the ultimate goal of communicating the news.

THE NATURE OF TV NEWS

In television, the picture comes first. After all, TV is a visual medium. People tune in to *see,* not just to hear. The fact that someone must write the words explaining just what it is that people are seeing is secondary to obtaining and broadcasting the pictures themselves.

In radio news, journalists may judge stories solely on the basis of their news value (although the quality of actualities does play a role in deciding how much air time to give a story). In TV news, the stories for which there are good pictures almost always get priority. Given the choice between two stories of equal news value, TV journalists give preference to the one with the more dramatic pictures. Hence, a flood gets preference over a budget vote in the city council, even though more people may be more profoundly affected by the latter than by the former.

The devotion to dramatic pictures permeates the entire process of TV news. When TV news producers meet to decide on the day's coverage, they discuss the picture possibilities of each developing story, and they allocate resources (camera crews, equipment, reporters, field producers, etc.) accordingly. Then, when the time comes to choose which stories to include in the final lineup (the ordered list of stories making up the newscast), they base their choices on the quality of the pictures as well as on the stories' news value; almost always, they opt for the stories with pictures at the expense of those without them. That is why your local 10 P.M. or 11 P.M. news is apt to dwell on a fire that barely makes the back pages of a newspaper or is told in 10 seconds on radio; the flames fill the TV screen and look "dramatic."

Television's preoccupation with pictures extends to the selection of personnel—both hiring and firing. A "good" TV reporter or field producer is one who knows how to get the pictures that will illustrate an assigned story; a "good" TV newswriter is one who knows how to make maximum use of those pictures in telling the story; a "good" TV producer is one who knows how to present a story, as well as an entire newscast, in visual terms.

It would seem to follow from all this that writing ability is only a secondary concern in TV news—and, in some newsrooms, that is indeed the case. In the main, however, writing ability and "visual flair" go hand in hand; the writer must be so adept as to be able to tailor broadcast-style language to suit the available pictures. This ability comes mainly into play when an assigned story includes videotaped actualities, NATSOT, or both. When, however, the story is accompanied only by a still picture or graphic, writing requirements are virtually identical to those in radio.

PICTURE COMPONENTS

Let's begin with the simpler components of video journalism, beginning with the TV screen itself.

Picture Area

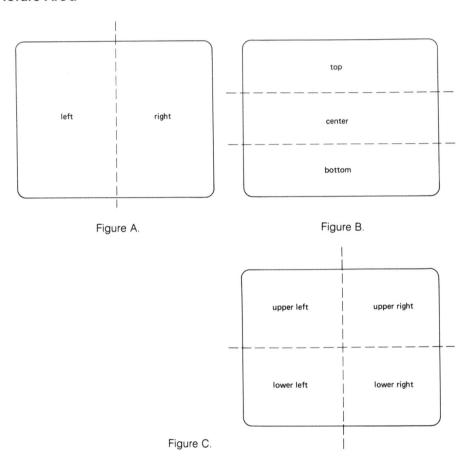

Figure A.

Figure B.

Figure C.

The sketches show the various ways of describing the geography of the TV picture (called the "frame"). Figure A divides the frame into right and left halves. Note that the terms apply from the *viewer's* point of view, *not* the performer's point of view. Figure B divides the frame into horizontal *thirds*. Thus, the word "top" refers to the top *third* of the frame and so on. And, finally, Figure C divides the frame into *quadrants*. The description "upper right" means the upper right *quadrant* of the frame. The significance of all this side-side, up-down will become apparent shortly.

How TV journalists write the news depends on how they want those picture areas filled. The simplest way to fill the screen is with a shot of the anchor:

That is called a *full-frame anchor shot.* It shows nothing but the anchor delivering the news from the center of the screen; there are no other visual elements of any kind.

News stories presented without videotape are called "readers" or "tell stories." Their written style follows *exactly* the style of radio news *in all major respects.*

The full-frame anchor shot is like watching someone deliver the news on radio. In the early days, that's pretty much what TV news was—radio news delivered on-camera. In modern TV news, however, the anchor-only shot is used comparatively rarely, usually as a means of providing a visual change from more common shots, or to create a sense of intimacy between anchor and viewer.

A much more common shot is this one:

Electronic Graphics

This shot places the anchor at screen left and inserts an electronic visual called a *graphic* in the upper right. (The shot can also be reversed, with the anchor on the right and the visual in the upper left.) The insertion of the graphic (in this case a map) is accomplished via computer-assisted electronic devices. As a journalist, you do *not* need to know how the devices work. But you *do* need to know that they are capable of inserting on the screen *whatever visual elements you choose.* In other words, the choice of what to put into that electronic window is an editorial decision made by a writer or producer.

Electronic graphics can be maps (to show the location of a story—the Where element); still photos of people or places (to show the Who, What, or Where elements); still frames extracted electronically from videotape; flags; corporate or governmental logos; charts; graphs; drawings; or original creations from a station's graphic arts department made on request of the newsroom. In short, they can be virtually anything a writer or producer feels will clarify, enhance, or pinpoint some element of the story being delivered by the anchor. Further, more than one graphic can be used per story; the first graphic can illustrate something in the lead sentence, the second graphic a later element, etc.

However many graphics are used, it is important to remember that an "over-the-shoulder" graphic occupies a relatively small area of the screen and must therefore not be too complicated or attempt to show a lot of detail; viewers might be forced to squint or be otherwise distracted from listening to the news copy itself. If it is important to show a detailed graphic, then it may be shown full-screen. This gives viewers a chance to study the visual details even as they absorb the facts of the story.

Stories delivered by the anchor and using graphics are also called "readers" or "tell stories," but, unlike stories without graphics, they are subject to slight modifications in broadcast style. First, because you can use maps to show a story's location, it is not necessary to spend a lot of time telling the Where element, the specific geography. If, for example, a brush fire is raging near the Arizona-Mexico border, it is unnecessary to say so in your news copy because people can see that in the graphic.

Second, it is unnecessary to describe someone's attitude or expression if viewers can see it in a photograph used in a graphic. For example, if the photo shows the governor to be smiling, it is unnecessary to write "A smiling (or happy) Governor Smith signed legislation today . . . ," etc.

In other words, the use of graphics allows you to tighten your written copy by omitting what people can clearly see. In fact, by *not* omitting obvious details, you are committing the sin of redundancy.

Electronic Titles

The other nonvideotape picture element you need to know about is electronic titling:

CBS Evening News   WBBM-TV, Chicago   NBC News

Electronic titles insert *textual* material into the picture—words and numbers. Produced by titling devices called *character generators,* titles are used mostly in conjunction with videotape to identify people and locations, itemize lists, give statistics, and spell out direct quotes. They may also be used to tell stories in conjunction with full-screen graphics (especially to give weather information or sports scores). Because the textual material in titles is meant for the viewer's eye, not the ear, it reverts to *print style:* "$1 million" instead of "one million dollars," etc.

Like graphics, titles enable newswriters to omit certain details from their copy, especially when writing to videotape (as we shall see in the next chapter). In tell stories, however, titles do *not* replace details in written news copy. Rather, they augment that copy by spelling out significant details *at the same time* as those details are being delivered by the anchor. For that reason, the text of titles must *closely match* the text of the news copy. Thus, for example, titles enable viewers to see and hear direct quotes simultaneously, and to see numbers that are simultaneously being reported orally. If news copy and titles are not closely matched, the mismatch of words and pictures can leave the audience confused and disoriented—which is just the opposite of the desired effect.

SCRIPTING

Television scripts are intended for many more pairs of eyes than are radio scripts. A TV news script contains not only the news copy itself but also instructions (called "cues") for the presentation of all audio and video components—that is, graphics, titles, and tape. Stories are typed on multicarbon "books" of script paper, with copies going to the anchors, producer, director, title machine operator, videotape playback unit, floor director (or "TD"—technical director), and teleprompter operator. (Some of these technicians may receive only a technical lineup rather than a full script.) Television newswriters are responsible for scripting the video cues as well as the news story.

It is unlikely that in your present setting you will have access to professional-style TV script books. They are expensive. Fortunately, they are easy to simulate with standard 8½-by-11-inch copy paper. Merely divide the page into roughly equal vertical halves, type video cues on the left half, and type the news copy and audio cues on the right half. Here are the specifics (refer also to p. 31–33):

1. Begin all video cues 5 spaces (Pica typeface) from the left edge.
2. Begin the news copy at the center of the page, and use a 35-space line (left margin = 42; right margin = 80).
3. Triple space between lines.
4. Follow the style set out in radio news to
   Type upper/lower case.
   Not divide words between lines.
   Not divide sentences between pages.
   Draw a bold arrow in the lower right to indicate "more."

One of the first odd things you'll find about typing TV pages is that the 35-space line is so short that on occasion you'll only be able to get in two or three words. So be it. In TV, the cost of script paper is infinitesimal compared to all other costs. Don't worry about it.

A few other things, pretty much standard in newsrooms everywhere:

5. The writer's last name (or initials), the date, and the time of the newscast go in the extreme upper *left* corner, just as in radio.
6. The slug goes in the upper part of the *video* column.
7. The timing of the story, rounded off to the nearest 5 seconds, goes just beneath the slug, circled.
8. Leave *at least 1 inch* of space between the foregoing information and the first video instruction and the first line of news copy.
9. Coordinate video cues with news copy by starting them *on the same line*.

Television script components such as electronic graphics and titles go by many different names, depending on the specific technology of each news department. Therefore, in this book's sample scripts, we shall use generic terms—

that is, *graphic, title, SOT,* etc.—for all audio and video cues. For now it is important that you learn the process of TV scripting; it will be a simple matter for you later on to learn your eventual employer's set of specific technical terms.

Naturally, the off-monitor photographs used in this book do not appear in actual scripts. They are included to demonstrate the type of TV picture that results from a specific script instruction.

One other thing before we proceed: You are about to learn new forms—repeat, *forms.* You may very well get the feeling that the forms divert your attention from the substance, namely the words you must write to tell a news story clearly and concisely. If so, that is an accurate reflection of the real world of TV news. The difference between a study setting and a professional setting is that here, in the classroom, you will have time and guidance to help focus your attention where it belongs—on the *words.*

Scripting without Graphics or Titles

As we've seen, the simplest TV news picture shows only the anchor as he or she reads a story on-camera. This shot is so standard that it does not require a specific video cue. In the absence of a cue for a graphic, title, or tape, the shot will be taken automatically. However, because most stations now use more than one anchor, it is necessary to specify which anchor is to deliver the story. This is accomplished by typing the anchor's name in the video column, adjacent to the start of the story in the audio column.

A sample script:

```
Smith                    ISRAEL
2/27, 8am
```

```
                Charles:            Israel says one of its warplanes

                                    was shot down today while attacking

                                    guerrilla bases in Lebanon.  The plane

                                    was one of four Israeli jets making an

                                    air raid on Syrian-controlled

                                    positions in the mountains around

                                    Beirut.


                                    ("Sunday Morning," CBS)
```

Scripting with Graphics

The inventiveness and originality of graphics depends both on the writer's imagination and the resources of his or her news department. At small stations and at larger stations with small news departments, the choice is limited to the graphics already on file, usually procured through companies that mail them out on a weekly basis. In large news departments and at networks, original graphics are made to order by staff graphic artists. A lead time of an hour or more is required for an original graphic.

A lot of care and preparation goes into a graphic element that may appear on the screen for only a few seconds. Indeed, it may take the writer longer to arrange for the graphic than to write the story it's to be used with. That is a normal condition in TV newswriting. At small stations, the writer simply combs through the file of prepared graphics and chooses the one that comes closest to his or her needs.

Whatever a station's resources, there will often be a number of choices available for each story. Let's say the story is that the U.S. House of Representatives cuts the defense budget. Among the choices for graphics might be

A photograph of Capitol Hill

A photograph of an aircraft carrier

A photograph showing some other type of military force or personnel

Lettering saying "Defense Budget Slashed" or something similar

A generic drawing showing an element of military might, such as a rocket or bomber in flight

And so on. You can probably think of several more possibilities. The main thing is that the graphic must somehow highlight the subject of the story. In so doing, it should neither contain too little information (such as wording like "Congressional Action") nor too much information (such as the exact dollar amount by which the budget was cut). The point is to enhance the anchor's words, not to detract from them by providing more detail that can be absorbed at a glance.

As for scripting, this, too, is usually straightforward and simple. Unless specified otherwise, the graphic will appear automatically in the upper right or upper left (depending on the news department's practice), over the anchor's shoulder. All that need be included in the video column is the word "graphic," followed by a word or two describing it:

Smith
2/27, NN

NOBEL

graphic -- Nobel Prize

An American won the Nobel Prize
for chemistry today, giving the United
States a clean sweep of this year's
Nobel science prizes. The winner in
chemistry: Henry Taube (TOW-bay) of
Stanford University.

("NBC Nightly News")

"Tell" stories using more than one graphic can be tricky. The changes should not come so fast as to be visually disorienting. Also, changes should follow both the written story structure and logical thought processes, which move from the general to the specific.

To change from one graphic to the next, script the video cue precisely adjacent to the line of copy where you want the new graphic to appear:

Smith
10/9, EN   ECONOMY

graphic -- economy

graphic -- indicators

The Commerce Department today
reported its main economic forecasting
gauge rose nine-tenths of one per cent
last month. That's the thirteenth
straight monthly increase for the
index of leading indicators, and it
pointed to continuing moderated
recovery. The report said five of
the available ten indicators rose in
September.

("CBS Evening News")

As noted earlier, a graphic you want the audience to be able to scrutinize in detail should be shown full-screen. This requires a different type of video cue—the addition of the word FULL right after the word "graphic" (see p. 226)

Full-screen graphics are often accompanied by electronic titles, the former serving as background for the latter.

Scripting with Titles

As with graphics, titles must be prepared well before airtime; there is seldom enough time while a newscast is in progress for the titling operator to type out the lettering that is to appear on screen. Instead, the texts of titles are stored in the character generator's computer, then recalled at the precisely correct time specified in the script.

There isn't enough room on the script itself to type out the full text of electronic titles, nor is it necessary to do so. All that's needed is the video cue "title" at the specific copy line where the title is to appear, specification of its location on the screen (FULL, BOTTOM, TOP, etc.), and a one- or two-word description of the text.

In practice, titles used to illustrate tell stories appear over a full-screen graphic. Without the graphic as background, the title would appear over the anchor's face.

The scripting would go as seen on p. 227.

Jones
5/12, 6pm

QUAKE

graphic -- quake   Walter: A major earthquake has struck

the northwestern United States,

killing two children, injuring an

unknown number of people, and causing

widespread damage in parts of Idaho.

The quake was centered near the

graphic FULL -- map

small town of Challis, Idaho, and was

felt in seven surrounding states and

Canada. It measured seven points on

the Richter scale -- a reading that

usually means very severe damage.

Several small towns in Idaho are

reportedly ~~devastated,~~ and two people

devastated,

are missing. The child victims were

crushed when a drugstore wall

collapsed right on top of them.

Rescue teams are being sent tonight

to remote areas of the state.

(WBBM-TV, Chicago)

Jones   CITY JOBS
11/4, 5pm

graphic -- court   Carol:

graphic FULL -- Murray plan
title FULL -- rehire

A compromise that would have at
least temporarily saved the jobs of 734
city workers slated for layoff...fell
through in court today.

Judge Thomas Murray proposed that
the workers be retained until the end
of the year. Then, if a re-evaluation
of the budget shows additional money
is needed to keep them on the payroll,
a city council majority would approve
a property tax increase to make up the
difference. But a spokeswoman for the
mayor said the proposed compromise is
"not feasible" under the current
budget deficit.

(WMAQ-TV, Chicago)

Our sample scripts so far have begun with the anchor sharing the screen with a graphic, then switched to full-screen graphics and titles. Although that is typical of most nontape stories, it is not always the case. Some stories may *open* with full-screen graphics and titles, then return to showing the anchor. Other stories, especially short ones containing statistics, can be presented *entirely* without seeing the anchor. An example:

```
Smith                    STOX
3/24, 5pm
```

```
graphic FULL -- stox bg    Walter:      On Wall Street today, stock

title FULL -- closing stox               prices were lower.  By closing time,
```

```
                                         the Dow-Jones Industrials were down

                                         more than 18 points.  The average

                                         share lost 30 cents, in trading that

                                         was active.
```

                                                  (WBBM-TV, Chicago)

Copy Appearance

Even moreso than in radio, a TV news script must be *clean*. In radio, newscasters can hunch over and squint at the script. In TV, the anchors have to *look* sharp as well as *sound* sharp. They must be able to read the news copy fluently just by glancing at it or by viewing it at a distance over a Teleprompter.

The director and other technical personnel, too, must be able to understand their cues at a glance. If you've ever been in a TV control room during a news broadcast, you know how chaotic things can get in the effort to make the newscast proceed smoothly. Scripts containing scribbles and strikeovers merely add unnecessarily to the chaos.

EXERCISES

1. Slug the following story VAN CRASH and write a 15-second tell story, using a map pinpointing Sweetwater, Texas, as an upper-quadrant graphic:

```
Team's Outing Ends in Tragedy
     MIDLAND, Texas (AP)--The young boys and girls of the
```

Midland Boys Club had spent the last week practicing for an out-of-town softball tournament, but their trip ended in tragedy.

Five lost their lives and 12 others in a Boys Club van were injured, four of them critically, in a collision Friday with a tractor-trailer near Sweetwater in West Texas. The Truck driver also was injured.

"It's truly a miracle any of them are alive," said Nolan County Sheriff Jim Blackley.

Midland Boys Clubs officials Saturday thanked people in the community for their sympathy and response during the tragedy.

"In particular, we are grateful to those who we do not know, whose faces we have not seen, those who provided swift medical attention to our children," said Chuck Clarkson, chairman of the board of the boys club.

Trooper David Gonzales said the van was nearly alongside the Coca-Cola truck when the van driver apparently dozed off and swerved onto a grassy median. The driver, attempting to regain control, oversteered the van directly into the path of the truck, Gonzales told The Dallas Morning News.

Gonzales said the van, with 17 passengers, was overloaded. He said there should have been no more than a dozen passengers.

The van was returning from a softball tournament in Abilene earlier in the day. Clarkson said the tournament was to cap the summer program for underprivileged youth in Midland.

"They had been practicing pretty hard for the softball tournament, and they were really excited about it," he said.

A memorial service was planned for Sunday afternoon.

The driver of the van and nine occupants remained hospitalized Saturday in hospitals in Lubbock and Abilene. The truck driver was released Saturday, but refused interviews.

2. Slug the following story TRIDENT PROTEST and write a 20-second tell story using two upper-quadrant graphics:

   1. the words "Protesters Arrested"
   2. a photo of a Trident submarine

   (Be careful. The choice of which graphic to use first depends on your decision how to lead the story.)

USS Pennsylvania Launched, Protestors Arrested

GROTON, Conn. (AP)--The U.S. Navy Saturday launched its 10th Trident nuclear-powered submarine, the USS Pennsylvania, as police arrested dozens of anti-war protesters.

"This ship is part of the strongest military deterrent force ever assembled," Rep. Joseph M. McDade, R-Penn, said at the launching at the Electric Boat Division of General Dynamics Corp. "This boat allows us the luxury of having no doubtful engagement."

The Pennsylvania, after it is fully equipped and

outfitted, a process that normally takes at least a year, will be the second ship in its class to carry the more accurate Trident II missiles. Each of the 24 missiles carries 10 nuclear warheads.

The boat, which was christened by Marilyn Kay Garrett, wife of Navy undersecretary H. Lawrence Garrett III, will have a crew of 154.

The Ohio Class Trident submarines are the largest and most powerful in the Navy fleet and are the heart of the U.S. sea-based nuclear deterrent. The boats measure 560 feet long and displace 18,750 tons.

The program was initiated in 1974, with the first ship, the Ohio, commissioned in 1981. Congress has approved funding for 15, of which eight are in service.

Fifty to 75 anti-war protesters demonstrated at the shipyard, and Joan Cavanagh, a member of the Coalition To Stop The Trident, said 32 people were arrested after they lay down in front of the gates.

A dispatcher with the Groton City Police Department said more than 20 people had been arrested on disorderly conduct charges as of Saturday afternoon and would be released on their own recognizance.

16

TV Writing: Videotape

We now come to what TV news prizes most of all: pictures that *move*.

It's true that even the standard shot of an anchor delivering the news does, in a way, show movement. And the insertion into the frame of graphics and titles also represents movement in the sense of varying the visual aspect. But what is really meant by "moving pictures" is videotape shot at the scenes of great and small events, showing us the "action."

Newswriting with videotaped story elements is perhaps the highest craft of TV journalism—and, for many newcomers, the hardest to learn. That's because moving images cannot be rearranged and juxtaposed as can still images; they cannot be edited as freely. Therefore, despite the craft of newstape editing, which is learned rather quickly, it is *language* that must be changed to suit the available moving pictures. This means that TV newswriters are not free to choose whatever words they like to tell a news story. Instead, they must choose words that compliment, explain, and put in context the moving pictures seen by the audience.

The problem of television as a news medium is that the pictures inherently compete with the words for the audience's attention. Experiments have repeatedly shown that, given a conflict between pictures and words, people consistently trust the pictures more than the words. The newswriter's task is to ensure that the competition is a beneficial one—that the result of the two combined is the audience's understanding of the story. If the writer fails in that task, the audience will remember the pictures without journalistic context.

Make no mistake about it, moving pictures do *not* speak for themselves. If you have ever looked through a camera lens or viewfinder, you know that the TV camera frames only a small portion of reality. Without the right words to put the pictures in context, TV journalists risk leaving the audience uninformed or, worse, with a distorted view of reality.

WRITING TO TAPE

Writing with videotaped elements is similar to radio writing with audiotape, in that it employs the same informal language of broadcast style and roughly the same structure of lead-in/sound bite/tag, or lead-in/report. There, however, the similarity ends.

The cardinal rule of writing to moving pictures is that copy and picture must be correlated. Not identical, *correlated.*

News copy delivered on-camera by an anchor or reporter is free from competing visual elements. Thus, it need not be tied to specific pictures because there are none on the screen (except, perhaps, for certain of the upper-quadrant graphics we looked at in the preceding chapter). But once the screen is fully occupied by a graphic, title, or moving pictures (whether live or on tape), the freedom of expression is lost. Copy must refer to what we are seeing, *at the time we are seeing it.*

This correlation between sound and picture is often called "referencing." News copy properly keyed to TV pictures is said to be "referenced." *Un*referenced copy is substandard; it disorients the audience.

This is absolutely fundamental. And it explains why so much money, time, and effort are spent on getting the right pictures in the first place. If the pictures show the elements of a news story specifically, the writer can combine tape editing and language to tell the news in whichever order and structure he or she thinks does the job best.

But things don't always work out that way. The "right" pictures aren't always on hand. Thus, the writer must find some way, some language, to tell the right news while incorporating the taped visuals that are available.

One option, of course, is not to use the tape at all if it doesn't show exactly what the writer wants to tell. However, in the real world (which is vastly different from the academic world), this option is rarely exercised. The name of the game is to exploit the medium's visual aspect whenever possible. In practice, this means going with whatever tape happens to be available (as long as it's related to the subject at hand). And for the writer, this means tailoring language to fit the situation.*

---

*It is absolutely forbidden to *misrepresent* a piece of tape (or still photograph, for that matter). For example, you may never show tape of a demonstration that took place the day before yesterday and say in your copy that this was "today's" demonstration, even though today's demonstration may have been very similar to the earlier one. This would be completely unethical and, in fact, could be grounds for a station's ownership to lose its FCC license.

The dictum never to misrepresent extends to even the smallest things. If your copy talks of "wheat fields" and if you only have tape of alfalfa fields, you may not use the tape, even though the chance of any viewers catching such a discrepancy is remote. "Truth in packaging" may not apply strictly to advertising, but it applies absolutely to TV news. No exceptions.

For example, let's say that Senator Piltdown, during a hot race for re-election, visits your town briefly as part of a whirlwind campaign swing. His visit amounts to little more than a quick stop at the airport for a speech at the terminal (the kind of "photo opportunity" politicians love to stage for the exposure it gets them in the local media). You have picturesque tape of the good senator waving as he exuberantly emerges from the plane and walks down the ramp. You also have excruciatingly dull tape of the senator's remarks (Piltdown is no Demosthenes). Your best picture is the ramp footage, so you are going to use it as a visual introduction, followed by a bite of Piltdown.

Your problem is this: It takes Piltdown 12 seconds to get down that ramp. That's how long the tape runs. There's no way to shorten it without a jump cut‡ making it look like Piltdown *tripped* down the stairs. So 12 seconds is what you've got—use it or lose it. That means you have to write 12 seconds of copy to cover the playing time, whether you like it or not.

And that copy should *not* say "Senator Orotund Piltdown smiled and waved exuberantly as he arrived in Ourtown today" because everyone can *see* him smiling and waving. Why be redundant? And it should *not* say, "Senator Orotund Piltdown said today" because we see him *smiling, waving,* and *walking down stairs,* not *saying*—a glaring mismatch of sound and picture.

You must somehow relate what we *are seeing,* the arrival, with what we *are about to see,* part of the speech, as you tell the news. Here's one way to do it:

```
Senator Orotund Piltdown, arriving

in Ourtown today on part of a

campaign swing, pressed the issues

that show him gaining in the opinion

polls: higher defense spending and a

crackdown on welfare fraud.
```

The italicized words explain the context of the picture we are seeing, and the rest of the words set up the sound bite that follows (which is on defense, welfare, or both). All the words together take 12 seconds to say. Bingo.

Now no one claims this is easy. It takes much trial and error. But after much practice, TV newswriters and reporters develop a kind of sixth sense for "writing to time." They are able, after looking at a tape just once, to tell a tape editor,

---

‡A technical explanation: As we've seen, radio's audiotape can be edited quite easily because only sound is involved. Provided the inflections sound natural, internal remarks, unwanted sounds, etc. can be edited out. However, editing videotape is not so simple. That's because, at the edit point, the pictures will not match. This mismatch (which you really have to see to appreciate) is called a "jump cut"—because, at the edit point, the image appears to jump from one place to another. This is visually jarring and disorienting. Thus, jump cuts are covered over visually by a short scene called a "cutaway"—usually a shot of spectators watching or a reaction shot of the TV reporter listening.

"Give me eight seconds of this, four seconds of that, six seconds of this, then a bite on the incue 'Mary had a little lamb,' to the outcue 'lamb was sure to go' "—and then go back to their desks and write the proper amount of copy without ever again looking at the tape.

This sort of newswriting cannot be haphazard. It requires discipline. It requires the writer to assess all the available elements—story points, picture, sound, plus the allotted air time—*before* sitting down to write.

Once at the typewriter, there are two general methods of correlating sound (copy) with picture (tape): scene-by-scene and as a flow.

Scene-by-Scene

This technique, which is easier to learn and is frequently used by field reporters to help guide tape editors in the choice and order of scenes, employs a key word or phrase that corresponds *precisely* with the appearance of a given picture:

```
VIDEO                           AUDIO

(victim's house)                The victim lived in this house on

                                Crescent Drive...


                                            -0-

(suspect's photo)               Police identified this man

                                -- 31-year-old Orotund Piltdown

                                Junior -- as the prime suspect...
```

The copy need not contain the demonstrative adjective "this" or "these"; the mere mention of a specific name or place will suffice. The technique requires a specific picture to appear at a specific time. For this reason, it is disliked by many "creative" tape editors who resent writers and reporters, in effect, editing their pieces for them. So be it.

As a Flow

By far the more difficult, more creative, and ultimately more satisfying technique is writing that lets thoughts and subject matters flow seemingly effortlessly one to another. In this technique, the references to specific pictures are more oblique, more off-handed, more like conventional storytelling.

```
VIDEO                           AUDIO

(victim's house)                From the outside, there was no hint

                                of what had taken place in the

                                victim's basement rec-room...
```

-o-

(suspect's photo)	And the man in custody tonight,
	31-year-old Orotund Piltdown Junior,
	is said by neighbors to have been
	one of the victim's frequent
	visitors...

Do you see the difference in styles? Scene-by-scene writing makes the audio-visual linkage the main business of the sentence. Flow writing makes the linkage seem incidental.

"Writing Away"

Now that I've stated the case strongly for tying news copy directly to the taped visuals, let me devote a few words to the inevitable exceptions. Sometimes, the most effective way to tell a story on TV is to let the picture speak for itself, or at least to let it show things not specifically described in the narration. Here, as an example, is some narration for a closing item (kicker) to a newscast:

(anchor on-cam)	And finally, there was an honored
	guest at today's commencement
	ceremonies at State
(tape)	University. Patty Cake, who
	followed a special curriculum on
	full scholarship, was graduated
	"magna-cum-banana." Patty had an
	outstanding academic record. Never
	once did she bite a professor. It's
	not known if Patty will attend
	graduate school. It's not even
	known what she'll do with the rest
	of
(anchor on-cam)	her diploma. Patty Cake was part of
	a language-learning experiment

underwritten by the American
Zoological Society.

Well, it's pretty clear from that copy that Patty Cake isn't human. But it *deliberately* doesn't tell you that she is a young chimpanzee or what is happening in the videotape. Here's what viewers *see:* the anchor introducing the story, then tape of Patty, wearing a cap and gown, being led by her trainer as she is handed a diploma and a banana, hugging her trainer, and then taking a bite out of the diploma instead of the banana, followed by the anchor back on camera (no doubt chuckling or smiling).

This kind of writing is called "writing away" (that is, "away" from the precise pictures). It deliberately uses language as a counterpoint to the pictures. Neither element, neither audio nor video, can stand on its own—the video because it doesn't tell us the context, the audio because it doesn't describe the pictures. But *together* they make effective storytelling on TV.

Of all television writing techniques, "writing away" is the most fun. But, as with many things that are fun, it's easy to overdo it. Thus, you should use the technique very rarely, and *only* when there is a strong picture.

"Visual Logic" (Sequential Writing and Editing)

In early chapters, we saw how and why the structure of a broadcast news story must follow a straight line instead of jumping back and forth as may a print story. Nowhere in broadcast journalism is this more true than in editing videotape and writing narration for it. That's because the tape, which is a progression of moving images, contains its own "visual logic" reflecting the natural order of the real world.

To illustrate, let's say we are doing a story on the space shuttle for the Late News. We have videotape of the following events, listed in the chronological order of their occurrence:

> The shuttle astronauts eating breakfast
> The astronauts boarding the shuttle
> The lift-off from Cape Canaveral
> The shuttle separating from the booster rocket
> The shuttle in orbit
> The astronauts getting a phone call from the president
> The astronauts conducting on-board experiments
> The astronauts eating dinner

After getting his or her lead paragraph out of the way, a print writer would be free to recount these events in any order, jumping back and forth, interweaving at will. He or she could, for example, describe the astronauts' dinner and then immediately contrast this with what they had for breakfast. Or the print writer could tell how calm a certain astronaut appeared, then tell how nervous that same astronaut had been before the launch.

But the TV newswriter who wishes to show any or all of these events on tape has no such freedom of movement. That's because to reverse the natural order of things, to show people eating breakfast right *after* dinner or someone preparing for space flight on the ground *after* we've already seen him or her in space, causes viewers to shake their heads in dismay. It *looks* odd to see things out of sequence, and *seeing* is what TV news is mainly about.

So here's a guideline for writing and editing: *Unless there's a compelling reason to do otherwise, always edit videotape in a natural sequence, and write your narration accordingly.*

Sequential writing and editing takes two forms: temporal and spatial. The foregoing space shuttle story, for example, can be told flowingly either by respecting a strict *chronological order,* showing things in the same order in which they occurred in real life, or by *location,* starting with what happened on the ground and then with what happened in space. Either way, however, there is *no going back.* Once we eat dinner, it's too late for breakfast. Once we're in space, it's too late to prepare ourselves for the launch.

Note that in either case, it is not necessary to show everything. You can pick and choose from the available tape, just as you can from the available facts. But once you do choose, you should follow the sequential order just described.

A typical handling of this story for TV would have the anchor open on-camera or with a graphic telling the latest or most important development, then go into tape for mission highlights seen and told chronologically, and then finally back to the anchor for a tag or the next story.

SCRIPTING WITH SOUND BITES

A TV news story in which the only taped part is a sound bite comes the closest to what you've already learned in radio. The basic structure is lead-in/bite, with or without a tag. Also like radio, the TV script page does not contain the verbatim text of the bite, but merely the audio and video cues necessary to get it on and off the air smoothly.

There is one big difference, however: Because electronic titles permit the *visual* identification of the speaker, it is not always necessary to identify the speaker by name or title in the lead-in or tag. This presents the writer with two options:

1. to identify the speaker in the lead-in and *not* use an electronic title, or
2. to omit identification in the lead-in and to give the speaker's name and title in a lower-third electronic title.

Either option is acceptable, although modern TV news practice greatly favors option 2. Remember, however, that you must do it one way or the other; the speaker must be identified in either the news copy or by electronic title.

To permit you to fully understand the script seen on p. 238, here is the text of the sound bit it incorporates:

```
Smith                    U.N.
9/11, 10pm
```

graphic -- U.N. HQ   Linda: The Soviets are charging that

American actions against Aeroflot, the

Soviet airline, are keeping the Soviet

foreign minister away from the U-N

session that is about to begin.

Those charges led to an American

suggestion: if they don't like it

here, they should consider removing

themselves from American soil. That

is diplomatic language for "Get lost:"

SOT (:17) -- FULL

title -- Lichenstein

ENDS: "...into the sunset."

                          Linda: The United States contributes

more to U-N operations than any other

country -- 879 million dollars in the

past year.

                                (WMAQ-TV, Chicago)

(Charles Lichenstein
U.S. Delegate at the U.N.)

We will put no impediment in your way. The members of the U.S.
Mission to the United Nations will be down at dockside, waving you a fond
farewell as you sail into the sunset.

(runs :17)

The circled time at the top of the page just under the slug—:40—is the total
running time of the story, derived by adding the tape time (:17) to the nontape
time (:24), rounded off to the nearest :05 seconds. Thus: :17 + :24 = :41,
rounded off = :40.

The cue "SOT FULL" means that the audio track of the tape will be played
at normal volume (rather than at low volume to permit the anchor to talk over it).
The time in parentheses—:17—is the total time of the taped portion only. As we
shall see, this is the correct time cue placement for the start of a piece of tape of
any kind.

The cue "title" calls for the titling operator to insert the identifying electronic title at the start of the tape. Normally, the title will be held on-screen for
several seconds before being dropped. (Sometimes it is necessary to script a
precise time for the title to appear—as, for example, when it would otherwise
risk appearing over a cutaway or other shot not showing the speaker clearly.)

In the audio column, the audio outcue is clearly set off from the body of the
script both to prevent the anchor from reading it aloud accidentally and to allow
him or her to know when to be looking back into the camera at the end of the
bite. At many stations, the practice is to circle the outcue instead of (or in addition to) setting it off by typed lines.

Many stories *end* with the sound bite—without a tag. As in radio, it is
essential that the outcue be precise and indicate applause, laughter, and so on,
where applicable, as well as any double outcues.

In television as opposed to radio, it is common to edit together (to butt)
sound bites from different speakers. Often one bite is a natural reaction or
corollary to the bite that precedes it. This works in TV (and not in radio) because
we can *see* that it's a different person. In such cases of multiple sound bites, the
tape time in parentheses is *one notation*—the *aggregate* time of all the bites together. And the outcue is the outcue of the *last bite only*. (The cue times for titles
will, of course, be different.)

SCRIPTING WITH ANCHOR VOICE OVER

Much more typical than stories with sound bites only are stories with tape narrated by the anchor. The tape is edited and timed under the writer's direction
and supervision, and a description of the individual scenes is *not* included in the
script. The anchor does not normally look at a monitor to coordinate the copy
with the pictures. That coordination is accomplished by the writer as he or she
tailors and times the news copy.

The following two scripts are competing versions of the same story as it was handled by local stations in Chicago. The only previously undisscused direction is AVO, which stands for "anchor voice over," meaning we see the tape while we hear the anchor's voice.

Jones
9/18, 5pm

SNOW

:20

graphic -- map

NATSOT (:15) -- AVO

Walter:

Four days of summer are left on the calendar, but some western states are already battling a major snowstorm.

As much as 17 inches of snow fell on parts of Montana last night, and by early today, half a foot was on the ground in parts of North Dakota, Wyoming, Colorado, and Oregon. Heavy snow warnings are in effect for much of the northern Rockies, and more snow is expected tonight.

(WBBM-TV, Chicago)

Smith
9/18, 5pm

EARLY SNOW

Carol: It's still officially summer for

four more days, but you might not be

able to convince the residents of

southwestern Montana of that.

NATSOT (:20) -- AVO

title -- Billings (TOP)

It snowed there today -- and it

snowed a lot. At last report, as many

as 17 inches were on the ground in

south-central Montana -- 14 inches in

the suburbs of Helena.

The snow as part of a fast-moving

storm out of Canada that hit Montana,

Wyoming, Colorado, and Washington --

where the temperature only yesterday

was 60 degrees.

(WMAQ-TV, Chicago)

The cue NATSOT (as noted earlier, shorthand for "natural sound on tape") tells the director that the soundtrack of the tape is to be played at a very low level, just loud enough to provide a "presence" under the anchor's voice. The cue AVO tells all concerned that the anchor will be reading news copy as viewers watch the tape.

In addition, the handwritten brackets in the audio column show the anchor the start and finish of the copy he or she will be reading off-camera. When an anchor comes upon a closing bracket, he or she knows to look back into the camera.

As for the content of these two competing stories, you may be wondering how it is that two entirely different news staffs can come up with virtually the same information and story structure. It's not a mystery. Both stations subscribe to the same news agencies. Both receive videotape from their respective networks. Both employ experienced professional newswriters. It's no wonder, then, that the major distinguishing feature is the language of the news copy.

SCRIPTING WITH AVO AND SOUND BITES

Television script cues must be short and precise. Otherwise, scripts would become cluttered and difficult to grasp at a glance. The addition of time cues as a new element in our next sample script requires some explanation. After all, you should know the technical reasons for the shorthand designed to reduce clutter.

The videotape portion of a story is edited onto a separate cassette, one cassette per story. Thus, by the time a newscast goes on the air, a stack of videocassetes, each clearly labeled and timed, has been assembled near the playback machines, ready to be loaded and aired at the director's command. Once a cassette is loaded and started, the tape *continues to play* to the end of the edited material—no stopping, pausing, or rewinding. Therefore, the only accurate way for everyone (technical and editorial personnel alike) to know the precise time to cue a title, full sound, or AVO is to keep a cumulative (or "running") time of the entire tape from start to finish. The reference point is thus the start of the tape, which is clocked as zero (:00) seconds. Every cue thereafter is notated cumulatively, so that once the director starts his or her stopwatch at :00, it does not stop until the end of the tape. The watch is then zeroed (reset at :00) in readiness for the next tape. Thus, as they edit videotape for broadcast, writers and tape editors use the same timing and cueing system.

The sample script of a typical story combining AVO and SOT FULL is on pp. 243–44. First the text of the sound bite so that you can follow the content of the story from start to finish:

(Dep. Chief Dave Clark
Des Plaines Fire Dept.)

When the crews arrived on the scene, we had a fire in the basement. Uh, the basement was full of smoke. We spent the first half an hour just evacuating the building. We got maybe 75 to 80 people out of the building.

(runs :16)

Running down the script:

- The handwritten and circled time just under the slug is, of course, the total time of the story, derived by adding the tape time (:55) and the non-tape time (:04 at the start + :03 at the end = :07) for a combined 1:02, rounded off to 1:00.
- The first cue, NATSOT (:55)—AVO, begins the tape and tells the director how long it runs. At this point, the director's watch starts running in sync with the tape. At the same time, the bracket in the audio column shows that the anchor is now reading voice-over copy.
- The next cue, for a title showing a street address to appear in the bottom third of the screen, is without a time cue, so the director will order it inserted, as intended, over the very first scene of the tape.
- The next title cue, however, does tell the director to insert the title "at :10"—which means at 10 seconds into the tape. Notice the progression of

Jones
10/2, 6pm

FIRE

graphic -- map   Ron:

NATSOT (:55) -- AVO

title -- address (BOTTOM)

title (at :10) -- this morn.(TOP)

SOT FULL (:22 to :38)

title (at :25) -- Clark

Suburban fire officials are
trying to determine the cause of this
morning's multi-alarm blaze in
northwest suburban Des Plaines...
...a fire that destroyed a
36-unit apartment building. Five Des
Plaines policemen, a volunteer
fireman, and one resident of the
building were treated for smoke
inhalation.

No one was seriously injured.
the pre-dawn blaze started in the
basement of the building...and spread
rapidly through stairwells and heating
ducts, up through the roof. Some
residents were trapped for a while by
the smoke and flames. They had to be
rescued by firemen using ladders going
up to the stories and balconies:

ENDS: "...out of the building."
                    (DOUBLE OUTCUE)

FIRE-2

AVO (:38 to :55)

Those residents left homeless by
the fire were housed in a temporary
shelter put up by the Red Cross at a
grade school. By early afternoon,
most of the burned-out families had
been relocated at nearby motels or put
up with friends and relatives.

    Officials are looking into the
possibility that the fire may have
been set.

                              (WMAQ-TV, Chicago)

visual information: The first title gives a specific place (Where), the second title a specific time of day (When). This is how electronic visuals should be used—to tell new information and reinforce earlier information, in coordination with the news copy.

- The cue SOT FULL (:22 to :38) tells the director not only that the sound-track should be boosted to normal volume but also that the anchor's mike should be shut off during the next 16 seconds. Note that the script does *not* show the time cue as ":16" because that timing has no meaning on a stop-watch that began 22 seconds earlier and is still running. But the script does tell the precise starting time (:22) and precise ending time (:38) of the bite.

- The next title cue, "title (at :25)—Clark," contains a specific time for its appearance. The director must respect this time cue because, not being able to see the tape in advance of airtime, he or she does not want to risk inserting the title over a cutaway shot.

- Looking now at the audio column, note first that the audio outcue contains the warning DOUBLE OUTCUE because the closing words "the building" are repeated in the space of a few seconds. As in radio, anchors must know precisely when the taped sound is done and when they should resume reading.

- Our old friend the arrow is back in the lower right of the page. As in radio, it indicates that the story continues onto another page.

- Note that page 2 of the script is indicated merely by the slug with a page number in the extreme upper left. That's all that's necessary.
- The final cue, AVO (:38 to :55), combined with another bracket in the audio column, shows everyone that the NATSOT continues for the anchor to read over. The closing bracket tells the anchor when to look back into the camera, just in case the director decides to cut back to the standard anchor shot instead of ending the story with the taped pictures.

(While we're on the subject of closing pictures, here's how to script a *video outcue*—that is, when a sound bite or NATSOT concludes with an action rather than words)

```
VIDEO                              AUDIO

Video out (at 1:18)                -------------------------------------

    (raps gavel twice)             (VIDEO OUTCUE: gavel raps twice)

                                   ------------------------------------)
```

Although it is standard practice to identify speakers heard and seen in sound bites either in news copy or by electronic title, there are times when individuals are not named. Such times are when the bites are of people whose participation in an event is clear from the context of their remarks, and when each bite is short. The bites are butted together, and the audio outcue is of the *last bite only.* Here's an example:

> (passenger #1)
> I could see it. I was sitting at the window. We flew right though a huge flock of sea gulls. We hit one in front, and one went right into the engine.
>
> (passenger #2)
> Well, I think we're pretty lucky. We're on the ground—both feet.
>
> > (runs :18 total)

(Script on p. 246)

In modern television, sound bites can be extremely short, lasting as little as 3 or 4 seconds apiece. Naturally, the content must lend itself to this rather abrupt treatment. It may seem foolish to spend hours (counting traveling time) to tape an interview and then to use only 4 seconds (or none) of it, but that's the way it works out sometimes. Many news managements like bites to be kept short because this gives "movement" to a piece that might otherwise appear static. "Keep it moving" is the advice they give writers and reporters, by which they mean "Keep the viewer's attention."

Summarizing the duties of writers in TV news:

Gathering the information for the story
Viewing and running down the tape from the field crew

Jones
10/14

NEAR MISS

(:45)

	Mike:

Mike: Some air travellers heading out
of Chicago got to their destination a
little late today -- but it could have
been a whole lot worse.

NATSOT (:37) -- AVO

title -- Midway (BOTTOM)

An Air Florida jet had to make an
emergency landing at Midway Airport,
just minutes after taking off for
Miami. A flock of birds, also heading
south, somehow got sucked into one of
the plane's engines:

SOT FULL (:12 to :30)

ENDS: "...both feet."

AVO (:30 to :37)

No one aboard the plane was
injured. The passengers were bused to
O'Hare Airport for a later flight to
Miami.

(WBBM-TV, Chicago)

Learning from the producer how much air time the story will get

Supervising the editing of the tape

Ordering the graphics

Ordering the titles

Noting the specific times in the edited tape that the sound bites and titles are to appear

Scripting the story, incorporating all the preceding elements

Reading it aloud (or giving it to the anchor to read aloud) to make sure that the AVO timing is right

Rewriting and rescripting as necessary

And, finally, handing the script pages to the producer

SCRIPTING LEAD-INS TO REPORTS

If a reporter is unavailable to oversee the editing of his or her own package or to write his or her own lead-in (reporters are often out on another assignment), that duty falls to a writer. The writer also orders any necessary titles and graphics, notes the time cues, and then scripts the lead-in to the report. In such a case, the actual writing represents only a tiny fraction of the writer's work. For in addition to the lead-in, the writer may have to prepare a cue sheet to go along with the script.

    The content of a lead-in to a report in television serves exactly the same purpose and follows exactly the same style as a lead-in in radio: It introduces both the subject of the story and the reporter, as it prepares the audience for what it is about to see and hear. It is either hard or soft, depending on the reporter's opening copy. It typically ends with a throw line such as "Joe Doaks reports:" or "We get details from Jill Jones:". But good writers try to weave the reporter's name and/or location into the rest of the lead-in copy. Here, for example, are competing network lead-ins to reports on a story about cocaine use by Major League baseball players:

```
Another big-league baseball player

is in the news tonight -- not

because of what he did ON the field,

but because of what he did OFF the

field.  Former Kansas City Royals

pitcher Vida Blue, once one of

baseball's best, pleaded guilty

today to possession of cocaine.  He

joins three other Royals in the
```

```
                              cocaine lineup.  And, as Jim Cummins

                              tells us tonight, there may be

                              others:
```

                                        (NBC Nightly News)

                                        —0—

```
                              It's a world apart from the World

                              Series -- an underworld of whispers

                              and pointed fingers and illicit

                              drugs.  But it's in the courts now,

                              and, as Frank Currier reports, the

                              scandal of "diamond dust" continues

                              to spread:
```

                                        (CBS Evening News)

To understand how a TV newswriter goes about scripting a lead-in and attendant cue sheet, it is necessary to go back a few steps. Even before the writer comes into the process, the producer and reporter will have discussed both the content and structure of the reporter's story, as well as how much airtime it will receive; the producer has the last word on these matters. The reporter then writes and records his or her narration, either in the field or back at the station. The reporter does *not* include specific times for sound bites or titles, for the simple reason that he or she cannot know such information until the report is edited.

Now the writer steps in. The producer assigns to the writer all the reporter's and camera crew's output: narration, videotape, handout material, and so on, as well as any wire copy or printed background information. The producer also tells the writer how much airtime is allotted to the story, including the lead-in.

The writer and a tape editor then edit the package (at small stations, the writer and tape editor are likely to be the same person), choosing the exact sound bites and noting the various cue times for requisite titles. Then the writer scripts the lead-in and cues.

Since the complete text of a reporter's package does not exist in scripted form, it is necessary to reproduce a transcript of one so that you can clearly understand what follows. Here is a report done for a local Chicago station (WMAQ-TV) about a potential environmental hazard. Although the text is self-explanatory, included in the video column are brief descriptions of the visuals:

(waste in ship canal)	v/o: Waste –– the product of more than 75 years of unregulated dumping... From the mills that have fed the economic life of the nation has come a hazardous legacy.
(reporter on–camera)	o/c: The Indiana Harbor ship canal is considered one of the most polluted waterways in the nation. The waste it holds includes the cancer–causing agent P-C-B. But now the canal must be dredged, and the problem is, where should the tons of waste be dumped?
(ship canal shots)	v/o: One plan would have it dumped in a giant holding container in Lake Michigan, just off Jorris Park in East Chicago. That's the plan Lake County commissioners approved. It's supposed to be safe. But some people here say such a holding container would become an environmental time bomb.
(East Chicago Councilman Frank Kollintzas)	(sound bite, Kollintzas) "It's impossible to give us the securrity that the toxics and many of the PCBs and the mercury that they're gonna be pulling out of the canal are gonna be able to be contained in one massive land fill."
(waste, dredging, & loading gear)	v/o: The canal must be dredged because it is filling in. Giant ships that

	haul the products and supplies of this area need a deeper channel. But, say some people here, there must be a safer way.
(East Chicago Councilman John Todd)	(sound bite, Todd) "My preference would be to put it on the land some place rather than in the water. It seems to me just reasonable that any problems occur, they would be far less of a catastrophe if it were on land – such as if the container were to break."
(beaches, Chicago skyline) v/o:	And, they say, the beaches of Chicago are not that far away.
(Todd again)	(sound bite, Todd) "We're playing with something here that is irreplaceable, the lake, and just the impact it could have on the health and welfare of the people throughout the southern lake area, possibly even the whole lake, and putting these things in a potential dangerous situation."
(canal again) v/o:	Indiana Harbor's ship canal <u>will</u> be dredged. It will take years and will cost millions. But there will be a fight if the dumping ends up out
(picturesque view of Lake Michigan)	<u>there</u> –– in the lake people here are trying to protect. Stephen Ray, Channel Five News.

That report, as broadcast with this text, ran 2:12. The cassette was labeled with the story slug, the reporter, the running time, and the show time: "Lake Fill—Ray—2:12—4:30pm." The writer's scripted lead-in and cue times went like this (the off-monitor photos are included for your benefit):

```
Smith                  LAKE FILL
10/27, 430p
```

graphic -- waste   Ron: Some East Chicago, Indiana,

officials are claiming a plan to clean

up the Indiana Harbor ship canal

threatens the future of Lake Michigan.

The plan, approved by Lake County

commissioners this week, would have

P-C-B's and other waste placed in

containers and dropped in the lake.

                                       Stephen Ray reports:

NATSOT FULL (2:12)

   (Stephen Ray)   ------------------------------------

                          ENDS: "...Channel 5 News."

                                       (WMAQ-TV, Chicago)

Cue Sheets

That script was comparatively easy to set up. But many reporters' packages in modern TV news are considerably more complicated. Often they contain such visual elements as full-screen graphics, electronic titles with statistics or quotations, and so forth. Each element requires a specific cumulative cue time in the script, possibly requiring the script to continue onto a separate second page called a cue sheet:

```
LAKE FILL-2          CUE SHEET
```

```
(at :05) title -- Ind. Harbor (BOTTOM)
```

```
(at :13) title -- Ray (BOTTOM)
```

```
(at :50) title -- Kollintzas (BOTTOM)
```

```
(at 1:17) title -- Todd (BOTTOM)
```

```
                              ----------------------------------------
out at 2:12                   "...Channel 5 News."
                              ----------------------------------------
```

Many small market stations do not have adequate staff or equipment for such electronic razzle-dazzle. This is probably a good thing for newcomers, who are thus less distracted from writing good copy at a time in their careers when they are on somewhat shaky ground.

EXERCISE

1. The following news agency copy, NATSOT, and sound bites constitute your raw material to write a TV script running a maximum of 1:15. Slug it GALLAUDET and be sure to familiarize yourself with all the available copy, sound, and picture elements before selecting those you wish to include in your story.

WASHINGTON (AP/UPI)--Gallaudet University's board of trustees today chose I. King Jordan to be the first deaf president in the 124-year history of the school for the hearing impaired, and announced that board Chairwoman Jane Bassett Spilman has resigned.

Jordan, dean of the school's college of arts and sciences, was chosen to replace Elisabeth Ann Zinser, a hearing woman, who resigned early Friday after protests from students seeking a deaf leader had virtually paralyzed Gallaudet's campus.

Spilman, who had come under fire from protesters for her handling of the crisis, will be replaced by Philip W. Bravin, one of the four deaf members on the board.

In a clean sweep for student protesters, Bravin announced that the board of trustees will form a task force to study composition of the board and institute a plan to ensure that a majority of the school's 20-member trustees panel was deaf. There will also be no reprisals against student protesters, Bravin said.

News of Jordan's selection was received with joy on Gallaudet's campus. There was pandemonium in the campus gym, where about 200 students had gathered throughout the day as the board met in a nearby hotel.

Before becoming dean of Gallaudet's largest undergraduate department in 1986, Jordan, 43, served as a psychology professor at the school. He becomes the seventh president of the nation's only liberal arts college for the hearing impaired.

Jordan's appointment comes after a tumultuous week in which clamor for a deaf president grew from an isolated campus protest to a national platform for deaf rights.

Students forced school officials to cancel classes Monday when they blocked all entrances to the campus and prevented faculty and staff from entering. Throughout the rest of the week, students boycotted classes, and on Wednesday, more than half the school's faculty voted to back the protesters.

NATSOT shows the following elements:

    Gallaudet campus exteriors

    Students in campus gym applauding at news of Jordan's selection

    File tape of students blocking campus entrances

    File tape of faculty meeting

    Still photograph of Jordan

Available opening graphics include:

"Gallaudet Student Victory"
Jordan photo
Gallaudet campus photo
"New Gallaudet President"

Available sound bites and running times:

I. KING JORDAN (at hotel where his appointment was announced):

1. In this week, we can truly say that we, together and united, have overcome our reluctance to stand for our rights and our full representation.

(runs :10)

2. The world has watched the deaf community come of age. We will no longer accept limits on what we can achieve.

(runs :09)

3. I must give the highest of praise to the students of Gallaudet for showing us all exactly how, even now, one can seize an idea with such force of argument that it becomes a reality.

(runs :13)

JANE SPILMAN (at same hotel, announcing her resignation):

1. I took this step willingly. In the minds of some, I've become an obstacle. I am removing that obstacle.

(runs :07)

PAUL SINGLETON, Gallaudet graduate student (in campus gym):

1. We love it. We know now the university is going to be ours.

(runs :05)

2. He (Jordan) is the perfect president, the perfect selection.

(runs :04)

(Remember to insert electronic title cues wherever necessary.)

Index